Streetsmart Financial Basics for Nonprofit Managers

Streetsmart Financial Basics for Nonprofit Managers

Third Edition

THOMAS A. McLAUGHLIN

WILEY

John Wiley & Sons, Inc.

Published by John Wiley & Sons, Inc., Hoboken, New Jersey.
Published simultaneously in Canada.

For general information on our other products and services, or technical support, please contact our Customer Care Department within the United States at 800-762-2974, outside the United States at 317-572-3993 or fax 317-572-4002.

Wiley also publishes its books in a variety of electronic formats. Some content that appears in print may not be available in electronic books.

For more information about Wiley products, visit our Web site at http://www.wiley.com.

Library of Congress Cataloging-in-Publication Data:
McLaughlin, Thomas A.
   Streetsmart financial basics for nonprofit managers/Thomas A. McLaughlin.—3rd ed.
      p. cm.
   Includes index.
   ISBN 978-0-470-41499-6 (paper/website)
   1. Nonprofit organizations—Finance.   2. Nonprofit organizations—Accounting.   I. Title.
   HG4027.65.M35 2009
   658.15—dc22

                                                                                    2009001910

10   9   8   7   6   5   4   3

To Gail, Paul, and Emily

Contents

Preface

Over the past two decades the nonprofit sector has grown at an astonishing pace. Today there are more than one million nonprofit public charities and hundreds of thousands of other nonprofit entities, and they are found in every community in this country. As important, the sector is beginning to figure prominently in public conversations as an acknowledged source of innovation and solutions to various social issues, especially in areas where government at all levels was formerly more active. This trend seems likely to continue and even accelerate in the years to come.

With greater prominence and more widespread acceptance come greater attention and more scrutiny. Nonprofit management is becoming a recognized specialty, and there is a growing recognition that nonprofit financial management is not just for profit financial management with a different name. The number of individuals and entities specializing in nonprofit financial management is growing as well.

With this growth in numbers comes a comparable growth in the demand for sophisticated management. The problem is that few nonprofit managers have any formal training in financial management. Almost everything they know is from on-the-job training, with a liberal amount of assumptions and conventional wisdom that may or may not be helpful. In some cases, these managers can rely on native instinct and clarity of thought, but most often they simply wing it and hope for the best.

Nonprofit organizations—and the users and funders of their services—deserve better, and they are getting it. It is not much of a stretch to say that the increased emphasis on financial management in nonprofits reflects a laudable striving for greater accountability. No longer is it enough just for one's financial records to be in order; one must be able to demonstrate good financial systems in order to meet all the other rising demands on today's nonprofit.

In my work as a nonprofit management consultant, graduate program faculty member, and nonprofit board member, I continue to find a widespread hunger for practical, immediately helpful financial information. That was the initial stimulus for this book, and it remains so today.

In this volume I tend to steer away from technical compliance-related matters, for two reasons. First, others can cover financial compliance subjects better than I. And second, my vision of financial management goes far beyond simple compliance to a stage that I fervently hope will be characterized by thoughtful, creative, and persistent management actions.

To support those who share my vision, I have tried to make this book as practical as possible. For example, most of my financial calculations and many examples are based on the IRS Form 990, the nonprofit "tax return." By using the only common financial reporting form, I hope to bridge the gaps between different types of nonprofit organizations so that the content will work equally well for a broad audience.

This third edition also contains many new items. I have added material on the proper financial roles of boards of directors ("Assets Are for Boards, Activities Are for Managers"), the Sarbanes-Oxley law, charity watchers, and many other subjects. New to this edition, I have told brief stories of nonprofit financial success (or lack thereof) at solving common problems. I have also double-coded and cross-walked all line items from both the old and the new IRS Form 990s, recognizing that the new version starting in 2009 will mean that for many years into the future analysts and students will have to work simultaneously with both forms.

In recent years I have seen a growing interest in the American nonprofit sector by people from other countries. From conversations with my consulting and academic colleagues, I know I am not alone. Foreign students and managers face the double challenge of learning financial concepts while also familiarizing themselves with cultural matters that are uniquely American. This is why I added an appendix designed to be a kind of cultural primer on practices, institutions, and policies that most Americans take for granted but that would be stumbling blocks to non-Americans' understanding.

As with the first edition, this book is not intended to be primarily a textbook. There are hundreds of thousands of people involved with nonprofits who need to know about financial management but who don't need another textbook in their lives. It is to them that I speak through these pages. At the same time, I have been flattered that many professors and academic programs throughout the country have adopted the book for use in the classroom, and I thank them. I only hope that their students do, too.

As a rookie executive director many years ago, I never dreamed that I might one day write a book that so many would find useful. Mainly, I was consumed with trying to figure out what seemed like a gargantuan task rapidly enough to avoid appearing foolish. In some very real way this book is a record of my personal journey through a sometimes confusing topic. The existence of this third edition is pleasing validation that many people have found my approach to nonprofit financial management helpful. I hope only that that will continue to be the case.

—*Tom McLaughlin*
December 2008

Acknowledgments

Many people helped with one or more editions of this book. I particularly want to thank Allwyn Baptist, Becky J. Cerio, Robert Cowden, Dennis Fusco, Jim Gambon, Robert Gardiner, Catherine Gill, Elizabeth Hart, John Joyce, Laura Kenney, Bill Levis, Marty McLaughlin, Jim Mecone, Clara Miller, Wayne Moss, James Nesbitt, David Orlinoff, Mary Plant, Joanne Sunshower, Shari Sankner, and Sherrell M. Smith. Catherine Gill at the Nonprofit Finance Fund supplied some of the vignettes. My editors at John Wiley & Sons, Marla Bobowick and Susan McDermott, provided support, feedback, and guidance in one or more editions.

As before, I want to thank my wife, Gail Sendecke, and my children, Paul and Emily, for sharing me with this ongoing project.

Note to Reader

Throughout this book, a Web icon (🖐) indicates that you should go the accompanying Web site for corresponding templates or examples. The Web site address is:

www.wiley.com/go/basics3E

Refer to Appendix C, "Using the Web Site," for the table of contents and detailed instructions for use of these templates.

Streetsmart Financial Basics for Nonprofit Managers

PART ONE

Analysis

CHAPTER 1

Organizational Structure: Programs and Corporations

The nonprofit industry is enormous. Tens of thousands of such organizations are created every year. Exhibit 1.1 shows the growth curve for the last several years. Nonprofit organizations in the United States spend over $340 billion each year. They employ nearly 7 percent of the total workforce and are responsible for 6 percent of the Gross Domestic Product. Universities, research centers, religious institutions, and museums produce priceless accomplishments. Nonprofit hospitals are major elements of our health care system and in many communities are the largest employer. Social service agencies provide a wide variety of services to those less fortunate citizens. Other nonprofits educate people of all ages and at all levels. Still others develop communities and support our social lives.

There are many ways to categorize this industry. The IRS's way is discussed later in this chapter. The traditional way is by the service provided and, to a lesser extent, the size of the nonprofit organization. This approach may not be particularly useful from a financial management perspective since services and even size alone do not necessarily say much about the nature of the financial management challenge, so we suggest a different way of thinking about the financial management challenge.

TYPES OF NONPROFIT ORGANIZATIONS

For financial purposes, a better way of looking at this industry is to sort it into categories according to the primary economic function the

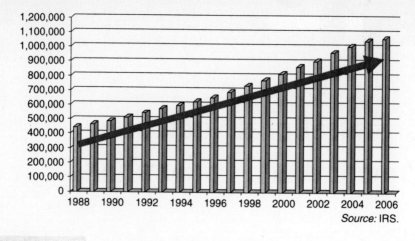

Source: IRS.

EXHIBIT I.I   Numbers of Nonprofit Public Charities 1988–2006

organizations perform. We suggest that there are six distinct types of non-profit corporations:

1. Direct service providers
2. Information managers
3. Resource distributors
4. Support and development providers
5. Grant makers or funders
6. Social organizations

Note that these groupings are chiefly for analytical purposes, and that the activities of many organizations can span several categories.

Direct Service Providers

These organizations are the classic nonprofits. Usually public charities, they are the hospitals, clinics, social service providers, and the like that provide some sort of direct and recognizable service to some or all of the public at large. Often major employers of professionals, these corporations provide a "hands-on" service.

Financial issues in direct service providers vary according to size and funding source. One characteristic that many share is the need to assemble a workable mix of funders, and to be careful about managing the relationships between funders' requirements. Complexities abound in their financial management profile because governmental and quasi-governmental entities are often major funding sources. More on that subject later. Due to the limitations of government funding, philanthropy must also often play a role in direct service providers' management, and the stakes are high if money is accounted for inaccurately.

Payment in this field has moved from the traditional reimbursement for costs incurred to a defined price for a defined service such as one often finds in the health care field now. Level funding and cutbacks for many years has been the norm.

Information Managers

Another large category of nonprofits are the information managers—universities, museums, advocacy groups, trade associations, and a variety of similar organizations. Their role is to accumulate information of a predefined sort and share it with selected users, often in the role of broker. A university, for example, can be viewed as a broker between professors and students, or between researchers and consumers of research. Information management agencies range widely in size from the very smallest advocacy group to multibillion-dollar universities with international branches.

Consumers of information management services are multiple and naturally quite independent of each other; their financial systems must be capable of handling unusually massive quantities of information. These types of organizations tend to have memberships; therefore, the financial systems must store information about the same people for retrieval and usage over a period of years. In effect, membership records are the financial data.

In practice this scenario dictates a financial system, especially the revenue tracking component, that is capable of handling large numbers of small or large transactions. Frequently, the financial task is paralleled by the program manager's need to communicate with hundreds or even thousands of people, members and nonmembers. Fast and effective data management often becomes the only thing distinguishing one information manager from another, laying a heavy burden on the administrative infrastructure of each organization.

Resource Distributors

Resource distribution agencies reached their zenith during the Great Society days of the 1960s. For a variety of political, psychological, and logistical reasons, the federal government did a lot of business directly with local nonprofit agencies, positioning them as the last stop before direct contact with eligible clients.

No doubt it was politically useful for these local players to wield ultimate distribution responsibility, thereby shielding the federal government from criticism. It was also smart to graft onto the organizations' existing formal or informal support systems rather than re-creating them from scratch. Community action organizations from the 1960s such as antipoverty programs and heating oil assistance services are good examples of resource distribution nonprofits.

The premiere financial demand of resource distribution nonprofits is strict accountability. In many ways, they serve as the social equivalent of general contractors, assembling a team of benefit or service providers in order to accomplish a coordinated job. In other cases, they act mainly as a final distribution point for transfer payments, usually as part of an entitlement program. Their work typically involves outreach, evaluation, and servicing of eligible clients. From the funders' perspective, however, their real value comes after the client transaction has occurred and they make their reports to the payments' source.

Owing to the demand for accountability, resource distribution nonprofits' financial systems will tend to be shaped by individual transactions and the funding source's rules. Most programs of this sort are expected to track the flow of money, not the effectiveness of the programs. Accountability in this context means careful accounting, not managerial success. Perhaps not surprisingly given their role as intelligent conduits, many resource distribution nonprofits end up looking a lot like the governmental unit that funds them.

Support and Development Providers

The fourth category of nonprofit corporations refers to support and development groups. These organizations are limited in number but play a major role in areas of the health and social welfare sector. In size and focus they are not unlike resource distribution nonprofits, except that they concentrate on leveraging resources rather than simply marshaling them.

Financial management for support and development groups will be unremarkable except when ownership or financing of capital projects is involved. The task in these cases often relates to properly valuing assets, estimating the percentage of a project completed, and properly accounting for and reporting on funds received. The difficult aspect of financial management in the property acquisition or rehabilitation environment is dealing with irregular flows of cash in and out of the corporation and keeping track of which expenses are of the current period and which expenses should be considered part of the capital project.

Grant Makers or Funders

One of the most common of all types of nonprofits, grant makers or funders can range from the very smallest fund-raising agencies to massive private foundations. Their task is to raise money and decide who should get it, and, in the case of private foundations, raising the money may consist chiefly of effectively managing a portfolio of equities.

One of the things that makes the funder's financial management job at least theoretically easier than many in the nonprofit field—foundation CFOs, block your ears—is that things like revenue management may have to be done by outsiders such as investment managers. No financial officer can be expected to have the skills to manage a major chunk of investments, nor would the responsible board expect it. Moreover, there are arguments for accountability that favor separating investment management from operational tasks.

On a broader level, to do the grant-making job correctly, the funder needs to operate in a planned, disciplined fashion. Happily, good financial management can thrive under the same conditions. In effect, a funder is engaged in the business of shaping and directing streams of money over a period of years. This is a profoundly different dynamic than most other nonprofit categories, and it should not be underestimated in the context of designing a financial management system.

For all practical purposes, funders are accountable to no one. While the technical aspects of fund-raising and grant-making must be handled properly, it is relatively easy to hire skilled staff to see to that. Beyond the minimal level of legal compliance in both the public charity and the private foundation worlds, no significant person or authority is in a position to routinely challenge the workings of a funder. Ironically, this can be as much a hindrance to good financial management as anything else, since there is the possibility that complacency will crowd out effectiveness.

Social Organizations

The final entry in the list of major nonprofit types is social clubs and organizations. Whether fraternities, lodges, sporting clubs, quilting associations, or any of a vast array of other entities, they share the common theme that they exist in order to further the social interests of their members. Funding comes almost entirely from members' dues and from business transacted with members (such as restaurant and bar sales at clubs), and occasionally from rents or investments.

Typically, the financial stakes are low in a social club. Members usually have little interest in the details of financial management beyond seeing that the dues are collected and the bills paid on time. As a result, two of the greatest threats to a club's financial health are sloppy record keeping and fraud. The need for fiscal accountability is just as strong as in other categories, but much of the focus is likely to be on cash. One thing that tends to be true for social clubs is that their financial prowess is never any greater than what the membership demands.

STRUCTURE OF NONPROFIT ORGANIZATIONS

Programs

Programs are the most visible and best understood aspect of the nonprofit form of business organization, and its chief means of carrying out its mission. Also called services, projects, clinics, divisions, departments, floors, or any one of a thousand other names, programs are the activities of the nonprofit organization.

Coming up with a fair and workable definition of a program is difficult. Here's an attempt: A program is a coherently packaged group of activities, usually associated with one or more specific physical locations, designed to accomplish a stated result.

Nonprofit organizations run all kinds of programs, and often more than one. Day care centers offer infant care programs, environmental groups operate recycling systems, museums run art appreciation courses, and so forth. The two keys to understanding programs are that they generally have some coherent internal structure, and they appear as distinct choices to potential users.

In most nonprofit organizations, programs are like little businesses, with a structure reinforced by nonprofit accounting rules and one that has immense if largely unnoticed consequences for everything from compensation to organizational effectiveness. They represent a delegation of responsibility from the chief executive officer, and so they are the engines of mission. It is at the program level where the organization's goals are accomplished or not, and therefore those in charge of programs carry heavy moral pressure to get the job done.

Notice the use of the word "moral" in the preceding sentence. Typically, the motivations of those who run nonprofit organizations are different from those who do the same thing in the for-profit world, and the motivations of program managers everywhere are often different still from their bosses. We'll explore some of those differing interests later. For the moment, we'll use the program as the smallest management unit of the nonprofit corporation.

Corporations

The next major level of nonprofit management is the corporation that "owns" or runs the programs. The corporation is a statutory entity established by the legally sanctioned actions of one or more individuals. As a legally approved entity separate from its constituent individuals, the corporation has its own continuing existence. In legal theory, corporations are treated as distinct entities just like individual people, and corporations have their own collection of responsibilities, liabilities, and powers.

Why a corporation? The answer is disarmingly simple: because it's easier for the rest of us. Corporations can be mentioned in the same legal breath as the individuals who use their services, work in them, or simply exist in the same state with them. All are on the same legal footing, in that respect. The complicated and narrower answer to the question has to do with such practical considerations as revenue sources and liabilities.

Revenue source regulations and political realities often nudge nonprofits in the direction of a specific type of organizational structure. Programs such as battered women's shelters almost of necessity start out as single-service corporations, while older and more established groups may have developed a multi-corporate structure.

There are also liability laws to consider when operating different types of businesses. Nonprofit public charities traditionally have been granted generous protection from state liability laws, although that tendency is beginning to change. It's a tradition growing out of English Common Law that

DROPPING OUT OF SCHOOL

The community center prided itself on being able to identify community needs and respond to them effectively over time. Unfortunately, their grand old 175,000-square-foot building had already chewed up substantial funding just to keep it running. They achieved their first operating surplus in years, but it was a tissue-thin $7,900 on a budget of $10,000,000. Projections for next year contemplated more red ink.

The most prominent program in their building was their Montessori school, which occupied only about 7% of their total space but represented half of their total employees. Moreover, it was running a regular six-figure deficit. As part of a strategic positioning process, the question arose: why are we doing this?

There was not an obvious answer. When a financial commitment of this size does not have a ready answer to this simple question, it is usually time for some re-thinking. Which the center did. As a result, the school was spun off as its own nonprofit public charity, with parents and teachers taking over the management. The happy ending is that the school now rents its space from the community center and is a steady source of earned income.

Ultimately, corporate structures are simply a way to organize programs and services in logical ways to achieve maximum results. What the community center realized was that a Montessori school, while obviously important to the community, was too much of a mission stretch for them. Re-casting the legal structures allowed the center to focus on the programs and services it was good at, while turning a management diversion into a source of revenue.

has been codified in many places around the country. Often there will be either an explicit limitation on suits or a prohibition altogether on the grounds that agencies funded by the public at large ought not to be siphoning resources into private hands via lawsuits. Liability considerations alone are not normally strong enough to determine a corporate structure, but the more favorable liability climate for public charities is clear.

The Role of the Internal Revenue Service

If programs sometimes seem fuzzily defined, there is no such problem with corporate structure. Unlike other forms of business organization, a corporation does not exist until certain governmental authorities say it exists. For nonprofit corporations, the lead voice in the chorus is the Internal Revenue Service (IRS). In matters having to do with nonprofit corporations, it is the IRS that giveth and the IRS that taketh away.

Corporations are organized according to the laws of individual states. Ordinarily, starting a corporation is as easy as filing the required paperwork and paying the necessary fees; in fact that is how all corporations must start. But government at all levels reserves the right to tax the profits of a business. In order to get the government to waive its right to tax—to allow a corporation to be *tax exempt*—a would-be nonprofit corporation must show that it has been created and will be operated with certain purposes in mind. It must do so according to preestablished guidelines spelled out in the code. Then it must wait for the IRS's decision on the application.

IRS acceptance of exempt status is the turning point. After this step, state government often must have its say about the organization's acceptability as a tax-exempt entity. Normally, state government is willing to follow the IRS's lead, so once the IRS has weighed in, it's usually pro forma thereafter.

In effect, the IRS considers all nonprofits to be taxable entities until they prove otherwise. The major thing that distinguishes a nonprofit from a for-profit corporation is that most nonprofits (including all charities) are not allowed to have shareholders with whom to share profits. Note that this is not a prohibition against profits, just against having shareholders with whom to share them. This is the reason why it is often said that the profits of a nonprofit are kept within the corporation—salaries, benefits, and perks notwithstanding.

The first permanent federal income tax was enacted in 1913, but affected less than one half of 1 percent of the population. Congress expanded the tax base in 1917, when it also initiated a deduction for charitable contributions.

Hybrid Corporations

In recent years there has been growing interest in what are sometimes known as "hybrid" corporations. These entities, approximations of which as of this writing exist in one state but not as a nationwide class of corporate entity, would combine the explicit profit-making and ease of capital formation characteristic of for-profit corporations with the social responsibility of nonprofits. Social enterprise practitioners are particularly interested in hybrid corporations because they often must create a basis for social responsibility in a for-profit, or manufacture ways to raise private equity (not donations) through a nonprofit. The compromises they must reach are unsatisfying or impractical, and that is what drives the search for a new form.

There is some precedent for these hybrid corporations, such as in England where the Community Interest Company form was approved in 2004, or in the United State where well-known groups such as Newman's Own or Ben and Jerry's Ice Cream have molded traditional for-profits into social enterprises. Even many nonprofits have experimented with for-profit-like structures and cultures. The difficulty is that these are one-of-a-kind ventures. Creative legal and financial advisors can often find ways to jerry-rig a structure that mimics a hybrid corporation, but until such options are well-defined, well-understood, and enshrined in law in all states, hybrid corporations will never really become widely accepted. This is the significance of the L3C form that first gained legal acceptance in 2008. This variation on the traditional LLC is specifically intended to support social enterprise and could become the first genuine prototype in hybrid structure.

An IRS Question: Private Foundation or Not?

Historically, Congress has disliked private foundations, which are a form of charitable organization, probably because of the abuses that occurred when they were first "created." In 1969, the U.S. Congress laid the groundwork for what we now call private foundations. In the process of paying attention to private foundations, however, a curious thing happened. The IRS actually developed a much clearer and better developed sense of what a private foundation is than what a public charity is. Consequently, it essentially regards public charities as nonprofit corporations that are *not* private foundations. This is why the IRS letter granting tax-exempt public charity status says that the applicant is a tax-exempt corporation that is not a private foundation.

The driving force around which the determination of private foundation or public charity status revolves has nothing to do with public mission, but rather is usually a product of that old-fashioned determinant, money and its control. Whereas a private foundation derives its initial or ongoing funding from limited private sources, regulators expect the charitable organization to get its funding from the public at large. For many public charities, that hurdle is set at one-third of total revenue, although in a few obscure legal cases that percentage could be lower.

It is not hard to infer the authorities' motivation here. Private foundations' sole source of revenue being a single individual or family gives the founders tremendous control over determining who gets the benefits of the tax-exempt activity. It could also lead to a temptation to abuse that power if not kept in check. By obliging public charities to derive a substantial chunk of their revenue from the public at large, the Congress has virtually guaranteed that a public charity's management could never exercise the same degree of control.

Another IRS Question: What Type of Nonprofit?

So far it may seem like the nonprofit organization's only choice about tax-exempt status is between private foundation and not a private foundation, but the range of choices is much broader than that. In fact, the familiar nonprofit public charity is only one of several possible options under which a nonprofit corporation can operate. In official IRS parlance, nonprofits are organized under Section 501(c) of the code. What all of these types of corporations have in common is that (1) they are exempt from federal and usually state corporate taxes and, in the case of public charities, (2) they are not private foundations. Significantly, only 501(c)(3) corporations—and a few others, under certain circumstances—can offer donors the right to deduct contributions from taxable income. (See Exhibit 1.2.)

EXHIBIT 1.2   TAX-EXEMPT ORGANIZATIONS AND OTHER ENTITIES LISTED ON THE EXEMPT ORGANIZATION BUSINESS MASTER FILE, BY TYPE OF ORGANIZATION AND INTERNAL REVENUE CODE SECTION, FISCAL YEARS 2003–2006

Type of Organization, Internal Revenue Code Section	2003 (1)	2004 (2)	2005 (3)	2006 (4)
Tax-exempt organizations and other entities, total	1,640,949	1,680,061	1,709,205	1,726,491
Section 501(c) by subsection, total	1,501,772	1,540,554	1,570,023	1,585,479
(1) Corporations organized under act of Congress	103	116	123	126
(2) Title-holding corporations	7,078	7,144	7,116	7,120
(3) Religious, charitable, and similar organizations [1]	964,418	1,010,365	1,045,979	1,064,191
(4) Social welfare organizations	137,831	138,193	136,060	135,155
(5) Labor and agriculture organizations	62,641	62,561	61,075	60,932
(6) Business leagues	84,838	86,054	86,485	86,563
(7) Social and recreation clubs	69,522	70,422	70,399	70,569
(8) Fraternal beneficiary societies	79,390	69,798	67,391	65,752
(9) Voluntary employees' beneficiary associations	13,066	12,866	12,567	12,206
(10) Domestic fraternal beneficiary societies	22,576	21,328	21,091	21,385
(12) Benevolent life insurance associations	6,662	6,716	6,718	6,738
(13) Cemetery companies	10,585	10,728	10,819	10,879
(14) State-chartered credit unions	4,338	4,289	4,083	3,976
(15) Mutual insurance companies	1,777	1,988	2,127	2,126
(17) Supplemental unemployment benefit trusts	468	462	448	438
(19) War veterans' organizations	35,132	36,141	36,166	35,982

(25) Holding companies for pensions and other entities	1,259	1,285	1,274	1,238
Other 501(c) subsections [2]	88	98	102	103
Section 501(d) Religious and apostolic associations	**138**	**141**	**146**	**162**
Section 501(e) Cooperative hospital service organizations	**39**	**38**	**37**	**37**
Section 501(f) Cooperative service organizations of operating educational organizations	**1**	**1**	**1**	**1**
Section 501(k) Child care organizations	**0**	**3**	**2**	**6**
Section 501(n) Charitable risk pools	**0**	**1**	**2**	**2**
Nonexempt charitable trusts	**138,999**	**139,323**	**138,994**	**140,804**

[1] Includes private foundations. Not all Internal Revenue Code section 501(c)(3) organizations are required to apply for recognition of tax-exemption, including churches, integrated auxiliaries, subordinate units, and conventions or associations of churches.

[2] Includes teachers' retirement funds [section 501(c)(11)]; corporations to finance crop operations [section 501(c)(16)]; employee-funded pension trusts [section 501(c)(18)]; black lung trusts [section 501(c)(21)]; multiemployer pension plans [section 501(c)(22)]; veteran's associations founded prior to 1880 [section 501(c)(23)]; trusts described in section 4049 of the Employee Security Act of 1974 (ERISA) [section 501(c)(24)]; State-sponsored high-risk health insurance organizations [section 501(c)(26)]; and State-sponsored workers' compensation reinsurance organizations [section 501(c)(27)].

Source: Internal Revenue Service Data Book, 2006. Tax Exempt and Government Entities SE:T:BSP

LOSS OF TAX-EXEMPT STATUS—THE MONSTER WITHIN

There is a monster loose in nonprofit land. It is a monster few have seen but many can describe, summoned up from nightmares to give body to commonly held, nameless fears. It has the power to terrorize whole boards of directors, senior staffs, attorneys, accountants, managers, and donors. It is the monster called "Loss of Tax-Exempt Status."

Like most monsters, this one's power comes not from what it does directly but from its ability to govern our thoughts and shape our actions in anticipation of encountering it. And it is in the latter dynamic that the uncritical mind is most vulnerable to the advice of those who would pretend to have glimpsed the beast.

Let us make the monster slink away into the night, discouraged by reality. According to the IRS, in many years the total number of those organizations that lost their tax-exempt status is around 100. In 2007 the IRS revoked 116 tax exempt statuses (although the pace increased in the first half of 2008, with 98).

If this surprises you, it might be well to remember that the business of managing the tax responsibilities of tax-exempt organizations is, at least at their initialization, largely a matter of trust. The IRS trusts that organizations that say they are organized to benefit the public good will do just that, and since the only return that they file (Form 990) doesn't determine the amount of money the government gets paid in taxes, there is little reason to systematically review it the way personal and for-profit corporate returns are handled. To put it another way, there's little payoff for the IRS to go looking for trouble in this sector.

Revocation Not Typical of Public Charities

When trouble finds the IRS and results in these yearly 100 or so tax-exempt status revocations, it tends to fall disproportionately on groups that are not public charities. These organizations are social clubs, trade associations, fraternal organizations, and the like that enjoy tax-exempt status but are not considered public charities in the same mode as the more familiar hospitals and universities.

By far the biggest reason for exempt status revocation is that the corporations violated the prohibition against private inurement, meaning that they used their tax-exempt status to illegally enrich individuals connected with the organization in some way. Public charities also tend to lose their tax-exempt status for political work on behalf of individual candidates, a strictly prohibited activity. Another major reason for loss of tax-exempt status in all types of tax-exempt organizations is a group's receipt of an excessive amount of income from an unrelated trade or business.

CHANGING TAX STATUS: A CASE HISTORY

The designations of tax-exempt entity are categories in the tax code for which each corporation must apply. The IRS has the final word on whether a corporation fits any given category. Organizations can change their selection of code if their mission or activities change. One organization, an association of nonprofit service providers, started life as a 501(c)(3). Why? The founder was candid, "We knew the options, but foundation grants were going to be critical."

Over time the organization changed its identity from that of charity to one involving considerable lobbying on behalf of its member corporations and others like them. Nonprofit charities that begin to do substantial lobbying, in addition to having to pay a tax on lobbying above the allowable limits, must rethink their tax code election. The clock was ticking, because the IRS has the right to examine the organization's performance over a four-year period and revoke its public charity status if they determine that the corporation never operated in a proper fashion.

Eventually, the association chose to change its status from a 501(c) (3) public charity to a 501(c)(4) social welfare organization. The tradeoff was explicit. In return for the opportunity to carry out considerable lobbying activity, the group gave up its right to receive tax deductible contributions. In this case, there was no real problem because they had long ago ceased seeking foundation grants and because increased lobbying was clearly in support of its evolving mission.

Here's the twist. That same organization realized that some of its activities such as running educational programs fit more comfortably in a public charity context. So, after changing their tax exempt status, they immediately created a *second* corporation, wholly controlled by the newly re-christened social welfare organization, for the sole purpose of running educational programs. This was a classic case of lodging the correct activities in the correct corporate structure.

Why should nonprofit board members care about IRS policy on tax-exempt status termination when so few organizations actually lose their privileged tax status? The answer to this question is rooted in the same reservoir of public trust and social spiritedness that gives rise to the privilege of tax-exemption in the first place. All of these are ways in which a tax-exempt organization behaves like something it is not, particularly when it acts as a vehicle for private enrichment.

The vast majority of nonprofit leaders are ethical, committed individuals who need not worry about their actions even remotely endangering the organization's tax-exempt status. This is the greatest counterbalance to the tiny fraction who would exploit the public trust.

But a more compelling and far more subtle reason for understanding the real risks regarding loss of tax-exempt status is to be in control of one's own organization. Citing a danger that doesn't exist, presumed experts can exercise undue sway over the actions of a board or management team, insidiously discouraging the assumption of prudent risk or the exploration of innovative financial directions. Well-meaning advisors can work in monstrous ways.

Mission: Managing Your Two Bottom Lines

It has become popular to refer to the bottom line in contexts far beyond the merely financial. The phrase has a certain ring to it, a suggestion of a no-nonsense philosophy that many find attractive. But the fact of the matter is that the bottom line isn't really, well, the bottom line. At least it isn't a bottom line in the sense of a definitive, live-or-die standard; any organization can lose money during any given year and still escape with relatively little damage. It can even do it several years in a row. For any kind of business entity, the real bottom line is the inability to get capital into the organization. For nonprofit corporations, that happens when no bank will loan any more money and no philanthropist will donate any more funds. For for-profits, it means no more credit and no one willing to buy the stock anymore. Large nonprofit groups rarely go out of business because it is usually possible to persuade one more source of capital to contribute.

Profit is the organizing principle in the for-profit world. It is the only commonly shared arbiter of conflicts and the enduring benchmark of all activity. It forces the recognition that a particular course of action should be chosen because it is in everyone's best financial interests. At the same time, profit alone is a weak organizing principle because the economics affecting it can change so easily. Athletic teams win the championship one year and explode the next, their players and coaches picked over by rival teams willing to offer individuals more money. Professional service firms constantly lose professionals who discover that they can make the same or greater profit offering the service on their own. Profit as a source of organizational discipline is the common strategy. Let's consider what alternatives serve when profit as the number one motivator is missing.

THE ROLE OF A VALUE SYSTEM

Without profit as a factor, nonprofits must find another way to move the organization forward. Typically, they find it in a shared value system. Formed properly, a shared set of values provides the kind of organizational discipline that the pursuit of profit would otherwise provide. For a variety of reasons it's not a perfect substitute, but as a lasting factor it is definitely

MISSION DRIFT CAN TAKE A TOLL

The family and children's services organization over the years had developed programs far from their mission such as home health care, employee assistance, and legal services. These programs, though valued by the community, were a clear case of mission drift—chasing services unrelated to the mission chiefly for their financial benefits. But over time many of these programs ran chronic deficits, constricting growth in other areas and limiting the organization's ability to fully serve their mission. The tensions and disconnection between the program management demands of these services and the more traditional offerings grew palpable until the board of directors finally decided to find a new home for each of the programs not squarely in their service model.

Transferring these services to another organization proved doubly problematic. First, no one entity was properly positioned to be able to accept and operate all three types of programs, so the organization needed to find different homes for each one. Second, feeling a commitment to their community, the board of directors was determined to operate the money-losing programs until qualified sponsors for each could be found. All together, this process took nearly three years, with the organization's net assets dwindling further each year.

Unexpectedly, at the end of this process and for the next two or three years, the organization faced a third task: convincing foundations and potential donors that the wind-down process was a deliberate, morally sound strategy rather than the dithering of a slow-to-react institution. Mission drift can have financial consequences.

superior. Incidentally, the very best for-profit corporations know the power of a coherent value system, and they know that it is stronger than the ups and downs of simple profit.

The role of shared values explains why certain nonprofit organizations can be contentious groups filled with infighting and rivalries. In a for-profit organization without a shared value system, sheer economics can carry things as long as times are good. But a nonprofit that loses its value system—such as through a change in the CEO—has no such backup. Strategic direction then becomes a matter of pitting one value system against another.

What does all of this have to do with managing the finances of a non-profit corporation? The connection is simple, yet powerful. Problems with finances mean problems accomplishing the mission. Missed payrolls mean dispirited, demoralized staff who cannot and will not give their service's consumers their full attention. A weak capital structure magnifies operational problems. Sluggish, inefficient systems retard growth, and so on. The very brightest of program service people cannot overcome poor financial performance and after a while they will leave. The opposite, however, is not as reliable. Poor program performance can exist indefinitely in spite of good quality financial performance. Good financial health can actually prop up a programmatically bankrupt administration. Mediocre program results carry little financial penalty even when they cause reduced income because managers can always ratchet spending down to adjust. Failure in service delivery, except in intensively competitive arenas, usually implies less for finances than failure in finances implies for service delivery.

It is easy to see why. Financial failure is measurable and clearly understood by outsiders. Many outsiders pay attention to the finances, which have to be drawn up in a standardized way to permit comparisons. Bankers holding a nonprofit's mortgage are motivated to monitor fiscal performance. Funding sources regularly demand reports that can spotlight a financial problem. Institutional donors demand financial profiles. On the other hand, who will demand to see measurable outcomes of program services in most fields? And does anyone really know what success would look like if it were achieved? The truth of the matter for some nonprofit services is that, from society's perspective, it is enough simply that the services exist and not that they be of some particular level of quality. Halfway houses for former offenders are a good example. The average compassionate citizen doesn't care much for the niceties of halfway house performance, just whether the program exists or not.

A former colleague once spent a few years in the highest ranking administration and finance position in state government. Having come from a health care background, he was pleasantly surprised by the state highway construction and repair department's approach to its budget review. For their yearly budget, they would request x amount of dollars in order to pave y number of miles of roads according to z specifications that could be expected to last a certain number of years. The output and the cost might vary due to blips in the economy, but for the most part their projections were reliable. Budget decisions were a simple yes or no that would result in a predictable amount of work getting done.

Because there is no comparable measurement for most nonprofit programming, program failure goes unrecognized. Worse, it goes unpunished. In for-profit environments, the market rewards entities with profit and survival. With financial profit relegated to a lower priority, and with the exit door effectively blocked by a combination of legal, political, and cultural factors, there is no equivalent judgment tool for nonprofits.

THE NONPROFIT'S DILEMMA AND HOW TO SOLVE IT

These facts in combination with nonprofits' typical reasons for creation lead to nonprofits' central dilemma and suggest the way that good financial management can help resolve it. To begin, consider the following stories:

> Around the turn of the century, the leaders of a medium-sized factory town acknowledge a major social problem deriving from the very success that their town's many factories enjoy. The factories, working at full production with early industrial methods, are so unsafe that they routinely injure or kill employees. In turn, this creates a growing population of orphans that the town's social systems are unable to support. In need of a solution, the leaders reach out to a religious order hundreds of miles away and ask that they establish an orphanage in town. The order agrees. Eighty years later, the orphanage that the nuns created has grown into a health care system that includes three hospitals, two nursing homes, a home health care agency, and the original orphanage, which has now become a school for special needs children.

During the nineteenth-century, state governments across the country began building large institutions for the mentally ill and developmentally
disabled. Over a hundred years later, for a variety of reasons including the
institutions' high cost and inflexibility, they began to be replaced by networks of much smaller programs called community residences or group
homes. Often operated by private nonprofit groups, these programs took
as a cornerstone of their philosophy that care for their clients should be
provided in the least restrictive setting possible, a direct criticism of the
institutions the homes replaced.

Each of these vignettes illustrates in its own way a core truth of nonprofit
organizations: Those that deal with the poor, the sick, or the disabled very
often come into being due to a dysfunction in some other part of society.
Orphanages were needed due to a combination of factors such as workplace hazards, social conventions, and economic pressures. When forces as
diverse as federal laws, labor unions, governmental workplace regulation,
and birth control came into play, the demand for what we had called orphanages diminished. Ironically, many of those original orphanages have
found a new role as educators of special needs children. Yet even here there
is consistency. What are "special needs" students except those for which the
conventional education system cannot or will not provide an education?

In these stories, we get a glimpse of the dilemma of nonprofit management: Organizations originally created to change society themselves become resistant to change *unless managed otherwise*. Unless, in other words,
managers pay attention to their two bottom lines. And it is hard for most
managers to meet one bottom line, let alone two. The result, in part, is the
mild irony that nonprofit workers are often far readier to hold liberal views
of the need for change in the external society than they are ready to accept
changes in their own organization.

This resistance to change takes many forms, not all of them immediately
recognizable as such. Some varieties masquerade as a commitment to "the
community," or a fierce dedication to the client. This tendency to focus so
narrowly makes the financial manager's job less complicated and therefore
easier—a seductive prospect—but in the end it sells the mission short. Visiting Nurse Associations (VNAs), for example, could have and should have
dominated the home care field for much longer than they did, but when
they got stuck in turf battles with similar agencies it allowed proprietaries
to seize new markets and eventually gain a permanent strategic advantage.

The VNA example also illustrates the way society must deal with whole industries that are unresponsive to change in either of their bottom lines. Society will demand services, and if any group of agencies is unmoved by the demands of either of its own bottom lines, society will create new organizations. Unfortunately, since the existing agencies rarely go out of business, the new and the old must exist together, in some cases sharing resources that are too lean to be shared. The lesson is that discipline must come from the financial bottom line, although not necessarily from the financial types.

The alternative is for program services to carve an unusually tough bottom line of its own, a very difficult task. One way to do this is through a philosophy of entrepreneurial management. The essence of entrepreneurial management in the nonprofit sector is a commitment to creating opportunity for everyone associated with the organization, and a willingness to disregard conventional wisdom. A chief executive can accomplish the same thing through sheer force of will. But under normal circumstances, the likeliest source of influence over the organization is financial.

Nonprofit financial management carries a burden with a twist. It is not the sole nor even the most important reason for the organization's existence. If it stumbles over a sustained period of time, there is little hope that the organization will truly fulfill its mission. On the other hand, the corporation's success depends on its ability to steer program services away from fiscal irrelevance, and for this job it has to achieve and maintain internal clout. There really are two bottom lines in the nonprofit corporation, and finance owns the first one.

CHAPTER 3

Accounting as a Second Language—A Nine-Point Program

Accounting was probably the furthest thing from your mind while you taught your students, managed works of art, or advocated changes in public policy. But now that you have some management responsibilities, it suddenly looks like a good thing to learn. Problem is, you don't want to become a CPA-in-training just to be able to find your way around a financial management system. If so, then this chapter is for you.

Welcome to a special mini-course in accounting as a second language. Not a comprehensive treatment of the subject by any means, it aims to give you a rudimentary grasp of some key concepts that will get you out of financial management trouble—or help you avoid it in the first place. Taken together, these nine concepts will span most of the conceptual ground that ordinary accounting covers. Most important, they'll give you a decent grounding in accountingspeak.

THE ENTITY PRINCIPLE

Begin with the nonstartling revelation that accounting books and records are kept for entities. This simple idea may not seem like much of a revelation, but think about it for a moment. Entities are legal vehicles such as corporations and partnerships that are established to carry out specific business purposes. The difference between entities and individuals is deceptively simple. Entities involve many people with different levels of accountability to each other, while individuals are accountable to no one but themselves.

Individuals don't really need much in the way of record keeping except lists. Entities such as corporations need some pretty sophisticated ways of keeping track of their financial affairs, so that's where most of the financial action occurs.

MONEY MEASUREMENT

Here is another non-news flash. Accounting records only show transactions that can be measured in monetary terms. Again, not a terribly radical-sounding pronouncement. But again, there is much more to it than might at first be apparent.

Limiting accounting records to those things that can be measured in money means that accounting cannot reflect admittedly important things like the staff's dedication, board members' business connections, or the CEO's energy level. The money measurement principle unapologetically forces a tunnel-vision picture of the organization.

As a result of this tunnel vision, accounting systems occasionally have to do some fancy footwork. Most notably, they sometimes have to attribute a monetary value when it's difficult to quantify a transaction at all.

The best example of this need to attribute monetary amounts everywhere is in something called goodwill. When a for-profit concern buys another for an amount higher than the actual value of the assets, accountants need to explain the difference in monetary terms. This difference between purchase price and book value is called goodwill, which will be carried on the purchaser's books for many years to come. Like any asset, goodwill is subject to a loss in value. For instance, if large numbers of products manufactured by the purchased company turn out to be defective, the goodwill that the transaction produced may not be so good anymore. In that circumstance, it must be reduced—or "written off"—to reflect the reduced value. The guideline that requires the write-off is the conservatism principle, described below.

CONSERVATISM PRINCIPLE

"Recognize bad news when it is reasonably certain to happen, good news only when it occurs." That's the nutshell summary of the conservatism principle. Now let's back up and see how we arrived at that summary.

To be effective, accounting records need credibility. People must feel that they are getting the straight financial story. One way to be sure that the records are credible is by making sure they don't overpromise good news. That is the role of the conservatism principle.

The for-profit world is super-concerned about one thing: equity. That is a polite term for ownership share which, it is hoped, is another word for "Ticket to Easy Street." The more equity one has in a company, the better. Thus, accountants can be forgiven if they express the conservatism principle in terms of equity. Records follow the conservatism principle if they recognize decreases in equity when they are reasonably likely to occur, increases in equity only when they are a fact.

To put it in nonprofit terms, an increase in equity would come about from things like the sale of a building. The book value (see below for an unnecessarily complicated definition of this concept) of a building may be $300,000 and the estimated market value $500,000. But until the sale is complete, that increase in equity of $200,000 is not real. Indeed, until the sale is complete, one cannot know for sure whether there will be an increase in equity at all.

LOSSES (OR GAINS) EVEN IF YOU DON'T REALIZE IT

The booming 1990s officially ended in March 2000 when the "tech bubble" burst and Wall Street companies began suffering losses. In 2001 and 2002 many nonprofits began reporting overall losses, yet many of those entities had adequate revenue and expenses that were well under control. How could these organizations have lost money? The same questions arose again starting in late 2008 after the sharp downturn in the second half of that year.

The answer lies in the difference between operating revenue and the profits or losses created by investments. Sound nonprofits with sizeable, well-managed endowments nonetheless suffered declines in the value of their holdings. When the value of an investment portfolio is lower at the end of a year than it was at the end of the previous year, the amount of the loss is considered unrealized and it is deducted from the operating bottom line. In many cases the operating profit the organizations created was not enough to offset the unrealized losses on investments, which led to a net loss. This created a misleading (though technically correct) picture of financial difficulty in some of these organizations.

Take a common situation as an illustration of how the conservatism principle treats decreases in equity. Suppose my organization leases space on a multiyear basis instead of owning it. The landlord agrees to send us a bill each month so that we can pay it and use the paperwork to get reimbursed from our funding source. One month, after many months of working properly, the system fails and we don't get our rent bill. That may be an interesting peculiarity, but the conservatism principle says that we must still recognize the expense as due because we are more than reasonably sure that the monthly rent is an actual expense.

> Debits must always equal credits. The tool for proving that all transactions' debits equal the credits is called the *trial balance*.

THE COST CONCEPT

Balance sheets need a reliable standard by which to record the value of an asset. Market value might seem at first to be such a standard. But what truly is market value? Amateur economists will respond that the market value of an asset is nothing more than what someone will pay for it. True enough. But this simple formulation hides two sources of huge complexity. First, which someone? Different buyers will respond to the chance to purchase an asset in different ways, almost always with different prices.

More important, the market price of an asset will vary over time. In periods of volatility, local real estate markets can swing a few percentage points in either direction. The same building that was appraised at a certain value nine months ago may today be worth 10 percent more or 10 percent less just because of quirky and wholly unpredictable swings in the local market. To record real estate assets at market value—which, after all, would more accurately reflect their worth—would require either a large degree of arbitrariness or an in-house appraiser doing the same appraisal monthly. It is for this reason, and a host of others, that assets are recorded at their cost of acquisition on the balance sheet.

GAAP TO BE REPLACED BY IFRS?

For years, American accounting has been according to GAAP—generally accepted accounting principles. In the future you may need to learn a new acronym—IFRS, or international financial reporting standards. In late 2008, the Securities and Exchange Commission announced that it was beginning a process designed to move publicly held companies away from the American GAAP standard to IFRS. The latter are principles-based, but they also demand specific treatments in many situations. The details of the change, including the final timeline, have yet to be approved. But don't panic yet. The initial timetable doesn't call for the smallest of publicly held companies to adopt IFRS until 2016. Any change, if it happens at all, won't likely affect nonprofit organizations until well into the next decade. Exactly how IFRS will—or will not—affect nonprofits will not be clear for a while.

The term *acquisition cost* is so simple that it's quite potent. The rule of thumb in determining the elements of acquisition cost is that anything that went into the acquisition of the property can end up being folded into the book value of the property. That means that if you are building a site for that new program, not only are the land costs included in the eventual book value but so are such easy-to-overlook things as architects' fees,

HOW TO TAKE ADVANTAGE OF A GAP BETWEEN COST AND MARKET VALUE

In Boston, the area around the statehouse known as Beacon Hill has become an increasingly toney place to live and work over the decades. Two different nonprofits originally purchased their office buildings many years ago when the area was much less desirable. Then, in the real estate boom of the late 1990s, they cashed in. Selling their buildings to developers at the height of the market, they were able to secure nicer spaces in areas of town closer to their natural client base—and pocket some leftover money. Why? Because of the cost concept, the book values of the buildings were much less than the value the market would bear. Talk about untapped wealth!

permits, the cost of demolition, landscaping, and many other items. The sum of these costs becomes the book value.

The cost concept only covers the front end of the transaction. Since everyone knows that large assets such as buildings don't stay unchanged once they are acquired, accountants need a way to reflect the fact that assets get gradually used up. This is the role of depreciation. In simple terms, depreciation starts with the assumption that a fraction of the asset gets "used up" (or expensed) each month. For nonprofits, depreciation is usually calculated by dividing the book value of the asset (less any anticipated end-of-its-life value) by the total number of months in the useful life of the category of asset. So if an asset is expected to last 20 years and cost $240,000, its monthly depreciation charge will be $1,000, or $240,000/ (20 years × 12 months).

THE MATERIALITY PRINCIPLE

Believe it or not, accountants don't necessarily like to dwell on details. For example, auditors know that some transactions are so small they wouldn't make a bit of difference in the overall financial picture no matter how they

HOW DEPRECIATION SHELTERS CASH

Depreciation is a noncash expense, which means that you don't have to write a monthly check to Depreciation, Inc. If your funding sources allow you to charge depreciation as a bona fide expense (and they should!), then by adding a depreciation charge to your books and records, you are building in a little extra cash each month. In the end, however, the theory is that that extra cash you get now should accumulate until it is time to purchase a replacement asset, when the cycle starts all over again.

The game is a bit more serious for for-profits. Why? Because for-profits are taxed on the basis of profit. Depreciation expense reduces profit, and reduced profit means reduced taxes. So, for-profits tend to like depreciation. A lot! Over time, they have figured out formulas and rationales for accelerating depreciation. This is why Washington lobbyists and some congresspeople wax poetic about accelerated depreciation schedules. Depreciation shelters cash *and* reduces taxes.

are treated. They know that it's better to concentrate their time and energy on the transactions that really matter. This is the source of what is called the materiality principle.

Auditors are the classic users of the materiality principle. Before starting an audit they establish a threshold of materiality for each organization they audit. It might be $10,000 in a small organization, or $200,000 in a very large one. They feel so strongly about the concept that they even refer to it in their opinion letters. Why? Because missposted transactions below a certain amount won't make any difference to a reasonable person reading the financial report. In fact, the previous sentence was a sneaky definition of the materiality principle.

There are two other groups that routinely use the materiality principle to determine their scope of effort. Internal financial people, especially those concerned with financial reporting, will have a different and probably much lower threshold of materiality. They are chiefly accountable to their fellow managers, and to mistakenly attribute a large expense to Department D instead of Department E will anger two department heads— Department Head D when the mistake is made and Department Head E when it's corrected at some later time after Department Head E has already committed the money that she thought she had. That's sure to put a damper on conversation at the office Christmas party, so the financial person needs to have a much lower threshold of materiality than the auditors do.

A third party with a distinctly different idea of materiality is the government auditor. Next time you come across a media story about waste, fraud, or abuse in some level of government, do a quick calculation. Divide the amount in question by what you would guess the total revenue of that level of government would be. Unless you're talking about a million dollar expense in a town of five hundred people, the amount alleged to have been wasted will almost certainly not be material to that unit of government. That is because government auditors usually have a threshold of zero: *anything questionable* is fair game for a government auditor. This is why some governmental audit reports will point out the $35 bottle of champagne purchased for the associate director's bon voyage party. Is this fair? Is it a good use of taxpayer's dollars to focus on such small amounts? You be the judge. Just hope no one saw you at the party.

GOING CONCERN

Assume permanence. That is what accountants and auditors like to do. It seems so self-evident that it's barely worth talking about, but the reality is that in the for-profit world the majority of new corporations go out of business within five or six years. With this kind of impermanence, it's no wonder that consumers of financial statements need to know whether the entity they are reading about is, in the opinion of its auditors, on the verge of oblivion.

✕◆   RED FLAG   ✕◆

THE GOING CONCERN OPINION

If you ever read an opinion letter and find a reference to a general concern that the entity may not survive beyond the next 12 months, let it be a red-flag event. This is a qualified opinion, and it means that the auditors have seen conditions that they believe may very well result in the organization's extinction before the next fiscal year begins.

The going concern assumption is one of those bedrock principles that lets you presume the entity about which you are reading will last for at least the next 12 months. If the auditors have reason to think that this is not the case, they must explicitly state their concern. They do this by inserting a statement, usually in the third or fourth paragraph of the opinion letter, to the effect that the statements have been prepared assuming the entity will continue as a going concern but that there is reason to think this may not happen. No reference to "going concern" anywhere in the opinion letter? Then you can take it for granted that those most in a position to know feel the organization will be around for a while.

GOING CONCERN OPINION NOT LIGHTLY GIVEN

No one likes to be a doomsayer, especially an organization's own auditors, who, understandably, would rather not bite the hand that pays them. It tends to chill the relationship, especially if it turns out to be premature, so the going concern opinion is not lightly given. Take it as the organizational equivalent of a fire alarm, and act accordingly.

DUAL ASPECT

This is the big one. Accounting is pretty cleverly designed, and this idea is at the base of a lot of that cleverness. Think of this principle as being like a law of Accounting Thermodynamics—every accounting transaction is composed of two exactly offsetting sets of changes to the books. One example: If I buy a building for $100,000 and pay for it in cash, I have *reduced* my cash account by $100,000—but I've *increased* my fixed asset account by the same $100,000. Two offsetting changes to the books.

SOFTWARE CAN BE HORIZONTAL OR VERTICAL

When software developers decide to write a program, they must first make a fundamental choice. If they plan to write software, which can be expected to appeal to a wide variety of buyers regardless of their industry, they are said to be attempting to reach a horizontal market. If they plan to write specialized software that will only appeal to buyers in a particular industry, they are said to be attempting to reach a vertical market. Spreadsheets and word processing programs are horizontal market software applications. Beauty parlor accounting software is a vertical application.

The choice they make is highly subject to the laws of economics. Horizontal software developers can reasonably plan to sell large numbers of their package, and so the cost of each package can be lower. By contrast, vertical software developers know that they will only get a share of a finite market, so they must price the software high enough to make a profit at the range of copies they expect to sell.

The consumer's trade-off, then, goes like this: low price, low functionality for their industry; high price, high functionality for their industry.

This is why off-the-shelf commercial accounting packages carry an attractive price tag but don't necessarily adapt well to the nonprofit sector. It's also why the vertical application you bought does exactly what you want it to do but carries a painfully high price tag.

An easy choice? No, but the laws of supply and demand never make things easy for you.

Another example of the dual aspect nature of accounting is the balance sheet itself. On the one side you have assets, the things of value that a corporation owns. On the other side you have liabilities, which are the claims against the corporation, and net assets, which represent the cumulative "net worth" of the corporation over time. Assets will always equal liabilities plus net assets, which has a lot to do with why they call it a balance sheet.

Accounting is so thoroughly based on the concept of balance that it pretty much grinds to a halt when it goes out of balance. If the bookkeeper entering the transaction described above forgot to increase the fixed asset account by $100,000, his accounting software would make a little "ding" or some other annoying sound and refuse to do anything else until the transaction was put back in balance. Don't you feel centered just thinking about it?

Realization Principle

This one will keep you out of a lot of trouble if you really understand it and act on it. The concept is disarmingly simple. It tells you that if you perform services that produce revenue, that revenue must be attributed to the time period in which the services were performed. So if your historical society runs five tours to five different places in June, the last month of your fiscal year, the realization principle requires you to show that revenue as having been earned in June, not July. Which means that if you are running a large

BUT CAN'T I DO IT JUST THIS ONCE? (I SAID NO AND I MEANT IT!)

What happens if you actually try to drag a big chunk of revenue from this June into July? Will the auditors catch it and object? Actually, your transaction massage shouldn't even survive long enough to catch the auditors' eye. Your own accountant should catch on and politely decline to participate. Is this being overly reliant on accountants' honesty? No, because the nature of bookkeeping is that it is so organically constructed that such a flagrantly unconventional gambit could make a mess of the accounting records, and your accountant would have to work harder to fix it all up again. So fear of accounting messes will win out even if morality wavers.

surplus this year but are a bit worried about next year's prospects and would like to push that revenue into July—too bad. This guideline gives financial records a certain integrity, since it ensures that managers and internal accountants must play by the same rules when reporting how the money has rolled in.

MATCHING PRINCIPLE

The other half of the realization principle is the matching principle. Whereas realization deals with revenue, matching deals with expenses. What this one says is that expenses associated with generating revenue ought to show up in the same time period as the revenue associated with delivering the services. Once again we have a deceptively simple-sounding concept that packs a real punch. In practice, it means that you can't soften this year's deficit by pretending some expenses really occurred next year.

REVENUE IS NOT THE SAME THING AS CASH

Just because you earned the revenue doesn't mean you got the cash. The realization and matching principles are accrual-based accounting concepts. If the cash didn't come in at the time the revenue was earned, it gets carried as an account receivable.

CHAPTER 4

Assets Are for Boards, Activities Are for Managers

One of the constant requirements of nonprofit management is to strike the correct balance between boards of directors and management in financial matters. The purpose of this chapter is to suggest a way to do this so that members of each group don't run into each other trying to do their jobs or, worse, leave something uncovered because each thought the other was going to handle it.

We suggest a simple guideline for all those pesky questions about roles and responsibilities: *Assets are for boards, activities are for managers*. To say it another way, boards of directors need to focus primarily on the balance sheet, while managers need to focus on profits and losses (note that the technical terms for these two reports are the "statement of financial position" and the "statement of activities," respectively).

Here's why. In legal and moral terms, the enduring assets and liabilities of an organization are the board of directors' responsibility. Their fiduciary duty is an explicit charge to oversee these things of value wisely. By contrast, the day-to-day affairs of procuring revenue and incurring costs are the province of managers. This conceptual razor slices the world of nonprofit accountability into two neat pieces that can be easily understood by everyone, from financial wizards to the numbers-challenged.

An important nuance here is that executives, as distinct from managers, share leadership responsibilities with the board. Executives must be firmly rooted in the board's asset work while being knowledgeable about the activities of their managers. The chief distinction between board member

EXHIBIT 4.1　PROPER AREAS OF FORM

Boards	Managers
Assets	Activities
Long-term focus	Short-term focus
Concepts	Details
Safeguard and grow	Produce and control

and executive in this regard is that there are usually more board members than top executives, but the executives are full-time.

Exhibit 4.1 summarizes some of the reasons why the assets/activities distinction works. The first element is related to the appropriate time frame for the two groups. Boards of directors, including executives, have responsibility for the long-term future of their organization. They are at the heart of the entity's leadership, and so they truly have to have a frame of reference measured in years if not decades. If the board of directors and their hired executives don't take a long-term view, who else in the organization will?

Program managers are too busy with the financial implications of things that have to be done now, tomorrow, and next week to worry about what will occur in the long run. Managers' focus (remember, for these purposes we're excluding executives from the management ranks) is properly on short-term execution. They constantly have to find the best balance between anticipating financial events and reacting to them, because if they spend too much time chin-stroking about what might happen, events will pass them by. And if they spend too much time reacting to things that have already occurred, they won't have time or energy for anticipating the future.

All of this explains why boards meet a few times each year, while managers meet frequently.

CONCEPTS VERSUS DETAILS

Another element of the difference between board and management is that boards need to operate in the conceptual sphere, while managers live in a world of details. This is consistent with the assets/activities differentiation, and it suggests what should be different about their approaches. Boards need to make their financial decisions based on concepts and strategy, while managers must make theirs based on a multiplicity of often conflicting details.

Dealing with assets is different from carrying out activities. The board typically safeguards the organization's assets and, it is hoped, grows them. This is why boards of directors must make decisions about the purchase and upkeep of large assets such as buildings and major pieces of equipment (should we invest in a bus or a building?). It is why the board should be charged with decisions about how to invest excess funds, and whether and how much of the resulting interest income should be used for managers' activities. In turn, managers have to produce revenues in the short term (think fund-raising, grant proposals, and fees for service), and they have to control the expenditures associated with them.

BOARDS INVEST, MANAGERS SPEND

This delineation of financial duties flows naturally from the assets/activities differentiation. Boards invest assets entrusted to them, while managers spend funds allocated to them. These are fundamentally different actions that have consequences for how each group sees the organization. Boards need to be primarily concerned with things of inherent value, and when one is given responsibility for things of inherent value, there is a natural tendency toward being conservative with them.

At their best, boards make investment decisions with the very long-term view in mind. One university board, for example, used a sliver of its institutional endowment to buy an operating railway yard. Why? The board knew that the tangled complex of railroad lines and spurs that existed a few hundred yards from the main campus was not feasible in that location in the long run. They knew that current economic forces were driving railway commerce from their neighborhood to the outlying suburbs, and that someday in the foreseeable future when the rail yard inevitably relocated, that presently ugly patch of land would become a beautiful new campus annex.

Managers, in contrast, are primarily occupied with costs. Unencumbered by items on the balance sheet, they see mostly things like needs and crises and opportunities to improve, all of which cost money. Both are legitimate perspectives, but the board's view is likely to triumph over time.

IF IT HAS TO BE DECIDED TODAY, IT'S PROBABLY THE WRONG QUESTION

A corollary to the invest/spend differentiation is that if a board ever encounters a major financial question that must be answered right now, it's either the wrong kind of question to come before the board or it's the right kind of question that was raised too late.

Big decisions of the kind boards must make have their own life cycles. Acquiring a building, trying to collect on a large outstanding pledge by an easy-to-anger donor, or changing investment policies are not suitable topics for 10-minute board discussions in most mission-based organizations. Nor are they usually discussions that have a narrow time frame for execution. These are important enough matters that they must be granted the proper time and background for due consideration. Making them into governance fire drills means treating them like short-term management matters.

BOARDS OWN THE CONTROLS, MANAGERS IMPLEMENT THEM

One of the changes demanded by the Sarbanes-Oxley law in publicly held companies that has begun creeping into the mission-based sector is that the responsibility for internal controls should be lodged with the board of directors. The thinking is classic assets/activities differentiation—those at the highest levels of the organization must see to it that assets are protected, while those at the activity level must develop and run the systems that accomplish this objective.

Arguably, this moves boards closer to the activities level since it's hard to be accountable for something without knowing about it in some depth. In a broad sense that was likely intentional, although in practice boards have little incentive to get deeply involved in the mechanics of the control systems.

The next few chapters go more deeply into the technical financial documents that board members and managers must use to do their respective jobs. Of necessity, this will be a narrowly focused discussion. But keep in mind a simple way to see all this in a larger framework that makes both conceptual and operating sense for both parties: Assets are for boards, activities are for managers.

CHAPTER 5

Balance Sheets:
How They Get That Way

More than any other single financial report, the balance sheet is a window into the fiscal heart of the nonprofit corporation. In one concise accumulation of numbers, the balance sheet shows an impressive array of data about the results of virtually every fiscal policy the organization has ever pursued. Unfortunately, its trove of information is often concealed to the untrained eye. In this chapter, we scrape some of the frost off that window and help the ordinary observer make sense of what's inside. 👆

The balance sheet is an ingenious device. On one side it places all the things of value of an organization, its *assets*. On the other side it places the claims of outsiders against those resources, otherwise known as *liabilities*. Whatever is left over on that side is considered equity or, in the nonprofit world, net assets (formerly fund balance). This leftover is essentially a form of ownership claim against the assets. Adding up the assets gives you exactly the same amount as the sum of the liabilities and equities. Now you know why they call it a balance sheet.

The rest of this chapter will explain all the balance sheet categories and describe how they behave. The numbers next to the line item name refer to the lines on the IRS Form 990. In all cases the old 990 line item number comes first in parentheses followed by the new number. Exhibit 5.7 and 5.8 (see end of this chapter) shows both the new and the old IRS 990 forms for an imaginary nonprofit organization, the Committee to Clean Up Amigosville (CCUA), that we will use in this and subsequent chapters to

EXHIBIT 5.1   FORM 990 VERSUS THE AUDIT: SUMMARY OF
              STRENGTHS

IRS Form 990	Audited Financial Statements
Standard definitions	Opinion letter is available
	Additional schedules
	Auditor judgments
Numbered format	Footnotes
Numerous types of governance, compensation, and leadership information (new 990 only)	Likely be more reliable and accurate than the 990, which is just for information purposes
Significant qualitative information not driven by accounting or financial practices	Will give more information on subsidiaries, especially taxable subsidiaries
Entities are considered on their own terms for tax purposes, apart from parent corporations	Controlled subsidiaries get rolled up (consolidated) into the parent, thereby giving a better view of the big picture

illustrate various points. We show excerpts from both the old and new versions in order to illustrate the contrasts between the two IRS approaches.

We have chosen to use the IRS Form 990 as the standard form for analyzing financial statements, rather than the auditor's report because, unlike the 990, auditors have some latitude in designing their financial reports. By contrast, the federal form is pretty rigid, a virtue when one is looking for standardization. It's not perfect, but for our purposes it works fairly well. But the two reports are not mutually exclusive. For a thorough financial analysis it is always best to look at both the 990 and the same year's audited financial statements. Exhibit 5.1 shows the advantages of each

CURRENT ASSETS

Although they are not labeled as such on the IRS 990, current assets are usually explicitly grouped as a multiple item category on audited statements. Current assets are defined as assets that could reasonably be expected to be turned into cash or consumed within a year. In certain for-profit businesses, the time frame for current assets will be longer because the natural business cycle is longer (a distillery, for instance), but that is not much of an issue for nonprofits.

Cash—Non-Interest-Bearing (45) 1

Easy to understand—cash is the green and silver stuff. Mainly, however, cash is what's in the checkbook after it is fully reconciled. This is the cash account you want to have the least money in, because it isn't earning you anything—it's lazy money, it's the kind that just hangs out all day playing video games and asking what time you'll finish preparing dinner.

Savings and Temporary Cash Investments (46) 2

Dollars parked somewhere for a short time. Certificates of deposit are a good example, as are money market funds, CDs, and United States Treasury bills. They're often called cash equivalents. Hey, at least these dollars are earning something.

Accounts Receivable (47c) 4

Some users of nonprofit organizations receive a service and then get billed for it. Those bills are official notices of money due the nonprofit. As such, they are worth something to the organization. Line 47 shows the total of all bills issued but not yet collected, called accounts receivable, or simply A/R.

ACCOUNT RECEIVABLE? OR FOND WISH?

Deadbeats are a reality of virtually all consumer-oriented businesses. One of the differences between for-profit organizations and nonprofits is in the matter of invoices issued for services delivered. When a nonprofit sends out an invoice for services delivered, it regards it as evidence of a near-sacred promise to pay. For-profits are more likely to see it as a fond wish.

Why? Most nonprofits deal with upstanding, highly accountable groups like foundations, governments, and other nonprofits. For-profits dealing intensively in the consumer industries recognize that not everyone is going to approach a business relationship with the same high morals and finely tuned sense of accountability.

Allowance for Doubtful Accounts (47b) no number

Even within organizations having good credit policies to prevent the delivery of services to customers who may not have the ability to pay, ultimately it may not be reasonable to expect all receivables to be collected. The amount of outstanding bills in this category is estimated in some sensible way by management and gets subtracted from the overall total of accounts receivable (A/R). This product is called the net accounts receivable and is entered in column B. Those accounts that never materialize at all are called bad debts (note: the new form provides no explicit allowance for doubtful accounts, expecting that this amount will instead be deducted from the total of all accounts receiveable and the "net" amount entered in line 4, as noted above).

Pledges Receivable (48a) 3

Same principle as accounts receivable, except that these are promises by outsiders to make donations to the nonprofit that have not actually materialized yet. A 1993 statement by the Financial Accounting Standards Board (FASB) requires nonprofits to recognize any unconditional pledge as an asset during the year in which it was made, no matter when the actual cash is received.

Grants Receivable (49) 3 [combined with line above]

Ditto, except that since pledges are made by individuals and grants by foundations, corporations, and government agencies, the latter usually don't produce many doubtful accounts.

Receivables Due from Current and Former Officers . . . (50a) 5

Occasionally—*very* occasionally, one hopes—nonprofits find it necessary to lend money to officers and directors. Since this kind of transaction depletes the resources available for the charitable mission, it can raise serious questions about the officers' execution of their fiduciary duties.

Receivables Due from Other Disqualified Persons . . . (50b) 6

This line is essentially the same as the one above, except that it refers to those insiders receiving loans who are not current or former officers of the entity.

Other Notes and Loans Receivable (51c) 7

Same principle as above, except that these are loans made to outsiders. Note the expectation that some of them will turn out to be doubtful in the same way as certain accounts receivable will be doubtful.

Inventories (52) 8

Only applicable in certain instances in the nonprofit world, inventories are the accumulation of raw materials, supplies, and the like that are waiting to be used in delivering services or making a product.

Prepaid Expenses and Deferred Charges (53) 9

These are, for the most part, benefits or expenses that have already been paid for and will be realized by the organization at some point in the future. Anyone who has ever paid a car insurance bill for a full year ahead of time understands a prepaid expense and therefore an asset. Often this category includes things like the unused portions of the value of fully paid insurance policies that cross fiscal years.

Noncurrent Assets

Assets in this category are harder to turn into cold cash on short notice. They are also nice assets to have, since they tend to be the kind that stick around for a long time.

Investments (54a+b) 11–13

For those groups lucky enough to have them, securities are debt or equity financial instruments (stocks, for example) that produce income and can be sold to raise cash. When nonprofit corporations have a substantial endowment, this is usually how it's held. Why would we consider securities to be a noncurrent asset if they can be sold at any time? In a nutshell, one would often not want to sell a security at any given moment, especially if it has declined in value or if it would be reasonable to expect it to gain value in the coming months. In that case it makes more sense to hold it until its value comes back. So it's not that one cannot turn a security into cash, because one can do that with a telephone call. Smart business practices often argue against it, so we regard securities as a noncurrent asset.

Investments Held as Land, Buildings, and Equipment (55c) [combined with (57c) 10 below]

Self-explanatory, except that these items are normally shown at the cost of acquiring them (minus the appropriate depreciation), not at the price they would fetch on the open market. This is usually a big difference. These properties, unlike the ones on line 57, are held chiefly for investment purposes, not operations.

Other Investments (56)

It's perfectly legal for nonprofit organizations to make investments in for-profit companies. It may even be smart although that depends more on the investment acumen of the nonprofit's managers than on anything related to its tax status. Increasingly, universities, research outfits, and others make these types of investments. Line 56 is a bit different from line 54 in that it usually indicates an investment in nonpublicly traded financial instruments.

ENDOWMENT? NO SUCH THING

You may be wondering why there is no line item called "endowment." That's because for accounting types there is no such thing. An "endowment" is just a normal person's term for what can be found on the balance sheet as "investments" and "land, buildings and equipment." The difference is that financialistas are more interested in the forms in which an endowment is held, not how much it totals.

Land, Buildings, and Equipment (57c) 10c

These are the operational holdings, distinct from the investment holdings of line 55. The new 990 does not make this distinction.

Intangible Assets (NA) 14

A new line referring to assets that do not fit neatly into one of the above categories because of their non-physical nature. Intellectual property such as patents or protected methods would be examples of this type of asset.

Other Assets (NA) 15

Research description and place accordingly.

CURRENT LIABILITIES

Like their counterparts on the asset side, current liabilities are obligations the corporation owes within the next year. These are the most immediate claims against the assets held by outsiders.

Accounts Payable and Accrued Expenses (60) 17

Just as there are receivables that can be expected to be converted to cash, so there are bills owed that will have to be paid within the same time frame.

Grants Payable (61) 18

For grant-making organizations, these payables were promised as of the date of the financial statements (or the tax return), but had not yet been disbursed.

Deferred Revenue (62) 19

Sometimes an organization gets money explicitly intended for use after the end of the fiscal year. Three-year memberships, for instance, still have two years' worth of value left after the first year, so a portion of them is considered a liability and therefore not rightfully the nonprofit's at this point.

NONCURRENT LIABILITIES

Noncurrent liabilities are less pressing claims against the assets.

Tax-Exempt Bond Liabilities (64a) 20

One of the distinct benefits of being a nonprofit public charity is that an organization can issue bonds whose holders receive favorable tax treatment and which therefore carry lower interest rates (often about 1.25 points less).

Escrow Account Liability (NA) 21

Financing mechanisms can require a nonprofit to put funds in escrow temporarily. While the funds are an asset, they are also a liability, and that is the function of this line.

Loans from Officers and Directors (63) 22

The flip side of the transactions described in line 50.

Mortgages and Other Notes Payable (64b) 23, 24

Here is where to put all the long-term debt incurred in order to renovate that day care center or buy that headquarters building. The new form splits this category into secured and unsecured instruments.

Other Liabilities (NA) 25

Research description and place accordingly.

Net Assets (67–73) 27–29

This is where it gets counterintuitive. First there's the matter of terminology. Like the word *profit*, the term *net worth* in a nonprofit context has perhaps been considered too jarring for the average set of ears, so we have developed euphemisms like *net assets*. No matter, it's the same thing.

Then there's the question of how the number gets calculated. Simple. If everything else has been accounted for and assets exceed liabilities, the amount it takes to get the two numbers identical is the net assets. When liabilities exceed assets, net assets become negative and one has then arrived at what a diplomat might call an extremely worrisome deficit position that may be the prelude to bankruptcy. Big trouble, in short.

What are net assets? In essence, net assets are nothing more than the accumulation of surpluses the corporation achieved since its beginning.

Extraordinary losses or gains aside, net assets are the cumulative sum of all the year-end pluses or minuses since the organization started out in its current form. If the profits outweigh the losses, the net assets will be positive; otherwise, net assets are negative and the fat lady has finished singing.

Now to completely confuse the matter. Managers will quickly pick up on the fact that one needs healthy net assets to remain a viable entity. Some who have studied the question briefly may even speak with pride about the size of the net assets they maintain. All in all, one gets the clear impression of net assets as a positive thing, which is true, in the context of financial management. But some go on from there to assume that it's a positive thing in the same way that assets are positive things.

Net assets are a form of claim against the assets of the nonprofit. Technically it's not the same as a liability, but for these purposes, it behaves similarly.

To put the question in a different light, think about who holds that claim. Let's start with a for-profit context. In a small business, the net assets equivalent would be "owner's equity" or "net worth." There the issue is much clearer. If the entity goes out of business and after final wrap-up the assets actually do exceed the liabilities, the owner walks away with the equity.

In the nonprofit public charity world there can be no "owners" in the legal sense even though the accounting operates the same way. So the surrogate "owner" of a nonprofit's equity is . . . society. Seems fair. After all, society via its government has voluntarily agreed to refrain from taxing the profits made by this type of corporation with the expectation that it will do some public good in return.

The way this "ownership" gets operationalized is usually through the organization's legal incorporation papers that state something to the effect that if the corporation ever goes out of business any leftover assets will be distributed to similar groups. In practice this is little more than a theoretical nicety, if only because relatively few nonprofits ever actually go out of business. Also, the practical workings of a nonprofit dissolution tend to be overseen by a state official such as the attorney general and unless a case is highly visible the harried executive branch of state government tends to focus its energies elsewhere. Still, it's a nice metaphor. On the positive side, it embodies the best of a nonprofit's mission to serve the public. On the negative, it reminds us that there is at least theoretical accountability for the privileges of nonprofit status.

Net assets is usually the hardest concept on the balance sheet to understand. This is probably because about every other item on the balance sheet can be traced to one or more pieces of paper in the accounting system. Cash deposits are documented in bank records, buildings have deeds, long-term liabilities have borrowing agreements. Net assets, on the other hand, is an abstraction. It exists nowhere except on the financial statements, and it carries its greatest meaning in combination with some other quantity, as we will see in Chapter 6. All things considered, it is not an instinctively easy idea.

Capital Stock, Paid-in Surplus, Retained Earnings (70–72) 30–32

A miscellaneous category for relatively rare holdings

MAKING THE BALANCE SHEET DANCE

It's time now to see how a balance sheet behaves. Happily, it turns out to be an entirely predictable organism, not to mention a clever one. Take the simplified balance sheet in Exhibit 5.2 as a starting point. Remember that whatever we do to one side of the ledger has to be balanced completely with an equivalent cumulative change on the other side.

Assume for a moment that we want to buy another set of buildings for $1 million, putting down half of that amount and financing the other half.

EXHIBIT 5.2   SAMPLE BALANCE SHEET

BALANCE SHEET AS OF 12/31/02 (000s)

Assets		Liabilities and Fund Balance	
Cash	$6,500	Accounts payable	$5,000
Accounts receivable	4,500	Mortgages	8,000
Land, buildings, & equipment	9,000	Other liabilities	2,000
		Net assets	5,000
		Total liabilities and	
Total assets	$20,000	fund balance	$20,000

EXHIBIT 5.3   SAMPLE BALANCE SHEET WITH PURCHASE
               OF BUILDING

BALANCE SHEET AS OF 12/31/02 (000s)

Assets		Liabilities and Fund Balance	
Cash	$6,000	Accounts payable	$5,000
Accounts receivable	4,500	Mortgages	8,500
Land, buildings, & equipment	10,000	Other liabilities	2,000
		Net assets	5,000
		Total liabilities and	
Total assets	$20,500	fund balance	$20,500

The transaction adds $1 million to the Land, Buildings, and Equipment account (call it LBE if you want to sound casually knowledgeable) and subtracts $500,000 from the cash account. Offsetting these are an increase of $500,000 in mortgage indebtedness as shown in Exhibit 5.3 (changed entries are in bold).

With a stroke of the pen and the help of financing, we have increased our asset base by half a million dollars. Notice that net assets did not increase because this was a financing transaction as opposed to a transaction that affected operations. The other half million simply transferred its place of residence from the cash account down to the LBE account when it was used as the down payment.

To go in a completely different direction, let's assume we have a nervous controller who doesn't like having bills sit around. She takes half of the available cash and pays off every bill she can find, leaving only a few that were hiding in the pipeline during her moment of madness. Starting with the original balance sheet, the new one looks like Exhibit 5.4.

Now let's go back to the original balance sheet and sprinkle efficiency dust over the billing system, causing $2 million of those original accounts receivable to be collected and not replaced. Watch the cash account balloon correspondingly in Exhibit 5.5.

Notice what doesn't change—everything else. Since improving the efficiency of the billing system meant getting the money owed to the organization sooner, that money went straight to the cash account. In effect, management transformed the form of the asset from one type (receivables)

EXHIBIT 5.4   SAMPLE BALANCE SHEET WITH PAID BILLS

BALANCE SHEET AS OF 12/31/02 (000s)

Assets		Liabilities and Fund Balance	
Cash	$3,250	Accounts payable	$1,750
Accounts receivable	4,500	Mortgages	8,000
Land, buildings, & equipment	9,000	Other liabilities	2,000
		Net assets	5,000
		Total liabilities and	
Total assets	$16,750	fund balance	$16,750

to another (cash). Since the measured levels of all assets didn't change a bit, there was no need to do anything else to the other (liabilities) side of the balance sheet.

Finally, consider one way to make net assets swell. Imagine that the agency made a profit of $500,000 last year, and that, for the sake of simplicity, the final amounts of all balance sheet accounts stayed unchanged. That being the case, if revenue was $500,000 greater than expenses, it could only mean that the cash account increased by that number. Something else has to increase on the liability side by the same amount and, since all other things are assumed to be unchanged, it's net assets that will increase, as shown in Exhibit 5.6.

EXHIBIT 5.5   SAMPLE BALANCE SHEET WITH MORE
COLLECTED FUNDS

BALANCE SHEET AS OF 12/31/02 (000s)

Assets		Liabilities and Fund Balance	
Cash	$8,500	Accounts payable	$5,000
Accounts receivable	2,500	Mortgages	8,000
Land, buildings, & equipment	9,000	Other liabilities	2,000
		Net assets	5,000
		Total liabilities and	
Total assets	$20,000	fund balance	$20,000

EXHIBIT 5.6   **SAMPLE BALANCE SHEET SHOWING THE EFFECT OF A PROFIT**

BALANCE SHEET AS OF 12/31/02 (000s)

Assets		Liabilities and Fund Balance	
Cash	$7,000	Accounts payable	$5,000
Accounts receivable	4,500	Mortgages	8,000
Land, buildings, & equipment	9,000	Other liabilities	2,000
		Net assets	5,500
		Total liabilities and	
Total assets	$20,500	fund balance	$20,500

TRANSPARENCY, THY NAME IS IRS FORM 990

When the history of transparency in the nonprofit public charity sector is written, it will be really boring except for the part about the new IRS Form 990. For many years the old IRS Form 990, a tax return required of public charities and other types of nonprofits, was a fiscal year-end ritual requiring the posting of virtually the entire quantitative contents of the audited financial statement, plus a good deal of additional information. Beginning in the late 1990s, the Web site Guidestar.org in collaboration with the IRS took on the massive task of digitizing all of the filed 990s and posting them for free public access.

Then the world changed. Enron collapsed, and suddenly stories about accounting were front-page news. A muted but steady drumbeat of media stories about the nonprofit sector's own versions of Enron that actually pre-dated the famous scandal eventually echoed in the ears of Washington policymakers. Somewhere deep in the underpolished hallways of the federal government the bureaucratic equivalent of a double-take was going on. Wait. The Form 990 is pretty good, but it's mostly about . . . numbers. And numbers don't tell the whole story. They don't tell about mission or governance or important corporate relationships or compensation policies for top executives. Eventually that double-take grew into a bona fide boomlet of energy, and a new Form 990 was born.

Seldom does a bureaucratic form shape the future. But when the Internal Revenue Service first released its new Form 990 it sent an unmistakable message about what it now considers most important for nonprofit public charities. That message can be summed up in three words: leadership, governance, and purpose.

While the form has only begun to be used as of this writing, it does seem safe to say that it will change many practices of many nonprofit organizations. To understand why, one need only put the old form 990 side-by-side against the new one and analyze the differences, as we do in Exhibit 5.1. The old form was truly a tax form, exactly as its lineage implied. Up-front information included numbers that would have been drawn directly from the audited financial statement such as types of revenue, total expenses, and net assets.

On the second page came the call for expenses and a thumbnail sketch of what the programs and services were all about. The balance sheet came next, and then some largely non-financial questions about an eclectic mix of subjects. In effect, the first three pages were a re-arranging and selective use of data from the audited financial statements. The underlying message was subtle but strong: Give us the numbers first and the soft stuff second, if at all.

The difference in the new form starts with the first line, which in the old form asks for total contributions. The new draft's first line asks for the mission. Although it's probably accidental, this change is a good test for any nonprofit manager because if you can't describe your organization's mission in the two lines provided it's time to create a new one. And in case you miss the point, the heading of the first ten lines is "Activities and Governance."

SWEEPING CHANGE

The magnitude of the change is sweeping. Those accustomed to the old form and its subtle messages ("tell us about the money!" the first page used to scream) will need to do some adjusting. By the time you've answered ten questions the subjects have ranged from mission to activities to unrelated business operations to executive and trustee compensation and their total number (including "independent" trustees, a term more familiar to the for-profit sector).

These first questions are just a hint of what's to come. The second page is entirely devoted to compensation received by executives, board members, and independent contractors. Alumni of these ranks get drawn in as well, since the questions specifically ask for data about people formerly in one of these positions. Smartly, it also asks for background information on the same topic from related entities. Then it goes on to ask Sarbanes-Oxley-inspired questions about whistleblower and records retention policies, board minutes, audit policies, collections of artwork, sponsorship of donor advised funds, and a whole range of other questions. Not until page 5 does it get around to asking the old front-page questions about revenue.

You get the picture. This form promises to dramatically alter what non-profits report and how they report it. To describe the changes succinctly, streetsmart CEOs will be paying a lot more attention to their organization's Form 990 than in the past. The relatively innocuous end-of-the-year ritual in financial reporting will become a whole-organization undertaking.

WHAT TO DO

The IRS suggests that the new form should not cause most organizations to experience a "change in burden." This seems a dubious proposition for many reasons, but in any case the nature of the existing burden will change for all. For those with complicated compensation practices and related corporate structures the IRS acknowledges that the burden may increase.

For small and/or relatively uncomplicated entities with modest financial operations, the change may not be troublesome. For example, the compensation disclosures generally apply only to levels exceeding $100,000 (the current cut-off is $50,000). For large and complex organizations it is hard to imagine the actual act of data collection will be difficult. Many of the requirements embody best practices that have been informally adopted anyway. But the real issue is not how easy or hard it will be to collect the data. The real issue will be the reaction to what is disclosed, and what the streetsmart manager can do about it in advance. Happily, following good practices will usually steer you clear of the potential gotchas.

For instance, there is a simmering tension about executive pay in all corporations, nonprofits included, and this form will fan those embers in the nonprofit sector. Several areas deal with executive compensation, but Part Two asks "Did the process for determining compensation include a review and approval by independent members of the governing body, comparability data, and contemporaneous substantiation of the deliberation and decision?" This is like a heavy-handed middle school history test, with the "correct" answer embedded in the question. The message is, do your homework on executive compensation. In practice that will probably mean a salary benchmark study by an independent party along with appropriate documentation of board deliberations on the matter.

Similarly, many of the mission, governance, and activity questions can be answered effectively if the organization has done some reasonably good thinking about its strategy. Other questions about how one makes certain documents and records available to the public can be answered simply by making them available on your Web site.

Enforcement is a lurking question in this form. The Form 990 was and is an informational return—there are no explicit financial stakes the way there are with a personal tax return. So if your mission statement is ill-conceived and poorly written, or if you don't have a written whistleblower policy, will the IRS do anything about it?

The answer has to be, probably not. It is inconceivable that the IRS would use its limited resources to pursue, say, a nonprofit that admits it doesn't have a written conflict of interest policy. More likely is that the form is meant as an implicit lesson in current thinking about nonprofit accountability, and that the real enforcers will be the outsiders who decide not to donate to you until you adopt these good practices. Also it cannot have escaped the IRS's attention that the new form provides a handy road map for data gathering by enterprising reporters who already have their suspicions about a particular nonprofit in their media market.

In the end, this is one of those situations where the inconvenience, extra work, and maybe even embarrassment for a few is the price that will be paid for strengthening the sector. Virtually every kind of institution in our economy gets publicly knocked down and dirtied every now and then, including nonprofits. A decline in reputation and financial well-being can come from this ritual roughing-up. The oil industry and the pharmaceuticals can absorb the blows well enough. Nonprofits usually can't, and if the increased disclosures mandated here can head off some public unpleasantness for some organizations and strengthen the rest, it should be a trade-off worth making. From transparency comes strength.

With the preceding as background, we can now get into the useful area of balance sheet diagnostics. It's possible to get a balance sheet (plus other parts of a financial statement) to give up some pretty impressive insights with only a little math; just another attribute of this most helpful of reports.

Form **990**	**Return of Organization Exempt From Income Tax**	OMB No. 1545-0047

Under section 501(c), 527, or 4947(a)(1) of the Internal Revenue Code (except black lung benefit trust or private foundation)

2007

Department of the Treasury
Internal Revenue Service

▶ The organization may have to use a copy of this return to satisfy state reporting requirements.

Open to Public Inspection

A For the 2007 calendar year, or tax year beginning _____, 2007, and ending _____, 20___

B Check if applicable:

☐ Address change
☐ Name change
☐ Initial return
☐ Termination
☐ Amended return
☐ Application pending

Please use IRS label or print or type. See Specific Instructions.

C Name of organization: Committee to Clean Up Amigosville

Number and street (or P.O. box if mail is not delivered to street address)   Room/suite: 527 Environmental Way

City or town, state or country, and ZIP + 4: Amigosville, Texas 77777

D Employer identification number: 44 : 4444444

E Telephone number: (555) 001 1000

F Accounting method: ☐ Cash ☒ Accrual ☐ Other (specify) ▶

● Section 501(c)(3) organizations and 4947(a)(1) nonexempt charitable trusts must attach a completed Schedule A (Form 990 or 990-EZ).

G Website: ▶

H and **I** are not applicable to section 527 organizations.

H(a) Is this a group return for affiliates?   ☐ Yes ☒ No
H(b) If "Yes," enter number of affiliates ▶ ....
H(c) Are all affiliates included?   ☐ Yes ☐ No
(If "No," attach a list. See instructions.)
H(d) Is this a separate return filed by an organization covered by a group ruling?   ☐ Yes ☒ No

I Group Exemption Number ▶

J Organization type (check only one) ▶ ☐ 501(c) ( ) ◀ (insert no.) ☐ 4947(a)(1) or ☐ 527

K Check here ▶ ☐ if the organization is not a 509(a)(3) supporting organization and its gross receipts are normally **not** more than $25,000. A return is not required, but if the organization chooses to file a return, be sure to file a complete return.

M Check ▶ ☐ if the organization is **not** required to attach Sch. B (Form 990, 990-EZ, or 990-PF).

L Gross receipts: Add lines 6b, 8b, 9b, and 10b to line 12 ▶

Part I   Revenue, Expenses, and Changes in Net Assets or Fund Balances *(See the instructions.)*

1	Contributions, gifts, grants, and similar amounts received:			
a	Contributions to donor advised funds	1a	599,110	
b	Direct public support (not included on line 1a)	1b		
c	Indirect public support (not included on line 1a)	1c		
d	Government contributions (grants) (not included on line 1a)	1d	375,590	
e	Total (add lines 1a through 1d) (cash $_____ noncash $_____)			1e 974,700
2	Program service revenue including government fees and contracts (from Part VII, line 93)			2 37,700
3	Membership dues and assessments			3
4	Interest on savings and temporary cash investments			4 5,000
5	Dividends and interest from securities			5 4,000
6a	Gross rents	6a	2,000	
b	Less: rental expenses	6b		
c	Net rental income or (loss). Subtract line 6b from line 6a			6c 2,000
7	Other investment income (describe ▶ _____)			7
8a	Gross amount from sales of assets other than inventory	(A) Securities	(B) Other	
		8a		
b	Less: cost or other basis and sales expenses	8b		
c	Gain or (loss) (attach schedule)	8c		
d	Net gain or (loss). Combine line 8c, columns (A) and (B)			8d
9	Special events and activities (attach schedule). If any amount is from **gaming**, check here ▶ ☐			
a	Gross revenue (not including $_____ of contributions reported on line 1b)	9a		
b	Less: direct expenses other than fundraising expenses	9b		
c	Net income or (loss) from special events. Subtract line 9b from line 9a			9c
10a	Gross sales of inventory, less returns and allowances	10a	40,000	
b	Less: cost of goods sold	10b	10,000	
c	Gross profit or (loss) from sales of inventory (attach schedule). Subtract line 10b from line 10a			10c 30,000
11	Other revenue (from Part VII, line 103)			11
12	**Total revenue.** Add lines 1e, 2, 3, 4, 5, 6c, 7, 8d, 9c, 10c, and 11			12 1,053,400
13	Program services (from line 44, column (B))			13 785,100
14	Management and general (from line 44, column (C))			14 130,800
15	Fundraising (from line 44, column (D))			15 103,500
16	Payments to affiliates (attach schedule)			16
17	**Total expenses.** Add lines 16 and 44, column (A)			17 1,019,400
18	Excess or (deficit) for the year. Subtract line 17 from line 12			18 34,000
19	Net assets or fund balances at beginning of year (from line 73, column (A))			19 43,800
20	Other changes in net assets or fund balances (attach explanation)			20
21	Net assets or fund balances at end of year. Combine lines 18, 19, and 20			21 77,800

(*Revenue* label at left side of lines 1–12; *Expenses* label at lines 13–17; *Net Assets* label at lines 18–21)

For Privacy Act and Paperwork Reduction Act Notice, see the separate instructions.   Cat. No. 11282Y   Form **990** (2007)

EXHIBIT 5.7   Sample IRS Form 990 (Old)

Form 990 (2007)   Page **2**

| **Part II** | **Statement of Functional Expenses** | All organizations must complete column (A). Columns (B), (C), and (D) are required for section 501(c)(3) and (4) organizations and section 4947(a)(1) nonexempt charitable trusts but optional for others. *(See the instructions.)* |

Do not include amounts reported on line 6b, 8b, 9b, 10b, or 16 of Part I.		**(A) Total**	**(B) Program services**	**(C) Management and general**	**(D) Fundraising**
22a Grants paid from donor advised funds (attach schedule) (cash $ _____ noncash $ _____) If this amount includes foreign grants, check here ▶ ☐	22a				
22b Other grants and allocations (attach schedule) (cash $ _____ noncash $ _____) If this amount includes foreign grants, check here ▶ ☐	22b				
23 Specific assistance to individuals (attach schedule)	23				
24 Benefits paid to or for members (attach schedule)	24				
25a Compensation of current officers, directors, key employees, etc. listed in Part V-A	25a				
b Compensation of former officers, directors, key employees, etc. listed in Part V-B	25b				
c Compensation and other distributions, not included above, to disqualified persons (as defined under section 4958(f)(1)) and persons described in section 4958(c)(3)(B)	25c				
26 Salaries and wages of employees not included on lines 25a, b, and c	26	508,400	423,400	65,000	20,000
27 Pension plan contributions not included on lines 25a, b, and c	27	5,000	5,000		
28 Employee benefits not included on lines 25a – 27	28	25,000	18,000	5,000	2,000
29 Payroll taxes	29	42,000	34,000	5,000	3,000
30 Professional fundraising fees	30	40,000			40,000
31 Accounting fees	31	10,000		10,000	
32 Legal fees	32	9,000		9,000	
33 Supplies	33	15,000	12,000	2,000	1,000
34 Telephone	34	28,000	22,000	4,000	2,000
35 Postage and shipping	35				
36 Occupancy	36	70,000	53,000	14,000	3,000
37 Equipment rental and maintenance	37	20,000	20,000		
38 Printing and publications	38	62,000	52,000	2,000	8,000
39 Travel	39	25,000	16,000	3,000	6,000
40 Conferences, conventions, and meetings	40	10,000	9,000	1,000	
41 Interest	41	1,000		1,000	
42 Depreciation, depletion, etc. (attach schedule)	42	26,000	24,700	800	500
43 Other expenses not covered above (itemize):					
a _____	43a				
b _____	43b	75,000	54,000	3,000	18,000
c _____	43c	5,000	2,000	3,000	
d _____	43d	28,000	26,000	2,000	
e _____	43e	15,000	14,000	1,000	
f _____	43f				
g _____	43g				
44 Total functional expenses. Add lines 22a through 43g. (Organizations completing columns (B)–(D), carry these totals to lines 13–15)	44	1,019,400	785,100	130,800	103,500

Joint Costs. Check ▶ ☐ if you are following SOP 98-2.
Are any joint costs from a combined educational campaign and fundraising solicitation reported in **(B)** Program services? . ▶ ☐ Yes ☒ No
If "Yes," enter **(i)** the aggregate amount of these joint costs $ _____ ; **(ii)** the amount allocated to Program services $ _____ ;
(iii) the amount allocated to Management and general $ _____ ; and **(iv)** the amount allocated to Fundraising $ _____

Form **990** (2007)

EXHIBIT 5.7   (Continued)

Form 990 (2007)   Page **3**

Part III	**Statement of Program Service Accomplishments** *(See the instructions.)*

Form 990 is available for public inspection and, for some people, serves as the primary or sole source of information about a particular organization. How the public perceives an organization in such cases may be determined by the information presented on its return. Therefore, please make sure the return is complete and accurate and fully describes, in Part III, the organization's programs and accomplishments.

What is the organization's primary exempt purpose? ▶ ....

All organizations must describe their exempt purpose achievements in a clear and concise manner. State the number of clients served, publications issued, etc. Discuss achievements that are not measurable. (Section 501(c)(3) and (4) organizations and 4947(a)(1) nonexempt charitable trusts must also enter the amount of grants and allocations to others.)

Program Service Expenses (Required for 501(c)(3) and (4) orgs., and 4947(a)(1) trusts; but optional for others.)

a Clean up with the stars: To prevent litter and Keep our communities clean, we use star Texas athletes to attract volunteers to community clean up days.

252,900

(Grants and allocations $ _____) If this amount includes foreign grants, check here ▶ ☐

b Don't Mess With Texas: This local version of the effective statewide program uses PSAs, print media ads, and innovative media appearances to reduce litter in our local cities and towns.

146,600

(Grants and allocations $ _____) If this amount includes foreign grants, check here ▶ ☐

c The committee holds recycling contracts with the 17 municipalities in Amigos County. Services range from weekly pickups to special recycling events.

375,600

(Grants and allocations $ _____) If this amount includes foreign grants, check here ▶ ☐

d Programs and seminars: The committee sponsors educational meetings to bring together government officials, businesses, and citizens to discuss new methods of trash collection, recycling, and litter reduction.

10,000

(Grants and allocations $ _____) If this amount includes foreign grants, check here ▶ ☐

e Other program services (attach schedule)
(Grants and allocations $ _____) If this amount includes foreign grants, check here ▶ ☐

f Total of Program Service Expenses (should equal line 44, column (B), Program services). . . . . ▶   785,100

Form **990** (2007)

EXHIBIT 5.7   (Continued)

Form 990 (2007)   Page **4**

Part IV   Balance Sheets *(See the instructions.)*

Note:	*Where required, attached schedules and amounts within the description column should be for end-of-year amounts only.*		**(A)** Beginning of year		**(B)** End of year
45	Cash—non-interest-bearing		12,000	**45**	29,000
46	Savings and temporary cash investments			**46**	
47a	Accounts receivable	**47a** 149,800			
b	Less: allowance for doubtful accounts	**47b** 10,000		**47c**	139,800
48a	Pledges receivable	**48a**			
b	Less: allowance for doubtful accounts	**48b**		**48c**	
49	Grants receivable			**49**	12,000
50a	Receivables from current and former officers, directors, trustees, and key employees (attach schedule)			**50a**	
b	Receivables from other disqualified persons (as defined under section 4958(f)(1)) and persons described in section 4958(c)(3)(B) (attach schedule)			**50b**	
51a	Other notes and loans receivable (attach schedule)	**51a**			
b	Less: allowance for doubtful accounts	**51b**		**51c**	
52	Inventories for sale or use			**52**	
53	Prepaid expenses and deferred charges		19,000	**53**	10,000
54a	Investments—publicly-traded securities ▶ ☐ Cost ☐ FMV			**54a**	
b	Investments—other securities (attach schedule) ▶ ☐ Cost ☐ FMV			**54b**	
55a	Investments—land, buildings, and equipment: basis	**55a**			
b	Less: accumulated depreciation (attach schedule)	**55b**		**55c**	
56	Investments—other (attach schedule)			**56**	
57a	Land, buildings, and equipment: basis	**57a** 55,000			
b	Less: accumulated depreciation (attach schedule)	**57b** 36,000	18,000	**57c**	19,000
58	Other assets, including program-related investments (describe ▶)			**58**	
59	**Total assets** (must equal line 74). Add lines 45 through 58		49,000	**59**	209,800
60	Accounts payable and accrued expenses		5,200	**60**	114,000
61	Grants payable			**61**	
62	Deferred revenue			**62**	18,000
63	Loans from officers, directors, trustees, and key employees (attach schedule)			**63**	
64a	Tax-exempt bond liabilities (attach schedule)			**64a**	
b	Mortgages and other notes payable (attach schedule)			**64b**	
65	Other liabilities (describe ▶)			**65**	
66	**Total liabilities.** Add lines 60 through 65		5,200	**66**	132,000
	Organizations that follow SFAS 117, check here ▶ ☐ and complete lines 67 through 69 and lines 73 and 74.				
67	Unrestricted		25,800	**67**	56,800
68	Temporarily restricted			**68**	
69	Permanently restricted		18,000	**69**	21,000
	Organizations that do not follow SFAS 117, check here ▶ ☐ and complete lines 70 through 74.				
70	Capital stock, trust principal, or current funds			**70**	
71	Paid-in or capital surplus, or land, building, and equipment fund			**71**	
72	Retained earnings, endowment, accumulated income, or other funds			**72**	
73	**Total net assets or fund balances.** Add lines 67 through 69 **or** lines 70 through 72. (Column (A) **must** equal line 19 and column (B) **must** equal line 21)		43,800	**73**	77,800
74	**Total liabilities and net assets/fund balances.** Add lines 66 and 73		49,000	**74**	209,800

Form **990** (2007)

EXHIBIT 5.7   (Continued)

Form **990**

OMB No. 1545-0047

Return of Organization Exempt From Income Tax

Under section 501(c), 527, or 4947(a)(1) of the Internal Revenue Code (except black lung benefit trust or private foundation)

▶ The organization may have to use a copy of this return to satisfy state reporting requirements.

Department of the Treasury
Internal Revenue Service

2008

Open to Public Inspection

A For the 2008 calendar year, or tax year beginning _____ , 2008, and ending _____ , 20 XX

B Check if applicable:	**C** Name of organization Committee to Clean Up Amigosville	**D** Employer identification number
☐ Address change	Please use IRS label or print or type. See Specific Instructions.	44 : 4444444
☐ Name change	Doing Business As C.C.W.A.	
☐ Initial return	Number and street (or P.O. box if mail is not delivered to street address) Room/suite	**E** Telephone number
☐ Termination	527 Environmental Way	(555) 001 1000
☐ Amended return	City or town, state or country, and ZIP + 4	**G** Gross receipts $ 1,053,400
☐ Application pending	Amigosville, Texas 77777	

F Name and address of principal officer: George B. Grinnell, Chairman

H(a) Is this a group return for affiliates? ☐ Yes ☒ No
H(b) Are all affiliates included? ☐ Yes ☐ No
If "No," attach a list. (see instructions)

I Tax-exempt status: ☒ 501(c) (3) ◀ (insert no.) ☐ 4947(a)(1) or ☐ 527

H(c) Group exemption number ▶

J Website: ▶

K Type of organization: ☒ Corporation ☐ Trust ☐ Association ☐ Other ▶   **L** Year of formation: 1992   **M** State of legal domicile: Texas

Part I   Summary

1 Briefly describe the organization's mission or most significant activities:
In 2008 we succeeded in raising recycling compliance to an average of 71% in the 17 municipalities of Pinchot County from 32% in 1998.

2 Check this box ▶ ☐ if the organization discontinued its operations or disposed of more than 25% of its assets.

3 Number of voting members of the governing body (Part VI, line 1a)	**3**	
4 Number of independent voting members of the governing body (Part VI, line 1b)	**4**	
5 Total number of employees (Part V, line 2a)	**5**	
6 Total number of volunteers (estimate if necessary)	**6**	
7a Total gross unrelated business revenue from Part VIII, line 12, column (C) .	**7a**	
b Net unrelated business taxable income from Form 990-T, line 34	**7b**	

	Prior Year	Current Year
8 Contributions and grants (Part VIII, line 1h)		974,700
9 Program service revenue (Part VIII, line 2g)		37,700
10 Investment income (Part VIII, column (A), lines 3, 4, and 7d) . . .		
11 Other revenue (Part VIII, column (A), lines 5, 6d, 8c, 9c, 10c, and 11e)		
12 Total revenue—add lines 8 through 11 (must equal Part VIII, column (A), line 12)		1,053,400

	Prior Year	Current Year
13 Grants and similar amounts paid (Part IX, column (A), lines 1–3) . . .		
14 Benefits paid to or for members (Part IX, column (A), line 4) . . .		
15 Salaries, other compensation, employee benefits (Part IX, column (A), lines 5–10)		40,000
16a Professional fundraising fees (Part IX, column (A), line 11e) . . .		
b Total fundraising expenses (Part IX, column (D), line 25) ▶		
17 Other expenses (Part IX, column (A), lines 11a–11d, 11f–24f) . . .		123,000
18 Total expenses. Add lines 13–17 (must equal Part IX, column (A), line 25).		1,019,400
19 Revenue less expenses. Subtract line 18 from line 12		34,000

	Beginning of Year	End of Year
20 Total assets (Part X, line 16)		209,800
21 Total liabilities (Part X, line 26)		132,000
22 Net assets or fund balances. Subtract line 21 from line 20		77,800

Part II   Signature Block

Under penalties of perjury, I declare that I have examined this return, including accompanying schedules and statements, and to the best of my knowledge and belief, it is true, correct, and complete. Declaration of preparer (other than officer) is based on all information of which preparer has any knowledge.

Sign Here

▶ Rachel Carson | April 21, 2009
  Signature of officer   Date

▶ Rachel Carson, CEO
  Type or print name and title

Paid Preparer's Use Only

Preparer's signature ▶ John James Audubon	Date 4/21/xx	Check if self-employed ▶ ☒	Preparer's identifying number (see instructions)	
Firm's name (or yours if self-employed), address, and ZIP + 4	John James Audubon, CPA		EIN ▶	
			Phone no. ▶ ( )	

May the IRS discuss this return with the preparer shown above? (see instructions) . . . . . ☒ Yes ☐ No

For Privacy Act and Paperwork Reduction Act Notice, see the separate instructions.   Cat. No. 11282Y   Form **990** (2008)

EXHIBIT 5.8   Sample IRS Form 990 (New)

Form 990 (2008)   Page **2**

Part III	**Statement of Program Service Accomplishments** (see instructions)

1   Briefly describe the organization's mission:

Our mission is to make Amigos County the greenest county in Texas.

2   Did the organization undertake any significant program services during the year which were not listed on the prior Form 990 or 990-EZ? . . . .   ☐ Yes ☒ No
If "Yes," describe these new services on Schedule O.

3   Did the organization cease conducting, or make significant changes in how it conducts, any program services? . . . .   ☐ Yes ☒ No
If "Yes," describe these changes on Schedule O.

4   Describe the exempt purpose achievements for each of the organization's three largest program services by expenses. Section 501(c)(3) and 501(c)(4) organizations and section 4947(a)(1) trusts are required to report the amount of grants and allocations to others, the total expenses, and revenue, if any, for each program service reported.

4a (Code: _____) (Expenses $ *252,900* including grants of $ _____) (Revenue $ *243,600*)

Clean up with the stars: To prevent litter and keep our communities clean, we use star Texas athletes to attract volunteers to community clean up days.

4b (Code: _____) (Expenses $ *146,600* including grants of $ _____) (Revenue $ *204,700*)

Don't Mess with Texas: This local version of the effective statewide program uses PSAs, print media ads and innovative media appearances to reduce litter in our local cities and towns.

4c (Code: _____) (Expenses $ *375,600* including grants of $ _____) (Revenue $ *520,000*)

The committee holds recycling contracts with the 17 municipalities in Amigos County. Services range from weekly pickups to special recycling events.

4d Other program services. (Describe in Schedule O.)
(Expenses $ *10,000* including grants of $ _____) (Revenue $ *6,400*)

4e Total program service expenses ▶ $ *785,100*   (Must equal Part IX, Line 25, column (B).)

Form **990** (2008)

EXHIBIT 5.8   (Continued)

Form 990 (2008)   Page **9**

Part VIII	Statement of Revenue			(A) Total revenue	(B) Related or exempt function revenue	(C) Unrelated business revenue	(D) Revenue excluded from tax under sections 512, 513, or 514
Contributions, gifts, grants and other similar amounts	1a Federated campaigns	1a					
	b Membership dues	1b					
	c Fundraising events	1c					
	d Related organizations	1d					
	e Government grants (contributions)	1e	375,590				
	f All other contributions, gifts, grants, and similar amounts not included above	1f	599,110				
	g Noncash contributions included in lines 1a–1f: $						
	h **Total.** Add lines 1a–1f ▶			974,700			
Program Service Revenue	2a		Business Code				
	b						
	c						
	d						
	e						
	f All other program service revenue			37,700			
	g **Total.** Add lines 2a–2f ▶						
Other Revenue	3 Investment income (including dividends, interest, and other similar amounts) ▶			9,000			
	4 Income from investment of tax-exempt bond proceeds ▶						
	5 Royalties ▶						
		(i) Real	(ii) Personal				
	6a Gross Rents	2,000					
	b Less: rental expenses						
	c Rental income or (loss)						
	d Net rental income or (loss) ▶			2,000			
	7a Gross amount from sales of assets other than inventory	(i) Securities	(ii) Other				
	b Less: cost or other basis and sales expenses						
	c Gain or (loss)						
	d Net gain or (loss) ▶						
	8a Gross income from fundraising events (not including $ .... of contributions reported on line 1c). See Part IV, line 18	a					
	b Less: direct expenses	b					
	c Net income or (loss) from fundraising events ▶						
	9a Gross income from gaming activities. See Part IV, line 19	a					
	b Less: direct expenses	b					
	c Net income or (loss) from gaming activities ▶						
	10a Gross sales of inventory, less returns and allowances	a	40,000				
	b Less: cost of goods sold	b	10,000				
	c Net income or (loss) from sales of inventory ▶			30,000			
	Miscellaneous Revenue		Business Code				
	11a						
	b						
	c						
	d All other revenue						
	e **Total.** Add lines 11a–11d ▶						
	12 **Total Revenue.** Add lines 1h, 2g, 3, 4, 5, 6d, 7d, 8c, 9c, 10c, and 11e ▶			1,053,400			

Form **990** (2008)

EXHIBIT 5.8 (Continued)

Form 990 (2008)

Part IX Statement of Functional Expenses

Section 501(c)(3) and 501(c)(4) organizations must complete all columns.
All other organizations must complete column (A) but are not required to complete columns (B), (C), and (D).

Do not include amounts reported on lines 6b, 7b, 8b, 9b, and 10b of Part VIII.	(A) Total expenses	(B) Program service expenses	(C) Management and general expenses	(D) Fundraising expenses
1 Grants and other assistance to governments and organizations in the U.S. See Part IV, line 21				
2 Grants and other assistance to individuals in the U.S. See Part IV, line 22				
3 Grants and other assistance to governments, organizations, and individuals outside the U.S. See Part IV, lines 15 and 16				
4 Benefits paid to or for members				
5 Compensation of current officers, directors, trustees, and key employees				
6 Compensation not included above, to disqualified persons (as defined under section 4958(f)(1)) and persons described in section 4958(c)(3)(B)				
7 Other salaries and wages	508,400	423,400	65,000	20,000
8 Pension plan contributions (include section 401(k) and section 403(b) employer contributions)	5,000	5,000		
9 Other employee benefits	25,000	18,000	5,000	2,000
10 Payroll taxes	42,000	34,000	5,000	3,000
11 Fees for services (non-employees):				
a Management				
b Legal	9,000		9,000	
c Accounting	10,000		10,000	
d Lobbying				
e Professional fundraising services. See Part IV, line 17	40,000			
f Investment management fees				
g Other	20,000	20,000		
12 Advertising and promotion	62,000	52,000	2,000	8,000
13 Office expenses	43,000	34,000	6,000	3,000
14 Information technology				
15 Royalties				
16 Occupancy	70,000	53,000	14,000	2,000
17 Travel	25,000	16,000	3,000	6,000
18 Payments of travel or entertainment expenses for any federal, state, or local public officials				
19 Conferences, conventions, and meetings	10,000	9,000	1,000	
20 Interest	1,000		1,000	
21 Payments to affiliates				
22 Depreciation, depletion, and amortization	26,000	24,700	800	500
23 Insurance				
24 Other expenses. Itemize expenses not covered above. (Expenses grouped together and labeled miscellaneous may not exceed 5% of total expenses shown on line 25 below.)				
a	75,000	54,000	3,000	18,000
b	5,000	2,000	3,000	
c	28,000	26,000	2,000	
d	15,000	14,000	1,000	
e				
f All other expenses				
25 **Total functional expenses.** Add lines 1 through 24f	1,019,400	785,100	130,800	103,500
26 **Joint Costs.** Check here ▶ ☐ if following SOP 98-2. Complete this line only if the organization reported in column (B) joint costs from a combined educational campaign and fundraising solicitation				

Form **990** (2008)

EXHIBIT 5.8 (Continued)

Form 990 (2008)   Page 11

Part X   Balance Sheet

			(A) Beginning of year		(B) End of year
Assets	1	Cash—non-interest-bearing	12,000	1	29,000
	2	Savings and temporary cash investments		2	
	3	Pledges and grants receivable, net		3	12,000
	4	Accounts receivable, net		4	139,800
	5	Receivables from current and former officers, directors, trustees, key employees, or other related parties. Complete Part II of Schedule L		5	
	6	Receivables from other disqualified persons (as defined under section 4958(f)(1)) and persons described in section 4958(c)(3)(B). Complete Part II of Schedule L		6	
	7	Notes and loans receivable, net		7	
	8	Inventories for sale or use		8	
	9	Prepaid expenses and deferred charges		9	
	10a	Land, buildings, and equipment: cost basis **10a** 55,000			
	b	Less: accumulated depreciation. Complete Part VI of Schedule D **10b** 36,000	18,000	10c	19,000
	11	Investments—publicly traded securities	19,000	11	10,000
	12	Investments—other securities. See Part IV, line 11		12	
	13	Investments—program-related. See Part IV, line 11		13	
	14	Intangible assets		14	
	15	Other assets. See Part IV, line 11		15	
	16	**Total assets.** Add lines 1 through 15 (must equal line 34)	49,000	16	209,800
Liabilities	17	Accounts payable and accrued expenses	5,200	17	114,000
	18	Grants payable		18	
	19	Deferred revenue		19	18,000
	20	Tax-exempt bond liabilities		20	
	21	Escrow account liability. Complete Part IV of Schedule D		21	
	22	Payables to current and former officers, directors, trustees, key employees, highest compensated employees, and disqualified persons. Complete Part II of Schedule L		22	
	23	Secured mortgages and notes payable to unrelated third parties		23	
	24	Unsecured notes and loans payable		24	
	25	Other liabilities. Complete Part X of Schedule D		25	
	26	**Total liabilities.** Add lines 17 through 25	5,200	26	132,000
Net Assets or Fund Balances		Organizations that follow SFAS 117, check here ▶ ☐ and complete lines 27 through 29, and lines 33 and 34.			
	27	Unrestricted net assets	25,800	27	56,800
	28	Temporarily restricted net assets		28	
	29	Permanently restricted net assets	18,000	29	21,000
		Organizations that do not follow SFAS 117, check here ▶ ☐ and complete lines 30 through 34.			
	30	Capital stock or trust principal, or current funds		30	
	31	Paid-in or capital surplus, or land, building, or equipment fund		31	
	32	Retained earnings, endowment, accumulated income, or other funds		32	
	33	Total net assets or fund balances	43,800	33	77,800
	34	Total liabilities and net assets/fund balances	49,000	34	209,800

Part XI   Financial Statements and Reporting

		Yes	No
1	Accounting method used to prepare the Form 990: ☐ Cash ☐ Accrual ☐ Other		
2a	Were the organization's financial statements compiled or reviewed by an independent accountant? **2a**		
b	Were the organization's financial statements audited by an independent accountant? **2b**		
c	If "Yes" to lines 2a or 2b, does the organization have a committee that assumes responsibility for oversight of the audit, review, or compilation of its financial statements and selection of an independent accountant? **2c**		
3a	As a result of a federal award, was the organization required to undergo an audit or audits as set forth in the Single Audit Act and OMB Circular A-133? **3a**		
b	If "Yes," did the organization undergo the required audit or audits? **3b**		

Form **990** (2008)

EXHIBIT 5.8   (Continued)

CHAPTER 6

Financial Analysis:
A Few Diagnostic Tools

Yes, you will need a calculator for this chapter. But not just yet, and when you do, it will be pretty simple stuff. Before we get into the ratios themselves, try the simplest yet most insightful piece of financial analysis possible. Run your thumb down the asset side of the balance sheet and find the largest number. Make a mental note of it. You have just learned a tremendous amount about your organization. Because *whoever controls the single largest type of asset controls the organization.*

Here's why. Suppose the organization in question is a university, and the largest asset is the endowment fund (investments). Whoever controls those investments controls the university. Sure, the professors make curricula decisions, the president and the deans decide who to hire and promote, and so forth. But whoever controls the investments sets the conditions and shapes the environment in which those other players make their operational decisions. Shrink or expand the endowment and the money-generating power that goes along with it and you dramatically alter the circumstances under which those decisions are made.

Finding and learning about how the largest asset is handled also tells you something about the organization's risk profile. It sounds like a tired cliché but it's true that your largest asset is usually your largest liability. Usually the largest asset is central to the service model the organization uses, so if something were to happen to that asset it could potentially severely hurt operations. For instance, a recycling program that holds the bulk of its assets as receivables from municipalities may be a free-standing operation, but it might as well add underneath the sign at its entrance "A wholly controlled subsidiary of local governments," because whatever the municipalities decide to do about those receivables will have a lot to say about the recycling program's future.

Although the following ratios cover a wide range of analysis, they are only a fraction of the ratios it is possible to calculate. What these particular ratios have in common is that they represent a good balance between analytical power and easy availability of the component numbers on the Form 990. Other diagnostic tools of the same or greater power may require a bit of inside information that does not have to be publicly disclosed. The intention of this chapter is to present a good set of tests that can be done by a total outsider to the organization as well as someone who has unlimited access to financial information.

FINANCIAL STATEMENT ANALYSIS FOR MATH PHOBICS

Math phobics, take heart. Crunching massive quantities of numbers isn't the only way to analyze a financial statement. In fact, you can learn a great deal about an organization without doing a single calculation. The secret lies in reading the words and knowing what they mean. Let's start from the beginning of the average financial statement.

Professional financial analysts often follow these steps when reviewing an audited financial statement of a new organization:

- Read the opinion letter.
- Read all notes and internal opinion letters, if any (particularly true for Office of Management and Budget Circular [OMB] A-133 audits).
- Review the numbers in the format presented.
- Calculate financial ratios as desired (optional).

Audit, Review, or Compilation?

Open the financial statement to the cover page, a letter signed by the certified public accountant or a CPA firm. The first verb you encounter tells you a lot. The sentence will read something like this: "We have (audited, reviewed, or compiled) the financial statements of XYZ Corporation . . ."

◇◆ YELLOW FLAG ◇◆

TIME NEEDED FOR AUDIT

Take a look at the date of the opinion letter. Compare it to the last day of the fiscal year. The first date is the last day the auditors spent on the corporation's premises doing field work, and it can be a rough guide to how smoothly things went. If the date is more than three months or so after the end of the fiscal year, it could indicate that the books and records were so disorganized that the auditors had to spend extra time just getting things into shape before conducting the audit. It could also say something about the auditors' level of effectiveness, although this is less likely. Either way, ask.

The difference between the three verbs tells the reader a great deal about the reliability of the financial statements. Technically, the financial statements are supposed to be the product of management, with the CPA's analysis of them offering three different levels of assurance. An audit is the highest form of reliability, since it involves careful analysis and testing of transactions according to the guidelines proscribed by various professional accounting societies and government regulators. A review, on the other hand, involves no such testing and merely suggests that the financial representations seem to make sense. Finally, a compilation is little more than a collecting and reformatting of raw financial records. Chapter 9 on choosing and using an auditor goes into greater detail on this subject.

The reader with a stake in the nonprofit will prefer an audited set of financial statements, and in fact many state and local governments—and most serious payers—require nonprofit agencies to obtain a full audit each year.

The Opinion

The next place to look is toward the end of the cover letter where the text should read "In my (our) opinion, these statements present fairly. . . ." This is the sentence for which the organization obtained the audit, and if the word *except* appears anywhere in this sentence, or if the auditor declines to express an opinion, alarms should go off in your head. Unless the exception refers to technical accounting disagreements with the way certain

⚑ **RED FLAG** ⚑

OPINIONS THAT MAKE YOU RUN SCREAMING FROM THE ROOM

ADVERSE OPINION

Sometimes the auditor wants to convey different information, such as their concern that the audited financial statements do not present the situation fairly. In that case, they would offer an adverse opinion, saying that the statements "do not present fairly."

DISCLAIMER OF OPINION

In this opinion the auditor politely says that they are unable to give an opinion on the financial statements. What the auditor really wants to be able to say is "Are you KIDDING ME??!? You called me in here to do an audit and all your records are still in SHOEBOXES! You call this a financial management system? Well, I call this a MESS. You should be ashamed of yourselves. I can't believe you thought we'd be stupid enough to try to fix this disaster area! I'm sick of this! You people have no respect for . . ."

information is presented, this is the auditor's place to reassure readers that things are pretty much as management says they are. As long as there are no exceptions or reservations expressed, the audit is considered to be an unqualified or "clean" opinion. Two of the most common reasons for qualified opinions are unspeakably bad records and the CPA's genuine fear that the organization may go out of business soon. Either one is cause for concern.

⚑ **YELLOW FLAG** ⚑

QUALIFIED OPINION

Some qualified opinions are a potential yellow flag, because the auditors considered some situation serious enough to put up front in the very place to which readers first turn for reassurance. Qualified opinions are not given lightly, so take their existence seriously.

Now skip all of the pages with numbers on them and turn right to the notes at the back. The back pages are like a bulletin board where accounting rules and conventions demand that certain important information be posted. Here you will find the following.

The Basis of Accounting

This note should say that the accrual basis of accounting was used in preparing the financials. There's just not much latitude here; nonprofit public charities beyond the very small or startup phase simply ought to be using the accrual method of accounting, not the cash method. If there's a good reason why an established nonprofit public charity should be using the cash method of accounting, we haven't thought of it yet. For more information on this subject, see the chapter on accounting. Also, note that both the old 990 and the new version ask for the basis of accounting. The old one puts the question up front on page one, while the new one buries the question on page 11—either way, for most organizations the box for "accrual" should be checked.

Related-Party Transactions

Sometimes a person connected with the organization, say, on the board or the management team, will also enter into some sort of transaction with the

---

✕ YELLOW FLAG ✕

"MODIFIED CASH BASIS"

Sometimes auditors need to say that their client is using an, ahem, less than standard method of accounting. Code words for that state of affairs would be things like "a modified cash basis of accounting," "a modified accrual basis of accounting," or some such equivocation. Whatever the terminology, it means that you can't read the financial statements with any degree of reliability. In that situation, the first thing you might want to do is ask why they are using a mongrelized system, and the second thing you might want to do is to head for the door.

corporation outside of his or her role. For instance, the chief executive officer (CEO) may own a piece of property that he or she rents to the corporation.

Related-party transactions can run the gamut from the perfectly innocuous to the sleazy. Or worse. It's not always possible to tell which is which on the face of it, so accounting rules require that related-party transactions be disclosed. Some funding sources require further detailed disclosure and some even attempt to eliminate all related-party transactions completely.

Why aren't related-party transactions banned altogether? Apart from the sheer impracticality of it we really, really believe in free trade in this country. Can you think of any type of transaction not involving fighter jets that the government bans or even tries to regulate? And even if we tried to ban certain transactions, what body would be charged with separating out the merely unwise from the sleazy, or the colossally stupid from the possibly criminal? So the best and only line of defense is sunshine. Related-party transactions, which should be identified in the routine course of an audit, get described in a juicy footnote and then the reader becomes the judge.

Borrowing Practices

Accounting rules stipulate that long-term indebtedness be disclosed in some detail, so this area can be a gold mine of information, especially for nonprofits that have borrowed a lot of money. Pay special attention to the following:

- *Lines of Credit.* Essentially, standing loans made by banks for balancing irregular cash flow in the short term. Is the line fully utilized as of the day of the statement? How much is it for? What is the interest rate being charged?

- *Interest Rates.* Often, the interest rate charged on borrowings says something about the organization. The prime rate is the interest rate banks charge their most favored customers, and few nonprofits fit that category, so you are likely to see a rate of "Prime plus" at least a percent. On the other hand, anything above approximately prime plus 1.50 percent may indicate lazy borrowing or a possible credit risk, and a red flag condition.

- *Purpose of the Borrowing.* The organization should match borrowing terms with purpose. That is, long-term borrowing should be used for long-term purposes such as investing in real estate, not supplementing cash flow. It's a yellow flag if purpose and terms don't match.

- *Patterns of Long-Term Indebtedness.* Typically, the footnotes will spell out future portions of long-term debt coming due. Since the year-by-year schedule of debt presents only what is currently obligated and does not include any planned long-term borrowing, the amounts shown should decline each of the future four or five years presented. If not, there may be a one-time payment, or a "balloon" payment, coming due during one or more years. This could be perfectly okay, but it should prompt the analyst to investigate the circumstances for the planned uptick in total long-term debt. Is it shrewd financing, or just putting off until tomorrow what they couldn't afford today?

- *Special Loan Covenants.* Occasionally, a lender will attach specific requirements to a loan, such as that certain outstanding bills will be payable directly to the lender under certain circumstances. The organization may have had to agree to the provisions to borrow the money, but it will limit future flexibility to a greater or lesser extent.

Lawsuits Pending

If someone has filed suit against the entity, it could eventually mean a significant alteration in its financial health if the suit is successful. Readers of the financial statements need to know that a suit is pending, so that fact is disclosed in the footnotes and should prompt further questioning. Management's evaluation of the suit will usually be included, and it will usually discount the merits of the suit. And why not? Wouldn't you have a very different reaction if they said, "Gee, those plaintiffs have a point?"

An unfortunate reality is that, once a nonprofit gets above a certain size (probably in the millions, certainly in the tens of millions), it is almost a certainty that it will have at least one lawsuit pending at all times. This is not necessarily a reflection on the organization as much as it is on the way we settle grievances in the twenty-first century.

Extraordinary Transactions

Every now and then something just plain unusual—good or bad—will happen to a nonprofit organization. Here's the place to talk about it. For example, if just after the fiscal year ends an entity restructures its long-term debt—say, by floating a bond that rolls up a number of pre-existing loans—this is the place that that will be noted. Kind of like movie trailers, except that you have to wait a year to see the movie.

Uncertainty of Future Funding

If the auditors feel that the nature of the organization's funding is shaky but they are not ready to ring any alarm bells on the opinion page, they may slip in a phrase about how unreliable future revenue streams are—especially if the money comes from the government. It signals an area worth looking into.

Subsequent Events

If a major event occurs after the last day of the fiscal year being audited and it can be expected to have a material effect on next year's financials—again, either positive or negative—the auditors will make a note of it.

Reading the opinion letter and the notes from a set of audited financial statements will tell even the novice a considerable amount about the organization. The words of a financial statement operate on two levels. The first is the obvious content expressed. The second level is open to veteran readers and can best be developed through experience. It consists of nuances such as the presence of an unexpected note or the cautious description of a pending lawsuit. Either one is accessible through simple reading—and not a single calculation.

Get Out Your Calculator

Now it is time to get out your calculator and refer to Exhibit 5.7. The following ratios use column B (End of year) from the 990 balance sheet for all balance sheet calculations unless indicated otherwise. Again, the old 990 numbers are in parentheses, the new ones are to their right.

CURRENT RATIO

Ratio: Current Ratio

Category: Liquidity

Formula: $\dfrac{\text{Current Assets}}{\text{Current Liabilities}}$

Form 990 Formula: $\dfrac{\text{Sum of lines (45 to 53)}}{\text{Sum of lines (60 to 63)}} \dfrac{\text{1 to 9}}{\text{17 to 19}}$

Sample Ratio: $\dfrac{(29,000 + 139,800 + 12,000)}{132,000} = 1.37$

What It Is

The current ratio is probably the most widely recognized measure of liquidity. This simple calculation—made easier since most audited financial statements have subtotals for both current assets and current liabilities—matches the short-term assets of an organization with the liabilities that it expects to face during the same period.

The power of this ratio lies in its simplicity. *Current* for most industries is defined as one year so, in effect, it selects a 365-day time frame and asks, "During this period of time, how do the resources that can be converted to cash compare with the liabilities that we know will be coming due during the same period?"

What It Should Be

This ratio should be at least 1.0, that is, for every dollar of liabilities coming due there should be at least one dollar of assets available to pay them. Ideally, the ratio will be higher—say, in the 1:5 to 2:1 range. Generally speaking, the higher the ratio the better—to a point. An excessively high current ratio can actually be a problem (and a sign of management timidity or inattentiveness) if it means that unneeded assets are being allowed to build up in short-term accounts instead of being invested for longer-term results. See Chapter 10 on cash flow management to determine how much cash should be readily available, and remember that cash needs can vary by industry and by time of year.

The nature of the nonprofit's need for cash is critical to a sensible interpretation of this ratio. Nonprofits with substantial amounts of complicated billing procedures need to have a stronger ability to meet short-term fluctuations in liabilities than those that get half of their revenues in cash at the door.

What It Is Not

This is actually a rather crude measure. Lumping a large number of asset categories into "current" masks the lack of meaningful liquidity that characterizes some of them. Inventories, for instance, do not typically get turned into cash easily—nor should the ongoing organization want to convert them, since they are presumably essential to continuing service delivery.

Fortunately, the inventory consideration is irrelevant for a large number of nonprofits and so the current ratio is as useful as anything one might need. For groups needing a more fine-tuned measure of liquidity where inventory is an issue, try the acid test:

$$\frac{\text{Cash} + \text{Receivables} - \text{Inventories}}{\text{Current liabilities}}$$

Working capital—you may have heard that phrase before—is simply current assets *minus* current liabilities. The "acid test" or "quick ratio" is the current ratio minus inventories.

DAYS' CASH

Ratio: Days' Cash

Category: Liquidity

Formula: $\dfrac{\text{Cash \& Equivalents} \times 365}{\text{Expenses} - \text{Depreciation}}$

Form 990 Formula: $\dfrac{(45 + 46) \times 365}{(44A - 42A)}$ $\dfrac{(1 + 2) \times 365}{(25A - 22A)}$

Sample Ratio: $\dfrac{(29,000) \times 365}{(1,019,400 - 26,000)} = 10\ \text{days}$

What It Is

Deprived of food, the human body proves surprisingly resilient. It slows its pace, shifts its focus, changes its systems. When the nourishment resumes, it readily returns to its former rhythms. The same is true for the nonprofit organization and its supply of cash. Deprived of cash, the entity adjusts its systems and compensates. This is a natural phenomenon, at least in a management sense, so the important question is, How long can it continue if the cash somehow gets completely shut off? The days' cash ratio gives that answer.

Think of days' cash as the number of days of average size cash disbursements the organization can withstand without any cash inflow. If a nonprofit spends $10,000 per day on average over a year and it has $200,000 of cash and cash equivalents on hand, it has 20 days' cash. Red flag range is 0 to about 10 days cash.

What It Should Be

To some extent, higher is better. However, by itself, the number doesn't tell us much, since it is pretty unlikely that incoming cash will be completely shut off for an extended period of time. What makes the number so useful is that it can be a good benchmark. In fact, the days' cash ratio is helpful mostly in the context of comparative analysis.

✂ YELLOW FLAG ✂

YOU CAN HAVE TOO MUCH OF A GOOD THING

Ever dream of raking up a big pile of dollar bills and then jumping in? If so, consider beginning therapy right away. For the rest of us, it's a silly dream. Because too much cash can indicate inattentiveness or a lack of understanding of cash flow management. Cash is the top-line way to hold assets. Once you've got enough, you've got enough. Make sure you push some of those assets down the line by making short-term investments (CDs, treasury bills, etc.) or long-term investments (equities or buildings). The exact mix of investments is up to you and will vary according to changing circumstances, but a mix is what you need.

What this means is that industry norms are essential to full usage of days' cash calculations. While some clear-cut inferences can be drawn from the ratio in a vacuum—Committee to Clean Up Amigosville (CCUA), for example, has little cash on hand by any measure—the deepest insights come from careful comparison with similar organizations. If nothing else, calculating this average helps focus management on how close to the bone their cash flow is running. Cash balances can be an eye opener, especially in a larger organization, but this number will cut through all of the fantasies and tell you exactly where you stand.

Days' Receivables

Ratio: Days' Receivables

Category: Liquidity

Formula: $\dfrac{\text{Accounts receivable} \times 365}{\text{Operating revenue}}$

Form 990 Formula: $\dfrac{47c \times 365^*}{(2 + 3)}\ \dfrac{4B}{2A}$

Sample Ratio: $\dfrac{139,800 \times 365}{(974,700 + 37,700)} = 50 \text{ days}$

What It Is

This is a multipurpose ratio if ever there was one. In one number, this measure not only says some very significant things about the size and nature of the bills owed to the organization at any one time, it also offers insight into the effectiveness of financial management systems as well as management philosophy.

---

*The idea here is to use only revenue sources that typically generate receivables. Lines 1 and 2 on the Form 990 also include grants, which typically are not considered receivable in the same way as invoices. However, "government grants" is a bit of an old-fashioned phrase that often means "government contracts," so it is usually safer to include line 1c. This part of the formula requires judgment.

Note: To get a more precise number, add the end of the year's net assets to the prior year's net assets and divide by 2. This gives a more accurate picture of the average net assets.

WHY CLOTHES COST MORE ON THE SHORE

Different industries use different ratios. In the retail clothing business, inventory turns are a critical measuring stick. To calculate inventory turns, divide the total sales by the average inventory throughout the year. If the store sells $4 million worth of merchandise and has an average inventory of $1 million on hand at any one time, it is said to have 4 turns.

Which, as it turns out, is about average. For a year-round clothing store to have four turns suggests that it pretty much sells out its entire inventory every three months, or once per season. Discount retailers make their money by achieving a higher number of turns, which is why some discounters seem to slice prices so furiously when an item has been hanging around too long. Volume of transactions is everything to them.

By contrast, a specialty retailer in a seasonal location such as a summer resort may only be able to achieve two turns per year. To make up for the lower volume of transactions, they must sell at higher prices. So buy your vacation clothing before you head to the beach.

You already knew this, of course, but now you know why you knew it.

To get the days' receivables, take the total amount of accounts receivable and divide it by the average amount of billings generated each of the 365 days of the year.

What It Should Be

Lower is better. Time is definitely money, and the less time it takes to collect one's bills the more cash one is likely to have on hand. In turn, that means more cash to be turned into another productive form of asset—such as investments—rather than being tied up in non–revenue producing receivables.

Days' receivables can offer a terrific window into management styles. A bloated number can mean bloated and inefficient billing systems (which probably implies some combination of poor personnel preparation and supervision, weak administrative systems, inadequate computer technology, or inattentive management). On the other hand, there's some fine irony here. A ratio at or lower than the industry standard in an otherwise lackluster set of ratios can actually mean not efficient management but a desperate, hand-to-mouth, beg-the-clients-we've-got-a-payroll-to-meet-tomorrow style of management.

CCUA sets a poor example by almost any standards, with a days' receivables ratio of nearly three months. On the other hand, a bit of careful reading reveals that they contract with 17 municipalities for recycling work. If that project produces most of the receivables, and that's a good guess, then at least the damage is confined to that single program.

A tip. Ballooning accounts receivable represent one of the best areas for a new manager to make fast progress in halting a financial slide. Most entities have little or no idea how long it takes them to collect their bills, and many don't understand how necessary it is to care. Or rather, they don't sense how important it is to keep receivables under control. Sometimes all it takes to improve the situation is to begin tracking the days in receivables (also called the collection period) and to set a lower target for the chief financial officer to hit.

What It Is Not

As presented, the days' receivables doesn't reveal anything about the quality of the bills. For that, one needs (a) access to the internal records, and (b) knowledge of the industry. To some extent one can count on the organization's auditors to insist that receivables that will never be collected get thrown out of the total count, but if the auditors don't understand the industry—or if management is determined to finesse them—the total amount of accounts receivable will be inflated.

CASH FLOW TO TOTAL DEBT

Ratio: Cash Flow to Total Debt

Category: Capital

Formula: $\dfrac{\text{Net income} + \text{Depreciation}}{\text{Total liabilities}}$

Form 990 Formula: $\dfrac{18 + 42a}{66b}$ $\dfrac{19 + 22A}{26B}$

Sample Ratio: $\dfrac{34,000 + 26,000}{132,000} = 0.45$

What It Is

Having liabilities means being obligated to pay them off. One of the quickest tests to use to understand something about the nonprofit's capital structure is the contrast between profit and depreciation as sources of cash and total liabilities. This ratio puts a slightly different twist on the idea of internally generated cash. What it asks is how much free cash is available each year to satisfy the liabilities on record. As will be seen in later chapters, profit creates cash for the nonprofit. Since depreciation is an expense that is not paid for in cash, it too leaves cash in the organization. Together, these two sources of cash are measured against the total liabilities of the organization.

What It Should Be

Higher is better. This is one ratio where most nonprofits will not score high because their net incomes are usually relatively low. Still, profit and depreciation are inescapable sources of cash regardless of tax status, so the ratio is a fair indicator of capital structure.

DEBT TO NET ASSETS

Ratio: Debt to Net Assets

Category: Capital

Formula: $\dfrac{\text{Long-term debt}}{\text{Net assets}}$

Form 990 Formula: $\dfrac{64a + b}{74} \dfrac{23B + 24B}{33B}$

Sample Ratio: $\dfrac{0}{77,800} = \text{NA}$

What It Is

Straight from the for-profit world (where net assets means equity), this ratio says something about the amount of long-term indebtedness an entity carries in order to do its business. Long-term debt means money loaned for any purpose with a payback period longer than one year, so the debt/ net assets ratio stacks an organization's total indebtedness against its accumulated net worth, or net assets. Another way to think about it is that it pits borrowed funds against "owned" funds. If an organization is highly leveraged—meaning that it has borrowed lots of money—you will see it here.

What It Should Be

This one is important for itself. Lower numbers indicate low debt loads. Since the number is expressed as a percentage, it's easy to compare it with other nonprofits' debt/net assets ratios. Industry ratios help put the answer in perspective, but the heart of the question is simply how high the number goes.

Perhaps not surprisingly, the best results here are under 1.00. Accumulated wealth is not as desirable in a nonprofit setting as it is in a proprietary one, yet it's still nice to know that the total amount borrowed is less than the corporation's "net worth," plus a little cushion for contingencies. CCUA is doing quite well in this department, with no long-term debt.

Again, some careful interpretation is necessary. Many nonprofits operate in fields where little capital investment is required, so the debt/net assets ratio could be low or even pointless to calculate. Sometimes the board is debt-shy and refuses to authorize any long-term debt if they can possibly avoid it. Other groups must invest heavily in equipment and usually have to borrow to do it, so the issue for them is more like the nature of the debt and how one nonprofit's debt load compares to its peers.

The other consideration here is what happens to this ratio over time. Look for the relationship between this ratio and the strategic direction of the organization. If conditions warrant expansion, expect the number to increase, probably for several years. If debt is declining or gets restructured, you'll also see some change. Remember that a significant change in *either* direction in debt load will translate into a significant increase or decrease in the dollars paid out of operations for interest.

Incidentally, you can reverse this ratio and get an equally useful number showing how many times net assets cover the long-term debt level.

TOTAL MARGIN

Ratio: Total Margin

Category: Profitability

Formula: $\dfrac{\text{Revenue} - \text{Expenses}}{\text{Revenue}}$

Form 990 Formula: $\dfrac{18}{12}\dfrac{19}{12}$

Sample Ratio: $\dfrac{34,000}{1,053,400} = 3.2\%$

What It Is

This is the bottom line, the one editorial writers point to with gusto, the one that tough, no-nonsense managers of all stripes supposedly focus on single-mindedly. It's what is left over after subtracting all the expenses from all the revenue, then dividing that number by all the revenue. It's the fundamental profitability indicator, and the Internal Revenue Service (IRS) requires you to show half the math just by filling out the Form 990 anyway.

What It Should Be

Higher is better, up to a point. While most nonprofit managers now recognize the necessity of at least trying to turn a profit each year, that accomplishment is merely a condition of nonprofit business, not the purpose of it.

The logical question is, "How much profit is enough?" The answer is, "What do you need it for?" Since most types of nonprofit corporations can't sell stock, and since most foundations are not keen on the idea of contributing working capital, profit is one of the few ways that the organizations can generate cash for investment, innovation, or capitalization. Generally speaking, the more stable and unchanging the organization, the less there is a need for profit. Nonprofits planning expansion, new ventures, or just trying to build a more reliable future will need higher total margins. Specific industry standards, if available, will give excellent guidance on exactly how much profitability similar groups enjoy.

OPERATING MARGIN

Ratio: Operating Margin

Category: Profitability

Formula: $\dfrac{\text{Operating revenue} - \text{Operating expense}}{\text{Operating revenue}}$

Form 990 Formula: $\dfrac{(2+3) - (13+14)}{(2+3)}$ $\dfrac{(12A - 1A) - (25A - 25D)}{(12A - 1A)}$

Sample Ratio: $\dfrac{(974{,}700 + 37{,}700) - (785{,}100 + 130{,}800)}{(974{,}700 + 37{,}700)} = 9.5\%$

What It Is

1,012,400

Push to the next level of analysis by calculating the operating margin. As useful as it is, the total margin can disguise some critical things going on in the organization. For instance, one organization experienced a giant deficit one year. Fortunately for them, that was the same year that some recently departed soul left them a more than giant bequest. One more than giant bequest minus one giant deficit equals one small profit. For one year, at least. But such good fortune masked a problem with their underlying economics that the operating ratio would have revealed.

What this ratio asks is that we compare all the revenue derived from operations against all the expenses associated with those operations. This means not counting any revenue gained from fund-raising as well as dividends, extraordinary income, and so on. To be fair, it also means eliminating identifiable expenses associated with that fund-raising. Sometimes this subtlety is not possible because data the outsider gets often does not separate out fund-raising expenses reliably (although the Form 990 does). This will tell us the true profit, minus all of that fund-raising noise.

What It Should Be

There's a funny thing about this ratio; old-timers, especially those serving on boards, often feel proud of a high level of fund-raising (i.e., a negative operating margin). And, indeed, doing a substantial amount of fund-raising is something to be proud about. But it means that the organization is extremely dependent on its contributors. Looked at another way, whoever contributes the operating revenue is unwilling or unable to pay full freight. The continued existence of the services is at the mercy of the tastes—and means—of those third-party contributors.

The answer to this dilemma only sounds evasive: The operating margin should be exactly where the organization wants it to be. Either the corporation willingly relies on fund-raising to supplement a chronically negative operating margin, or it uses fund-raising to pay for the difference between merely good programs and great ones. It's an individual choice—no one size fits all—but it should be a conscious, deliberate choice.

ACCOUNTING AGE OF PLANT/EQUIPMENT (OR LAND, BUILDINGS, AND EQUIPMENT)

Ratio: Accounting Age of Property/Plant/Equipment

Category: Miscellaneous

Formula: $\dfrac{\text{Accumulated depreciation}}{\text{Depreciation expense}}$

Form 990 Formula: $\dfrac{57b}{42a}\ \dfrac{10b}{22A}$

Sample Ratio: $\dfrac{36,000}{26,000} = 1.38$ years

What It Is

Imagine being able to read a set of financial statements in Atlanta and describe the qualitative aspects of a nonprofit's buildings and equipment in Oregon—and be right 90 percent of the time! This little trick gives you some special insight into a major aspect of a nonprofit's financial profile.

Average accounting age of plant is a pure index, even though it is measured in "years." Assets are always depreciating (i.e., wearing out), so dividing the total depreciation charged on the current tangible asset inventory by the amount charged in any one year gives an idea of how young or old the property, plant, and equipment is.

What It Should Be

Lower is better. What's really being measured is not age per se, but the rate at which plant and equipment get used up and replaced. This is another ratio that will tell you something about the organization in isolation, and even more in comparison with others in the same field.

Knowing what it takes to get the nonprofit's job done is the starting point for making use of this calculation. Hospitals, for instance, must invest in expensive equipment and keep their large buildings in good repair just to stay even with the changes in medical technology, so this is a particularly telling number for them. Success in this area means better positioning to attract the best physicians, which means more referrals, which means more revenue. Failure to keep one's investment program current even for a few years in this type of environment may take its worst toll several years later and can quickly lead to the erosion of operating results.

What It Is Not

Little depreciation activity does not allow the analyst to draw meaningful conclusions, except to venture the safe guess that the organization rents all of its sites (which could be inferred from the lack of any entry on line 57a of the Form 990 anyway). It also does not allow you to separate out the mix of items producing the depreciation charges, so a very old building could boost the number artificially even if all the equipment had come out of the box yesterday.

A FOOTNOTE

Ratios can give enormously powerful insight into a nonprofit's financial well being. Rarely does a single ratio offer reliable insight, but an integrated package can do just that, painting a picture of financial health that can be quite revealing. Most of these ratios are at their best when compared with something else such as a target value, a previous year's value, or an industry standard. Unfortunately, industry standards are hard to acquire for nonprofits. The lack of uniformity in programming, an historic lack of appreciation for the power of quantitative comparisons, and lagging computer technologies are just some of the reasons why standards don't exist in large numbers.

Happily, the picture is changing. More and more managers are beginning to realize the value of benchmarks such as these, and logical suppliers of industry averages such as associations, universities, and financial advisors are beginning to provide them. Resources like Guidestar.org are also helping out. It may very well be possible to obtain meaningful local standards from one of these types of sources. Even in their absence, however, it is worth calculating the amounts solely for internal purposes.

PART TWO

Accounting

Nonprofit Accounting: Acknowledging the Strings Attached

I f the measurement of profitability recedes as a driving force for non-profit accounting, accountability comes to the foreground. Entities whose mission is to make a profit for their owners do not have to care very much about where their money comes from or how it is used, except for some fairly broad requirements imposed by lenders or the rules of securities exchange. By contrast, nonprofit corporations often need to be scrupulous about tracing both aspects of a transaction. Beginning in 1994, the way that organizations did that began to change significantly due to the adoption of the Statement of Financial Accounting Standards (SFAS) 117, a pronouncement governing nonprofits' financial statements.

Prior to 1994, a practice called fund accounting had evolved to fulfill the more stringent standards of nonprofit accountability. In financial terms, it was the single greatest inherent difference between the two sectors in accounting and financial management. The term *fund accounting* refers to a loose collection of practices typically found in tax-exempt organizations years ago in which five separate groups within the tax-exempt field developed their own versions of fund accounting: government, hospitals, colleges and universities, health and human services agencies, and a mix of miscellaneous tax-exempt entities.

There were also at least five types of funds, and a potentially confusing presentation of the financial statements that had the effect of fragmenting the overall financial picture of the organization and making it difficult to get a coherent picture of its financial health. Imagine not just one balance sheet but several—how does one keep track of everything in that environment? The answer is, not very easily.

Initial efforts at standardization occurred within each of the industry categories, leading to a patchwork of accounting practices. Of the five, government fund accounting grew so complex and self-referencing over the last three decades that in the 1980s it became a separate category of accounting in itself, with its rule-making and standard-setting functions separated from those of commercial accounting and the rest of fund-accounting users. This field is called Generally Accepted Government Auditing Standards, pronounced gag-us, a fact that we did not make up.

NET ASSET CATEGORIES

According to the Financial Accounting Standards Board (FASB), the purpose of SFAS 117 was to "enhance the relevance, understandability, and comparability of financial statements issued by" nonprofit organizations. The pivotal consideration for SFAS 117 is the presence or absence of donor restrictions, that is, the strings attached to a nonprofit's resources. The explicit intention of SFAS 117 was to make nonprofit financial statements as readable and usable by stakeholders of the nonprofit organization as they are for commercial entities. It was effectively a recognition that former accounting practices in this field were more restrictive—and for no identifiably productive purpose—than in the commercial sector.

Now there are only three funds: (1) unrestricted; (2) temporarily restricted; and (3) permanently restricted (think of these as funds for now, funds for later, and funds forever). These groupings apply only to the net assets (formerly fund balance) of the organization.

Permanently Restricted Net Assets

These comprise the portion of net assets that result from contributions or other types of inflow of assets whose use is limited by restrictions placed by the original donor. For an asset to be permanently restricted, there needs to be a condition imposed by the donor that can never be met or that simply does not expire with the passage of time. Net assets can also be permanently restricted as a result of reclassification of other classes of net assets due to donor requirements.

Temporarily Restricted Net Assets

Net assets are classified in this fashion if it can reasonably be expected that the organization can meet the donor-imposed conditions or that the restrictions simply expire after a certain period of time.

Unrestricted Net Assets

This portion of net assets is unencumbered by any restrictions placed by donors and can therefore be used freely by the nonprofit.

OTHER PROVISIONS

SFAS 117 also standardized nonprofit financial reporting by defining what should go into the financial statements. Previously, there was a great deal of variability in the way that nonprofit organizations reported such things as cash flows and expenses. Now, a complete set of financial statements is defined as including the following:

- A statement of financial position (balance sheet)
- A statement of activities (changes in net assets)
- A statement of cash flows
- Accompanying notes
- A statement of functional expenses (voluntary health and welfare organizations only)

WHAT IT ALL MEANS

The effect of fund accounting was to treat each of the fund groups as though it were its own separate entity, with separate assets, liabilities, and net assets. The sum of the funds for each organization was the total for the corporation as a whole. Exhibit 7.1 shows a highly simplified presentation of a balance sheet under fund accounting for a hypothetical organization. Exhibit 7.2 shows the same balance sheet presented according to the stipulations of SFAS 117.

EXHIBIT 7.1   NONPROFIT BALANCE SHEET—FUND ACCOUNTING PRE-SFAS 117

	Unrestricted	Restricted	Land, Buildings, & Equipment	Endowment	Trust	Total All Funds
Assets						
Cash	$100,000	$10,000		$ 500,000	$50,000	$660,000
Accounts receivable	75,000					75,000
Securities				3,000,000		3,000,000
Land, buildings, & equipment	—	—	$500,000	—	—	500,000
	$175,000	$10,000	$500,000	$3,500,000	$50,000	$4,235,000
Liabilities						
Accounts payable	$ 50,000				$50,000	$ 100,000
Notes payable	125,000					125,000
Long-term debt			400,000			400,000
Fund balance	—	$10,000	$ 100,000	$3,500,000	—	$ 3,610,000
	$175,000	$10,000	$500,000	$3,500,000	$50,000	$4,235,000

EXHIBIT 7.2   NONPROFIT BALANCE SHEET AFTER SFAS 117

Assets	Total
Cash	$ 660,000
Accounts receivable	75,000
Securities	3,000,000
Land, buildings, & equipment	500,000
	$4,235,000

Liabilities	Total
Accounts payable	$ 100,000
Notes payable	125,000
Long-term debt	400,000
Net assets	
Unrestricted	3,600,000
Temporarily restricted	2,500
Permanently restricted	7,500
	$4,235,000

The difference is clear, even to the untrained eye. Fund accounting was complex and hard to follow and focused much more on the component parts of an agency's finances, all to get a precise picture of how the funds with strings attached have been used. Now statements treat the organization as a whole entity and only spell out restrictions for net assets. This allows everyone to view nonprofits as integrated, whole organizations rather than as the sum of many smaller parts.

That said, we must distinguish between the nature of external reporting governed by SFAS 117 and the internal needs of management. Because of the frequent demands of funding sources to account for their particular donation, nonprofit accounting must still be capable of "drilling down" to the level where the funds are being used, that is, the program level.

This higher level of accountability, the equivalent of Toyota routinely making detailed revenue and expense information available for its Prius model, comes at a price. One element of the price is that a nonprofit's accounting system needs to be able to handle that additional dimension, which tends to make it more expensive than systems that need to deal only with the corporate level.

A second element of the additional cost is that one must be able to allocate costs fairly and efficiently across the board. For example, if an individual is in charge of two programs, the accounting system must be able to reflect the fact that the cost of paying the individual should be spread across two programs. For-profit corporations have the same kind of need, but in that context it is called a *cost accounting system*. It usually supports the pricing function without any of the legal and public accountability built into the average nonprofit's financial reports.

The complications of financial accountability do not stop here. Programs rarely have a single funding source, and those programs with multiple funding sources need to match some portion of program funding with some portion of program expenses. In short, because there is a second level of data gathering and reporting, there must be a third level, as follows:

Corporate Level
Program Level
Program Funding Level

The interaction between program funding level information needs and the nature of nonprofit accounting itself gives nonprofit organizations the characteristics of operating as though they were a collection of independent businesses. That sense of independent internal entities is actually pretty close to the mark and was encouraged by traditional fund accounting. It is also one of the reasons why accounting software developers were relatively slow to develop packages that could serve nonprofit users.

One side effect of the need for program-funding level accountability is that it sets a good foundation for management accountability as well. The chapter on management controls explains this idea further.

A negative side effect is that it complicates the accounting task. A for-profit company with two or three different products producing a million dollars of revenue will probably have internal financial statements that do not distinguish between the products in any way. For that type of information, they would have to rely either on a cost accounting system or, more likely, the general manager's intuitive sense and a few quick calculations by the bookkeeper. A comparable nonprofit, on the other hand, would be likely to have to report its expenses and probably its revenues by program at some point, which means that its accounting system for the same revenue level would have to be more sophisticated.

To make things more complicated, the most scrutinized spending area is typically personnel. As long as a given individual works in only one program, his or her expenses can be charged directly to that program. But as soon as one individual is assigned to two or more programs, his or her

COST REPORTING VS. COST ACCOUNTING

Distinguish between cost reporting and cost accounting. The former is usually a creature of some sort of regulated environment such as in the federal Medicare program. It consists largely of submitting information on costs in a standardized format that is then used by a governmental agency or some sort of other payer. Financial accountants generally handle cost reporting, because it is so tied to the accounting records. Cost accounting, on the other hand, is a management function that attempts to collect information in some consistent fashion so that managers will know or at least be able to estimate the cost of decisions such as increasing services delivered or adding a major capital asset. Management accountants and analysts tend to run cost accounting systems.

overall cost has to be shared ("allocated") among the programs, and the task gets complicated.

Devising a reasonable and workable set of allocations and maintaining them is difficult enough under any circumstances, but if the accounting system is flawed in any way, the job could be hopelessly muddied. One $2.5 million antipoverty agency had several thousands of dollars in questioned costs as a result of one audit. The problem was that they had faithfully kept time and attendance records to support the payroll, but at some point a year's worth of allocation formulas and worksheets had disappeared.

Although they could prove that employees had in fact worked the hours that they were reported to have worked, using attendance records, they couldn't reconstruct how employees who crossed program lines had been allocated. Ninety-five percent of the total revenues came from government, and the auditors never questioned whether payroll payments had been made as recorded. The only reason the costs were questioned was because the organization was unable to show how it allocated costs to the various government funding sources. Ultimately, the organization suffered serious problems with their government funders.

Historic changes in nonprofit accounting simplified a previously complicated reporting style. Policy makers in the field now seem to recognize that nonprofit financial statements should convey useful information similar to their for-profit counterparts; but the strings-attached nature of nonprofit accounting, especially for public charities, will continue to demand a relatively higher degree of financial sophistication than that typically necessary in the commercial world.

CHAPTER 8

Cost Accounting:
How Much Does It Cost?

How much does it cost to provide your services? There are many answers. But the one thing that all responses to the question have in common is that they must first answer the equally important question, "Who cares?"

The theoretical answer to this resonant question is easier than the practical one. Speaking from the moral high ground, everyone connected with a nonprofit has a reason for caring about the cost of services in order to make sure that they are delivered as efficiently as possible. Certainly, boards of directors should know the true cost of services as part of their fiduciary responsibility.

In practical terms, however, the real answer to the question "Who cares?" is rooted in economics rather than the public good. Historically, some non-profits must care a great deal about the cost of their services while others feel little economic pressure to do so. Beginning with the 2008 recession, it is safe to say that virtually all nonprofits have had to pay more attention to this area.

For any nonprofit, there are many reasons beyond the moral and narrowly financial to have some type of cost accounting information. To the extent that any proposed programming resembles an existing service, it is always extremely helpful to have cost information while building a planned budget. Cost information allows comparisons between services both inside and outside of the nonprofit organization. It can also be useful for political and grant-winning purposes to be able to show an actual cost per unit of service delivered.

In the past, especially in health and human services, cost accounting was important because of the way it produced information requested by government purchasers in order to set rates. The implicit assumption was that providers would be nonprofit, and, unlike for-profit companies, they would only be concerned with recouping their costs.

With changing economic conditions and the rise of simplified, prospective payment systems, the role of cost accounting as the source of compliance with regulations has diminished but, ironically, management has begun to value it more as a tool for internal decision making. Did a particular program make money last year? Why or why not? If we keep a losing program open, what will it do to our fiscal health? Why are these two very similar programs' costs behaving so differently? Cost accounting can help answer questions like these, and it can also provide the raw material for much deeper analyses. Even if a nonprofit gets all of its funding from non-contract sources, it will have to have a good understanding of its cost structure to succeed in the future.

A FORM OF MANAGEMENT ACCOUNTING

Cost accounting is a form of management accounting. In order to do it right, the underlying financial accounting must be sound. One of the distinguishing features of financial accounting is that its records are or could potentially be subject to verification. Cost accounting, on the other hand, while its mechanics are just as mathematical and logical as financial accounting, rests on concepts that tend to be unique to an institution. For that reason, cost accounting information rarely has much meaning outside of an organization unless the definition and treatment of costs are standardized.

Cost accounting would be a lot simpler if the only costs incurred to deliver a product or service were clear-cut and directly attributable to that service. In fact, if that were the case, it wouldn't exist at all. Costs that can be readily identified with a particular service using a reasonable amount of effort can be handled via accounting systems. These are called the direct costs of producing a service. Since the vast majority of nonprofits produce services rather than manufactured products, we will use the term *service,* although the principles would be the same for product manufacturing. Some examples of direct costs might be the following:

- Salaries of employees delivering the service
- Their supplies
- Their equipment
- Their telephone calls
- Expenses of the physical space they use

But what about the expense of keeping the financial records associated with the service? What about the cost of the organization's CEO or president? The legal advice the corporation receives? The sign in front of the institution's office? These are all legitimate indirect costs of doing business that must be taken into consideration in identifying a meaningful cost. If the nonprofit corporation provides only a single service, and does not conduct its own fund-raising, then effectively there is no such thing as indirect costs. But as soon as it provides two or more distinct services, or conducts its own fund-raising, its management and possibly its funders will want to know the answer to the question, "How much does it cost?" and only a cost accounting system can provide the answers.

In any organization, there are two types of activities—the services the institution is in existence to provide, and those activities that support the delivery of those services. For instance, in the Committee to Clean Up Amigosville (CCUA), such things as recycling and public education are the reasons the organization was established in the first place. Bookkeeping and marketing staff, even though they may work very closely with recycling or public education staff, exist solely to support the latter.

There is no single accepted set of names for these two categories of activity. CCUA's recycling and public education programs might be called mission centers, direct services, program centers, line programs, or the like. Bookkeeping and marketing might be called service centers, support services, or administrative services. Whatever the names, the distinction between these two types of costs will pop up later in significant ways. We will use the terms *program* and *support*.

In keeping with our central premise that this is a book for consumers of financial information rather than producers, we will not get into the specifics of setting up and maintaining a cost accounting system. Instead, we will focus on how to evaluate an existing system or how to think about a new one.

There are two things that the average nonprofit cost accounting system has to do well if it is to provide managers with useful information: (1) distinguish between direct and indirect costs, and (2) assign certain support costs to other support costs before the entire cost of support gets divided among all direct services. (Note that this is for internal management purposes only since the American Institute of Certified Public Accountants [AICPA] guides and the IRS Form 990 instructions do not permit it for external reporting.)

INDIRECT COSTS

In most instances, the difference between direct and indirect costs is easily handled by the accounting system. In fact, if the accounting system is unable to identify indirect costs, take it as a wake-up call to find out what's wrong. The real issue with indirect costs is how they are defined. For reasons that we will discuss later, indirect costs are inherently slippery characters. No one seems to define them in exactly the same way, unless they are operating in a very tightly regulated environment.

The effect of this free-form definition of indirect costs is that comparisons among many types of nonprofit organizations are pointless. Unless the chart of accounts and related procedures for two organizations are extremely similar, comparing indirect costs will be misleading at best and counterproductive at worst. Nevertheless, comparisons for internal purposes can still be valuable and are the basis for calculating actual costs of providing services.

CERTAIN SUPPORT COSTS GET ASSIGNED TO OTHER SUPPORT COSTS

If the cost accounting system can distinguish between direct and indirect costs, it passes its first test. Next comes the hard part. Some indirect costs are rightfully borne by both program services and support services. For example, occupancy costs such as heat, lights, and air conditioning must be carried by all types of services whether they are engaged in providing program services directly or supporting them. The principle is that each type of support service that makes use of another support service must take on its share of that support service before being broken up and distributed across the program services. Exhibit 8.1 shows a brief example of how this might work for CCUA.

EXHIBIT 8.1 ALLOCATION OF COSTS

Expense or Program Category	Total Costs	Management & General	Fund-Raising	Total Cost	Total Units of Service	Full Cost	
Management and general	$ 130,800						
Fund-raising	103,500	$ 15,235					
Volunteer teams	252,900	37,226	$ 38,247	$ 328,373	11 Teams	$29,852	Per Team
Public education/seminars	156,600	23,051	23,683	203,335	32 Seminars	$ 6,354	Per Seminar
Recycling	375,600	55,288	56,804	487,692	1,500 Days	$ 325	Per Day
Totals	$1,019,400	$130,800	$118,734	$1,019,400			

The structure of this analysis bears explaining. The ultimate goal is to get a number under the total cost column that is the sum of the total direct costs of each program plus all of the support costs shown on the lines to the right. In effect, as the total direct cost for each program marches to the right, it passes through each column of support costs, where it picks up its fair share of those costs. The sum of all these direct costs and pieces of support costs then gets divided by the number of units of service the program has delivered to arrive at what can be called the "fully loaded" cost. More on each of these elements later.

There is an important logic here. The columns are arrayed in a very specific order, starting with those support costs that affect the greatest number of other service centers and support costs. For CCUA, the first support cost to be distributed is the cost of management and general activities. All direct services take management resources, but so do support activities such as fund-raising. The result is that every type of activity must carry its share.

Fund-raising is next because it affects all other departments except management. Notice that the sum of fund-raising costs has increased from $103,500 in the original budget to $118,734 in this analysis because fund-raising was just assigned its share of management resources of $15,235. This newly swelled fund-raising cost then gets broken down according to some reasonable basis for allocation among the three direct service programs. In this example, we have assumed that the rough size of each program's expenses is a reasonable guide to allocating management and general costs. The result is a "fully loaded" cost because each direct cost has picked up its share of the load of each type of support service.

Deciding how to allocate portions of costs is always tricky. Sometimes there is an obvious basis, such as using cost per square foot to allocate occupancy expenses. Even with such a straightforward basis, however, there may be complications. For example, it may be theoretically easy enough to measure the square footage used by each department, but common areas such as halls and stairways and the copy machine alcove must also be factored into the equation.

Percentage of payroll is a popular basis for allocation, the theory being that the demands on management and general resources can be expected to roughly parallel the percentage of total staff a particular program uses. This may be generally true, but when it fails as a standard, it fails miserably. For instance, setting up a new service typically demands extraordinary management resources yet rarely provides additional reimbursement for those expenses. Or some programs may use a disproportionately high number of staff but prove to be relatively easy to run, while smaller programs may necessarily require a lot of administrative support. Using the program's total revenue as a percentage of the nonprofit's total revenue may also be an acceptable method for allocating costs, but this choice is susceptible to the same pitfalls as payroll percentages. For CCUA, we relied on percentages of the total spending amounts in question rather than any more complicated basis such as personnel hours. Parenthetically, actual time reporting is often the best source of guidance about how to charge time, and for staff exempt from federal fair labor standards, this can be accomplished as easily as using time studies done randomly throughout the year.

Visually and mathematically, this cost analysis has a distinguishing characteristic. Each of the two columns being allocated starts at a point one line lower than the previous column. In a larger organization with a more complicated cost analysis, the series of downward steps might stretch clear across the page, looking very much like a neat set of stairs. This is why Exhibit 8.1 symbolizes the essence of what is called a *stepdown analysis*. Each column picks up its share of costs from the one to its left, then steps itself down to the remaining columns to its right until all indirect costs have been allocated.

This exhibit is nothing more than one version of a cost analysis for one organization. Different organizations will chose different methods for entirely different and valid reasons. Whatever the method chosen, it should meet four criteria (see Box). First, it should be consistently applied across the entire organization and over a period of time. Second, it should be a reasonable method of allocation, meaning that it should not use tortured

THE FOUR TESTS OF A COST ALLOCATION SYSTEM

1. Consistently applied over time
2. Reasonable choice of allocation bases
3. Flexible and practical
4. Conforms to applicable industry standards

logic simply to support a predetermined outcome. Third, it should be flexible in the sense that it should fit all programs' cost accounting needs without significant reworking just to arrive at a fully loaded cost figure. Finally, it should conform to prevailing standards for the particular field of nonprofit endeavor, if any.

Readers with a fondness for simplicity will ask why we do not simply allocate a share of fund-raising costs and a share of management and general costs to each of CCUA's programs rather than go through this exercise. The answer is that we could, if we were willing to accept a less precise calculation of costs. Managers make that kind of calculation frequently for rough planning purposes, but if one is going to go through the effort of analyzing costs, it makes sense to get them as precise as possible.

A brief digression to highlight the obvious: CCUA needs a cost accounting analysis because it offers different types of services. If it were a single-service nonprofit, there would be little point in analyzing costs since a few simple calculations as just described would be enough to get a cost per unit of service. What this cost analysis does is to differentiate the three types of service and load each one with the appropriate mix of indirect costs. Even if CCUA were a single-service organization with several different departments or program units delivering the service, it would require this kind of cost accounting.

Be aware that Exhibit 8.1 is a completely backward-looking exercise. The fiscal year is over, the expenses have been accumulated, and all we are doing here is putting these well-behaved figures in their proper columns. There is an implied orderliness in these calculations that simply is not real. To give the cost accounting some punch, one might go back, say, three years in order to see how costs behaved over time and to draw at least some tentative inferences about how they will behave in the future.

BREAKEVEN ANALYSIS—ANOTHER USE FOR COST DATA

The practical usefulness of knowing a nonprofit's true costs cannot be underestimated for planning purposes. Building next year's budget or evaluating a potential new program is much easier with good cost information. Especially when considering a new program, there are multiple uncertainties. How many units of service should we plan to deliver? At what price?

How will we know if the new program is financially healthy? Is there a financial point below which we should consider terminating it? These questions can all be answered by using the output of a cost accounting system.

The classic form of cost planning is called *breakeven analysis*. Done properly, breakeven analysis can give practicing managers a simple yet powerful tool for estimating the impact of new ventures. Breakeven analysis starts with the presumption that there are two types of costs in any organization: (1) those that stay fixed regardless of what happens to the program, and (2) those that vary according to the volume of service the program delivers.

Fixed costs are easy to understand and relatively easy to identify. They are the expenses of "opening the doors," the costs that one must incur just to be prepared to provide the service regardless of whether one actually delivers one unit of service or a thousand. Typically, fixed costs are considered in the context of a particular service or program, so that in CCUA's recycling program some fixed costs would be equipment rental agreements, occupancy costs, and depreciation for whatever assets the program is assigned. Each of these costs is inescapable if CCUA wants to run a recycling program. The organization must expect to spend that money no matter what kind of revenue the program produces.

Other costs will vary with the volume of service provided and therefore are called *variable costs*. Many of the other expenses fall into this category. For example, the cost of supplies can be presumed to increase in roughly direct relationship to the amount of service delivered.

Unfortunately, many other costs are not so neatly categorized because a part of them is fixed and another part is variable. Salaries and wages are a good example of this type of expense, since a certain number of positions can be expected to be necessary just to open the doors, but an increase in volume will necessitate additional staff. A recycling program will need at least a telephone line or two, the installation charge and basic service for which is assumed as part of a contract and consequently is fixed. But the rest of the telephone bill will be for usage, and that presumably will go up or down in an approximate relationship to volume.

These other costs are called semifixed or semivariable, depending on which is their dominant character. One way to think about them so as to allow them to co-exist with the concept of fixed costs is to regard them as variable (or fixed) *within a certain range of volume*. Over the long run, all costs are variable because whatever gives them their fixed nature is usually only true for a defined period of time. Occupancy costs, which seem fixed for the moment, will change once the rental agreement is renegotiated or when the program changes in size so much that it needs new quarters. Depreciation is fixed for a year at a time, but even that will go up should new depreciable assets be acquired. With this understanding, we can proceed to the fundamental breakeven formula:

Breakeven volume = Fixed costs + (Variable costs × Units served)

The same idea in traditional formula format looks like this:

$$B = F + (V)(U)$$

Where

B = Breakeven
F = Fixed costs
V = Variable costs, expressed per unit of service
U = Number of units served 👆

For example, if a child care program knew its fixed costs for an after-school program were $132,000 and its variable cost was $1,100 per child, its breakeven point for a 100-child program would be:

$$\$242,000 = 132,000 + (1,100)(100)$$

Revenues of less than $242,000 would be inadequate to cover the program's costs. Revenues over this point would result in a profit.

Practically, breakeven analysis is more often used to determine the desired level of utilization, or the number of children in this case. It can also be very helpful in determining an appropriate price level in those cases where the nonprofit is free to set its own prices. Leaving any one variable unassigned to a value and then performing elementary algebra will yield the recommended amount for that quantity.

If you carefully analyze the whole idea behind breakeven analysis you will see its manufacturing heritage. The implicit assumption is that it is based in an environment characterized by linear behavior—the breakeven graphic sketched by the formula above is a cost line rising from southwest to northeast on an X-Y graph. It is more or less intuitive and visually pleasing, and for the manufacturing economy of much of the twentieth century it made a great deal of sense.

It makes less sense in a multiple-product environment—at least, it makes less sense to expect an individual without access to fancy business planning software to produce a breakeven analysis. It also makes even less sense in the provision of services, which is of course what nonprofits usually provide. So breakeven analysis has its limitations for nonprofits. It is most likely to be helpful in planning programs that have a production-like feel to them, which is why it worked well in the child care example above. It can also work well as a rough guide to organization-wide planning. For example, just calculating one's estimated fixed costs and variable costs can guide planners' thinking about the management demands of an organization with a large fixed cost, such as a symphony orchestra's concert hall.

COST ACCOUNTING VERSUS COST REPORTING

A final word about the difference between cost accounting and cost reporting. Cost accounting is almost purely a management exercise, while cost reporting has legal and contractual implications. One must have at least a basic cost accounting system in order to report costs accurately to an external party such as a funder. However, the cost reporting function is often so structured and carefully laid out that the pressure is on the financial person to master the reporting system rather than produce anything of value to management. That is why a nonprofit operating in a heavily regulated cost-based field will still need a separate cost accounting system in order to make informed decisions.

Even a modest cost accounting system can offer the nonprofit manager a powerful tool for managing programs. For any given period, it can reveal the underlying economics of programs in as much detail as desired. It can show, in a standardized fashion, which services are financially viable and which are not. As a planning tool, it can help suggest which service directions are most promising and which should be deferred. Without exaggeration, it is probably the single most potent analytical tool the average manager can use for decision making.

Which is why the output of a nonprofit cost accounting system may need to be ignored. Cost accounting in a for-profit organization rightfully offers more value than it does in a nonprofit setting, because a for-profit organization needs to stick with its winners and tolerate its money losers only if they show promise of making money or at least adding value eventually. In nonprofits, the crucial measure is whether a program supports the mission and not solely whether it has a positive bottom line. Sometimes carrying a money-losing program is simply the right thing to do, and that alone is a legitimate reason for keeping it.

Cost accounting can be useful even when it delivers bad news about a losing program. For one thing, it will document that the program's economics are out of sync, and that alone may be enough to tease some additional dollars out of a funding source. For another, managers are always better off knowing the precise location and reason for a problem rather than having to guess about it. Finally, a cost accounting system can help identify other programs better able to subsidize the occasional money loser through higher profits.

So the real message is that a cost accounting program is worse than useless if it becomes the sole measuring standard for deciding whether to keep a program. Mission should rule, not the activities designed to support mission. To paraphrase Oscar Wilde only slightly, a cynic is a person who knows the cost of everything, and the value of nothing.

CHAPTER 9

Auditing:
Choosing and Using an Auditor

Time to rush into an area where angels fear to tread as we consider the role, selection, and use of outside auditors. Independent audits are ingenious transactions. Here you have one party, usually some type of funding source, requiring a second party, the nonprofit corporation, to hire outsiders to examine the organizational equivalent of personal possessions and then file a public report on their findings. What's more, the whole thing is an entirely private arrangement, with no direct government involvement in the actual inspection.

Read the opinion letter in Exhibit 9.1 carefully. It says exactly what it means, not surprisingly, since the conventional wording has been tested and revised continuously for many years. The auditor says that he or she has inspected the books and records and found them to be adequate enough to generate the financial statements that are attached to it. More important, the auditor says explicitly that those financial statements convey reliable information.

Let's be frank, shall we? Most practicing managers, on the whole, would rather not have external audits. They take up valuable staff time, disrupt operations anywhere from a few days to several months, cost money, and may produce unpleasant surprises (ever notice how most financial surprises are unpleasant?). Sure, they can and should provide some valuable suggestions for improving things, and the process can even help shape an organization's future. But few managers would voluntarily submit to an audit once every year solely on the basis of these benefits.

EXHIBIT 9.1   SAMPLE INDEPENDENT AUDITORS'
OPINION LETTER

Dear ___:

We have audited the accompanying balance sheet of ___ as of June 30, 20xx, and the related statements of public support, revenue, and expenses and changes in fund balances, statements of functional expenses, and cash flows for the year then ended. These financial statements are the responsibility of the Company's management. Our responsibility is to express an opinion on these financial statements based on our audit.

We conducted our audit in accordance with generally accepted auditing standards. Those standards require that we plan and perform the audit to obtain reasonable assurance about whether the financial statements are free of material misstatement. An audit includes examining, on a test basis, evidence supporting the amounts and disclosures in the financial statements. An audit also includes assessing the accounting principles used and significant estimates made by management, as well as evaluating the overall financial statement presentation. We believe that our audit provides a reasonable basis for our opinion.

In our opinion, the financial statements referred to above present fairly, in all material respects, the financial position of _____ as of June 30, 20xx, and the results of its operations and its cash flow for the year then ended in conformity with generally accepted accounting principles.

Regards,

[Name]

[Title and Affiliation]

The audience for that letter, then, is outside the nonprofit organization. Presumably, management already knows that their financial systems and practices produce reliable information, but who is really going to believe them? Too many opportunities to do a little self-promotion might obscure the real financial condition of the organization. Outside third-party observers without the same self-interested incentives can be trusted more.

Why would those other than management care about internal financial matters anyway? The answer is the same for both nonprofits and for-profits: money. In one form or another, suppliers of funds have the most influence over whether and how auditors do their work. In the for-profit environment, those suppliers are banks, investors, and stockholders. Nonprofits' equivalents are banks, foundations, donors, and the government as a purchaser of goods and services. Each interest-holder has a different motive for wanting reassurance about financial conditions.

AUDIT, REVIEW, AND COMPILATION

The practice of outside accountants looking at an entity's financial records has coalesced into three distinct levels: audit, review, and compilation. Each type of report offers a different mix of complexity of the analysis, time required for its completion, and strength of assurance given (Exhibit 9.2).

A compilation is the lowest end of the continuum, involving little more than the gathering together of various financial records into a standardized, readable format. The accountant expresses no opinions on the material presented and does no tests to confirm its veracity.

A review goes one step beyond a simple compilation. In a review, the accountant compiles the information into standardized formats and then performs some quick analyses to see if it seems to have internal consistency. The accountant offers no opinion, only what is called negative assurance: "I'm not aware of anything that would materially alter these statements." The report reader gets information presented in traditional formatting in addition to the comfort of knowing that an intelligent set of eyes has reviewed the material for extreme inconsistencies or significant gaps in data.

The audit is the deepest, most intensive examination of a set of books possible. Auditors test management's representations in many different ways according to preestablished protocols. In addition, prolonged exposure to the books and records gives auditors greater opportunity to spot errors and omissions and to make suggestions for improvement.

At the same time, there are no guarantees. Unless one second-guesses 100 percent of all transactions, there is no basis to certify the absence of fraud or material misstatement—and even then there would need to be a lot of additional second-guessing in other areas. Instead, the audit opinion offers assurance that skilled accounting professionals have examined the

Compilation	Review	Audit
Low		High

Degree of: Complexity
Time Required
Assurance

EXHIBIT 9.2   The Three Levels of Reporting

financial records and feel that they can be relied on. In short, an audit offers exactly the level of reliability that the opinion letter says it does.

Who Uses What

Because the market for auditing services is driven by who wants the assurance, different types and sizes of nonprofit organizations need different types of work. Compilations tend to be favored by small, relatively unsophisticated private for-profit companies. For a variety of reasons, they are not an option for most nonprofits. Reviews are an alternative to a full audit for certain nonprofit corporations, although state laws may make this choice available only to groups with the smallest revenues. By contrast, reviews are a popular choice for many privately held for-profit businesses since they give some minimal level of outside evaluation at a lower price and with less disclosure than an audit.

Whenever maximum accountability is required, managers must choose a traditional audit. This is why most larger nonprofit public charities will be audited. In a sense, the various governmental and other regulations stipulating audit types are just affirming what a prudent public charity manager would do anyway. The public's trust in a charity is so fragile and yet so critical to its functioning that independent audits are a natural means of gaining that assurance.

The Audit Equation

There is a dynamic at work in nonprofit audits that rarely gets spoken of directly between the organization and its auditors. We call it the audit equation, and it is the balance between auditing and bookkeeping shown in Exhibit 9.3. The former is the auditors' job, the latter is the responsibility of management. If both parties labor quietly at their respective chores with little effective communication between them about this central expectation, the result can be a mutual misunderstanding or even a breakdown in the relationship. Remember that the audit is supposed to be an opinion on the reliability of *management's* financial statements. That means that management is expected to prepare the statements, and the outside auditors will analyze them and the systems that produced the information so as to offer an opinion on their collective reliability. When management fails to do things like

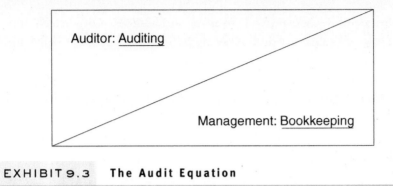

EXHIBIT 9.3   The Audit Equation

reconcile bank statements, prepare depreciation schedules, and even enter basic accounting data, the auditors have to do it instead.

When the outside auditors have to do this type of work, it increases the audit cost for the organization since the auditors must also act as bookkeepers. More important, if it happens to a significant extent, the auditors find themselves effectively auditing their own work. This impairs their independence and in extreme cases can even prevent the issuance of an opinion.

The simple way to avoid these problems is to keep the audit equation in mind. This has become easier since the advent of the Sarbanes-Oxley law and the updated GAO regulations. Management must always be careful to do all operations in its corner, leaving the auditors to concentrate on their corner. In addition to being a good idea, this formulation has the newly added benefit of being consistent with the new laws and practices in the field. The disk accompanying this book gives an audit self-test for clarifying this question.

THE AUDITOR MARKET

Like all other professions, auditing services have their own distinct and definable market. Individual CPAs are the professionals qualified and licensed to give an opinion about the financial health of business entities. They exist in many different forms, from the part-timer who works out of a spare bedroom to the sole practitioner employing a dozen or more staff, to one of many professional personnel in an international firm. These professionals can be found on just about any type of engagement, from nonprofits to start-up proprietary businesses to individuals.

Each type of audit firm tends to shape its clientele in predictable ways. Small firms and sole practitioners, as might be expected, handle small local audits and reviews. When an organization grows too large or too sophisticated for this level, or needs consulting services, it will often gravitate to smaller national or large regional firms where it can find more nonprofit specialists and access to the latest industry knowledge. Large national public charities often use one of the Big Four, the nickname for the largest auditing firms.

Elements of Auditor Choice

Most nonprofit managers regard the yearly financial audit as a commodity. There is some debate over this point among auditors themselves, but in economic terms if most buyers see something as a commodity, that's the way the market will behave. What truly distinguishes one audit from another is when it is carried out by auditors with deep knowledge of the industry they are auditing. Even if the results are the same, the audit done by industry experts is far more likely to go smoothly and quickly and to teach management a thing or two in the process. Research shows that one of the prime reasons for making an auditor change is industry familiarity, and auditing firms with marketing savvy are beginning to organize themselves to offer that feature to the industries in which they specialize.

Who chooses the auditor? In truth, this is one of those instances where the textbooks say one thing and real-world practice says another. For the record, the board should make the decision. Further, the board should meet with its auditors at least once a year to get a firsthand account of the agency's financial status, and it ought to maintain at least an informal dialogue in the interim.

In reality, some boards are either too busy, too uninterested, or too intimidated to take the lead in an auditing relationship. It then falls to the CEO, who often delegates it to the CFO. By itself, there's nothing fatal about this scenario. It just means that the agency's fiduciaries have voluntarily given up a means of ensuring accountability. When this single step is part of a larger pattern of refusing to demand accountability from management, it can mean that an important element of leadership is lacking.

One effect of the Sarbanes-Oxley law (see Chapter 19) is that boards of publicly held companies have been forced to take more responsibility for the relationship with the auditor. As individuals with private sector experience serve on nonprofit boards or become nonprofit financial executives, it is quite likely that the pendulum will swing back in the direction of greater board accountability in this area.

HOW TO PURCHASE AUDIT SERVICES

Auditing services are professional services. Once a minimum level of technical competence is established, the primary goal of a professional services procurement is to determine the fit between the professional service provider and the service user. Resist the urge to demand responses with fine-point specificity, as though the answers were going to be placed side-by-side on a spreadsheet for comparison. That's how you buy wheat, apples, milk, and other commodities, not professional services.

The traditional way to solicit auditing services is through a Request for Proposals (RFP). There is no single correct way to design an RFP, but here are some things to keep in mind:

- *Describe the organization thoroughly.* What is your mission? When were you founded? Are you a 501(c)(3) or some other type of nonprofit? What are your services? Are there special circumstances the auditors should know about (e.g., this is the first financial audit after a merger)? It is helpful but not necessary to include a copy of audited financial statements at this stage—you can make them available during preproposal interviews—but do include summary financial information such as revenues and their sources and balance sheet data.

- *State what you need.* State explicitly what you need the auditing firm to do. Some nonprofits want their auditors to audit the financial statements, complete the tax return(s), and file various financial reports, while others want only the audited financials.

- *Request qualifications.* Request that the auditors describe their qualifications to audit your organization. Explicitly link your needs with their qualifications, such as "Must have experience performing OMB A-133 audits."

- *Describe your timetable, decision process, and selection criteria.* Detail how you will make a decision, when, and on what basis. A

(Continued)

(Continued)

formula with points for various criteria is bureaucratic but probably harmless. Best to be straightforward here. *Note:* By all rights, the auditors report to the board, so they should be the ultimate decision makers even if staff does most of the work.

As much as possible, send the RFP to practitioners and firms you know to be skilled in your industry and appropriate providers of service. Be prepared to meet with each candidate in person (if they don't request a personal visit, ask yourself why). Give plenty of time for all parties concerned to do their jobs—four to eight weeks should work—and plan to put in at least as much time managing the process as any single candidate will in responding to you. Use the process as a management tool.

GETTING VALUE FROM THE AUDIT

The Management Letter

At the end of the audit process, the audit team has accumulated a tremendous amount of knowledge, new or updated, about how the nonprofit runs its affairs. The team will put some of that information into its final report, but a good measure of it will never see the inside of a financial statement and yet is extremely valuable to management. The solution to this dilemma is the management letter.

The point to remember about a management letter is simple—*get one.* You deserve it. You and your staff put in the time, you worked through the entire audit process, and now it's payback time. The hours that these informed outsiders spent looking at the nonprofit from the inside out can produce valuable insights about what areas need improvement. The letter should include both findings and recommendations for action, so it's like the first step of a how-to course. Take advantage of it.

Specialized Reporting

The federal government has auditing requirements for groups receiving federal funding of any sort. As a result, very specific audit guidelines now exist for universities, hospitals, governmental entities, and public charities

THE CHILL ON THE MANAGEMENT LETTER

A subtle chill has crept into the practice of issuing management letters in recent years. It started when government funders learned about management letters and decided that they liked the idea so much that they wanted to get a copy of it for themselves. In geographic areas where this has happened, one can imagine the effect it's had on the content of the management letter. An auditor wishing to communicate various problems with a client's financial system is going to be a whole lot less willing to put into writing anything that might put that client in a bad light, especially if there are less formal ways of communicating the information. So it appears that there has been a gradual move toward including only those things that must be communicated, and a search for less damning ways of communicating other material.

Another reason for the gradual diminution in importance of the management letter has been computerization. Many of the comments about sloppy or inconsistent practices from 10 and 20 years ago that might otherwise have shown up in an average management letter tend to be eliminated by good accounting software.

receiving direct or, in some cases, indirect federal funds. In addition, professional standard-setting societies in the accounting field have established standards for auditing and for the training of personnel who work on these types of audits.

Some of these requirements include Office of Management and Budget Circular A-133 (OMB A-133), the Single Audit Act, the Guide to Audits of Nonprofit and Governmental Entities (the "Yellow Book"), and various pronouncements of the Financial Accounting Standards Board and the Governmental Accounting Standards Board.

These governmental requirements tend to shift more of the burden for examining recipients of federal funds from the government itself to private auditors. For example, OMB A-133 dictates a series of signed opinion letters from the auditors on matters ranging from the effectiveness of the internal controls governing federal funds to compliance with certain federal laws. In a different time and place, this type of certification would very likely have been done by the government itself. Today, government requires that the private sector do it.

As a result, governmental and nonprofit auditing is becoming more standardized and a bit more technical. This raises the hurdle for auditors wishing to get into the field or stay in it. For instance, there are now minimum continuing education requirements for those who work on these types of audits.

The implication is that it is no longer practical for small-to-medium-sized firms to do just one or two such audits since they will have to invest a minimum amount of time in learning the rules and staying current. In turn, this will cause firms to pull out of incidental nonprofit auditing relationships or to make a larger specialization of it. At present, the nonprofit auditor market is fragmented. In part, this is because nonprofits tend to be smaller organizations more likely to come to the attention of small, local audit practices. This is an industry practically begging for consolidation, so as average agency size and complexity increase, the total numbers of audit firms active in the field will decrease.

One can see the same patterns at work in varying degrees across the nonprofit field. Universities, for example, are now so large and complex that relatively few audit practices are able even to consider taking one on as a client, whereas domestic violence agencies are so small and diverse that it is highly unlikely that there will be a concentration of audit talent in a few firms. As the government's demands on auditors rise, and as the various categories of nonprofits themselves mature, the potential number of nonprofit auditors will decline. This diminished choice should be offset somewhat as the quality of services provided by those who do choose to specialize in the field increases, meaning an overall increase in value for consumers.

Conclusion

Yearly financial audits are a necessary part of nonprofit financial management. The motivation for outside inspection in this field has more to do with accountability than the protection of investment characteristic of the for-profit world. Still, the process holds the potential for great usefulness to managers if it is handled effectively. All it takes is a little bit of time, skill, and knowledge of the industry to make it a mini-asset of the nonprofit corporation.

Operations

CHAPTER 10

Cash Flow Management: Why Cash Is King

C ash is king in the nonprofit realm as elsewhere. Those who have it can do just about anything. Those who do not, stagger. Adequate cash allows the organization to pay its bills. More than adequate cash gives the organization a source of additional revenue, an operating cushion, and liberation from some of the daily grind of financial existence. Much more than adequate cash confers something more: power.

Some of the most powerful of all nonprofit institutions are hospitals and universities. The major versions of each almost always have a solid cash position, derived from a number of sources, which they can use either in operations or investments. Their power comes with their control of capital, and controlling a sizable portion of cash means controlling some potent capital. (For more on the role of capital in a nonprofit organization, see Chapter 11 on capital structure.)

Nonprofit organizations with adequate cash can do two critical things: survive crises and take advantage of opportunities. Few crises are true threats to an organization's existence—even if it may seem that way at the time—as long as the group has the resources to respond. It takes more than cash, of course, but cash can make an effective response immeasurably easier. Similarly, it takes cash to buy a building, start up a program, or do some research, and all of these things can be an *investment* in the nonprofit's future. Organizations with inadequate cash are shut off from those potential investments and easily trapped by crises.

The need to manage cash flow is particularly acute in a nonprofit setting because few nonprofits operate as cash businesses. Not only is this inherent in the services—as distinct from, say, a bar or a pizza shop—but funders like the accountability that it brings. And, naturally, no nonprofit is immune from the effects of forces as diverse as economic swings, abrupt changes in market conditions, or natural disasters.

The job of managing cash flow consists of creating cash or moving assets toward a liquid, or cash, state and incurring the right liabilities. The trick is knowing when and how to do this.

UP THE BALANCE SHEET

The simplest way to "create" cash is to change an asset from a less liquid form to cash. Think of the different classes of assets as being like the different states of water. Down at the bottom of the asset side you'll find land, buildings, and equipment—very tangible assets. These are like ice. They are cold, stiff, unchanging, and not responsive. Toward the middle of the continuum are things like stocks and bonds. These assets are a lot like water—they'll move when you arrange for it to happen, but left on their own they'll just puddle. At the top is cash, which is like steam—fast moving, constantly changing, and quickly disappearing.

To keep the metaphor going, part of the job of cash management consists of knowing when and where to apply a little heat to the assets. Running out of steam? Heat up some water/investments. No assets in this category? Turn to the ice.

Let's look at the example in Exhibit 10.1. Suppose that the organization represented here had yearly expenses of $3.5 million. With those kinds of numbers, the balance sheet shows a pretty skimpy cash total. Ignoring the effects of depreciation (which we don't know), they need a little less than $9,600 per day to survive ($3,500,000/365 days). At this rate, they have less than two days in their cash account as shown on line 45 ($16,190/9,600).

If this manager needed cash, the first stop would be to turn the heat up under line 46, savings and temporary cash investments. There are more than 10 days of cash here ($102,929/9,600). That will help a great deal, and it shouldn't be much of a problem to pull the cash from its temporary investment state. If management is smart, they will have parked those

Form 990 (2001)   Page **3**

Part IV   **Balance Sheets** (See Specific Instructions on page 24.)

		(A) Beginning of year		(B) End of year
Note:	Where required, attached schedules and amounts within the description column should be for end-of-year amounts only.			

			(A) Beginning of year			(B) End of year
Assets	45	Cash—non-interest-bearing	141,462	45	16,190	
	46	Savings and temporary cash investments	104,674	46	102,929	
	47a	Accounts receivable ... **47a**				
	b	Less: allowance for doubtful accounts **47b**	339,753	47c	376,205	
	48a	Pledges receivable ... **48a** 41,515				
	b	Less: allowance for doubtful accounts **48b** 16,500	47,401	48c	25,015	
	49	Grants receivable	23,858	49		
	50	Receivables from officers, directors, trustees, and key employees (attach schedule)		50		
	51a	Other notes and loans receivable (attach schedule). **51a**				
	b	Less: allowance for doubtful accounts **51b**		51c		
	52	Inventories for sale or use	381,424	52	502,722	
	53	Prepaid expenses and deferred charges	21,405	53	12,675	
	54	Investments—securities (attach schedule). ▶ ☐ Cost ☐ FMV	34,560	54	23,324	
	55a	Investments—land, buildings, and equipment: basis **55a**				
	b	Less: accumulated depreciation (attach schedule). **55b**		55c		
	56	Investments—other (attach schedule)		56		
	57a	Land, buildings, and equipment: basis **57a** 7,710,806				
	b	Less: accumulated depreciation (attach schedule). **57b** 685,719	1,668,665	57c	18,506,767	
	58	Other assets (describe ▶ _____)		58		
	59	**Total assets** (add lines 45 through 58) (must equal line 74)	17,781,189	59	19,565,827	
Liabilities	60	Accounts payable and accrued expenses	344,493	60	779,426	
	61	Grants payable		61		
	62	Deferred revenue		62		
	63	Loans from officers, directors, trustees, and key employees (attach schedule).		63		
	64a	Tax-exempt bond liabilities (attach schedule)	5,096,648	64a	7,311,327	
	b	Mortgages and other notes payable (attach schedule)		64b		
	65	Other liabilities (describe ▶ _____)	1,525,178	65	1,531,164	
	66	**Total liabilities** (add lines 60 through 65)	6,966,319	66	9,621,917	

Organizations that follow SFAS 117, check here ▶ ☐ and complete lines 67 through 69 and lines 73 and 74.

Net Assets or Fund Balances	67	Unrestricted	10,123,969	67	9,942,855	
	68	Temporarily restricted		68		
	69	Permanently restricted	690,901	69	1,055	

Organizations that do not follow SFAS 117, check here ▶ ☐ and complete lines 70 through 74.

	70	Capital stock, trust principal, or current funds		70		
	71	Paid-in or capital surplus, or land, building, and equipment fund		71		
	72	Retained earnings, endowment, accumulated income, or other funds		72		
	73	**Total net assets or fund balances** (add lines 67 through 69 OR lines 70 through 72; column (A) **must** equal line 19; column (B) **must** equal line 21).	10,814,870	73	9,943,910	
	74	**Total liabilities and net assets / fund balances** (add lines 66 and 73)	17,781,189	74	19,565,827	

Form 990 is available for public inspection and, for some people, serves as the primary or sole source of information about a particular organization. How the public perceives an organization in such cases may be determined by the information presented on its return. Therefore, please make sure the return is complete and accurate and fully describes, in Part III, the organization's programs and accomplishments.

EXHIBIT 10.1   Sources of Cash

savings in the same bank where they keep their cash, so in all likelihood a phone call will do it.

Next Stop, Accounts Receivable

Still, 12 days' cash isn't a lot. They will almost certainly need more. The next stop on the continuum is usually the most promising of all, accounts receivable (A/R). This enduring reservoir of money owed to the corporation offers a lot to cash-hungry managers with the right approach.

Begin with the fact that quantifying A/R is more art than science. If it were possible to peer deeply into the anatomy of this line, you would see, depending on the size and nature of the organization, hundreds or even thousands of individual transactions in varying stages of completion.

Some are simply taking a bit longer to process (and thus turn into cash) than average. Some are stretching a bit, perhaps because the person owing the money sent the check to the wrong address or has temporarily forgotten about the debt. Some are practically nonexistent and are on the verge of being ignored completely because, for whatever reason, they will never be paid. And perhaps a few are dead beyond any doubt, don't belong here at all, and just haven't yet been removed (or "written off").

Incidentally, it's a bit troublesome that the presenters of this balance sheet feel that they will eventually collect 100 percent of their outstanding bills, a fact we can infer because they have made no allowance for doubtful accounts. If the nature of their business is such that their receivables line consists of a few big invoices due from, say, the federal government, fine. But in the absence of this type of situation, it is virtually inevitable that some amount of these accounts will never be collected, and management's estimate of how much that will be should be shown here.

To sum up—all semivibrant, quivering, or near-death accounts traditionally get lumped into this single line as an asset of the corporation, and the manager seeking cash is well advised to look here early and often. There are several strategies for turning A/R into cash. Here are a few worth considering:

- *Prevent transactions from landing in A/R in the first place.* Once an individual bill ends up as an A/R, there's nothing preventive you can do about it. But if you can learn what put it and others like it here, maybe there are some things you can do differently next time. For example, encouraging more transactions to be done in cash up-front will keep down the receivables. Simply requesting cash as payment is a start, and offering a discount for it works, too. For some nonprofits, prevention might mean checking payment sources more carefully or assigning a staff person to work with consumers to locate and verify payment sources.

A/R FIRE DRILL

The long-term CEO of the community transportation nonprofit passed away unexpectedly after a short illness. The interim CEO was a transplant from private industry via a local masters program, and he set about the task of learning the organization. After a few months, that distant-sounding gloomy message from the bookkeeper came into sharper focus when the CEO realized that the dial on the cash flow gauge was somewhere between "Empty" and "Stop Kidding Yourselves."

The scramble for cash was on. The interim executive turned to the line of credit first, but the organization owed $320,000—on a line of credit with a $300,000 limit (they owed interest charges in addition to the $300,000 they borrowed). Next stop was the list of accounts receivable. He targeted the receivables outstanding for 60 to 90 days and called the organizations directly. Most were either cities and towns or direct service providers. His message was simple: we're in a cash crunch, but if we can collect the money you owe us quickly your elderly consumers won't be out of a ride.

It worked. Many of the groups owing money forwarded at least some of it rapidly. Some paid the bill in full, and those who do so agreed to and generally followed an accelerated payment schedule.

The interim director here achieved success through sheer force of will and personal energy. But it is fair to ask how the organization got to this point. Maxing out on a line of credit doesn't just happen overnight. The presence of significant unpaid interest reinforces this point. Did the previous CEO know what was happening, and why? Was the board aware? Was the bookkeeper ignored previously, or did she first start feeling free to speak out with the appointment of an interim CEO? In this case a single individual made a big difference, but avoiding a crisis by ensuring that everyone fulfills their responsibility is preferable to heroic actions to solve it.

- *Tell the business manager to reduce A/R.* Even if you can't do anything about current A/R, reducing the rate at which future accounts flow into A/R won't take long to have a positive effect on cash flow. Without exaggeration, this one should be good for at least a 10 percent reduction in A/R. What gets measured gets done, and as soon as you make it clear that you are measuring your billing department and the person responsible for it according to the number of days in receivables they report (see Chapter 6 "Financial Analysis: A Few Diagnostic Tools" for a definition of days in receivables), you are almost certain to see an improvement. Make average days in receivables a component of your business manager's yearly evaluation.

Improve Invoicing Technology

Incremental progress is the theme here. Again, there's nothing to be done about accounts already languishing in A/R, but often you can find a way to tweak the billing system's technology without spending money and yet still get reduced receivables. Groups working on contract, for instance, may find that their payment source will deposit payments directly into their corporate bank account, saving a day or two in transit time. It may not seem like much, but after a while that kind of money turns into improved cash.

TRY THIS TEST IN THE PRIVACY OF YOUR OWN MIND

Here's a quick way to learn a lot about any organization. Scan the asset side of the balance sheet. Let your eye come to rest on the single largest asset. Find out who controls that asset. You have just discovered who probably has the most to say about how that organization is run.

For example, suppose an organization's largest asset is its A/R. If most of those receivables represent invoices presented to, say, Medicaid, that funding source will have a huge influence over the entity. Not only is it likely to represent the largest portion of the organization's revenue, but if Medicaid slows down its payments or disallows a major portion, the entity will be in serious trouble.

Borrow Against or Sell Receivables

Sometimes a bank will lend money against solid receivables. Though it doesn't happen often, this is a way to turn receivables into cash a bit sooner. In certain for-profit industries (the garment industry, for instance), it is commonplace to sell one's receivables to another company for a percentage less than 100 percent of expected value. The other company then chases the payments and pockets the difference between what they paid and what they collected. This is called *factoring*, and although there isn't any factoring in the nonprofit sector, there is a variation.

Many hospitals will sell their old receivables to such a company for a deep discount, and the company will then attempt to collect on them. At least one consultant has developed a kind of quarter-in-the-washing machine practice in which he attempts to collect old bills sent to government health insurers. He and the health care provider split the proceeds in some fashion: Since he can focus exclusively on the old bills, he almost always collects something from them. By contrast, the provider's regular billing staff are highly unlikely to make good on a collection. Maintaining a billing function is a daily affair, and once a packet of bills falls off the speeding train, there is a strong temptation to leave it behind.

At the hypothetical $3.5 million volume with no depreciation cost assumed, this organization has about 39 days of cash tied up in receivables ($376,205/9,600). On the face of it, this seems unremarkable. Without knowing more about the nonprofit's business and without some sort of standard for comparison, there is no reliable way of evaluating this record. This may already be a reasonably tight billing system with only marginal room for improvement.

Pledges Can Be Promising

Not every organization is lucky enough to have uncollected pledges sitting on its books, but these folks have $25,015 (line 48c). Two things are noteworthy here. First, this amount is what remains after subtracting $16,500 in doubtful pledges; management apparently has greater doubts about its pledges than its bills. Second, they routinely have pledges outstanding, last year's amount totaling $47,401.

These people know how to secure and collect on pledges, and this fact gives hope for another potential source of cash. It is possible that one or more pledges could be hurried up to produce additional cash: check with the development person.

Other Receivables

Grants receivable (line 49) are similar to pledges receivable, although they may be slightly more collectible than pledges since they tend to come out of a formalized process rather than from individuals. In theory, receivables from insiders and other notes and loans (lines 50 and 51c) may be collectible, but for internal political reasons they are not usually worth considering.

Inventories

Most readers can skip this section. Since most nonprofits carry no appreciable inventories (line 52) in connection with daily operations. For those that do, a single operative principle applies: Inventories can almost always be smaller than they are. Few companies, for-profit or nonprofit, are willing to state publicly that they manage their inventories well, and for good reason. Inventories of raw materials *or* finished goods (the former being more applicable here) are messy. They are hard to track, difficult to value, and prone to shrinkage. It takes great skill, better technology, and lots of experience to do it well.

Valuing inventories is inherently tricky, and whole careers in accounting theory have been dedicated to the task. Real-world twists also have a pesky way of intruding. In methadone clinics, whose service is tightly regulated by the federal government, accounting conventions stipulate that the methadone inventory be listed at acquisition cost, which tends to be low. Were a clinic manager to make decisions solely on the basis of acquisition costs, he or she would miss the fact that the street value—and therefore the security risk—of a methadone inventory is many, many times the nominal price.

The one thing certain is that, accounting questions aside, *inventories cost money to acquire.* Therefore, the smaller the inventory (especially of raw goods, the most common kind in nonprofits), the less expenditure of cash required. As with A/R, the secret is not to let transactions go into inventory in the first place.

Prepaid Expenses and Deferred Charges

As a source of ready cash, forget these amounts (line 53). Ever tried to get a deposit back from your telephone company? Though a current asset, this cash is iced over.

Investments

Investments in various financial instruments (lines 54–56) are unquestionably one of the most fertile sources of cash since they can usually be sold quickly. Two caveats apply: (1) dumping securities to produce cash should always be part of a planned process and not an emergency fix, and (2) it may not be as easy as it seems anyway.

In many nonprofits with large endowments held in securities, the actual instruments are under the control of a second party. Typically, this second party is a professional money manager of some sort. Not only do professional money managers not want the gates to the money swinging open and shut like a screen door in a heavy breeze, but they are often under explicit instructions from the board of directors regarding transfers of funds. Getting a cash infusion in this situation is guaranteed to take some persistence.

Land, Buildings, and Equipment

Down here in the ice section of the balance sheet (line 57c) is the classic use of tangible assets for raising cash—as sales or as collateral for loans. This is one of the best reasons for adequate capitalization in a nonprofit organization, since lenders like a good base of real estate as backup for operating loans. Be aware, though, that turning tangible assets like these into cash takes time and effort. At the very least, it requires prearrangement with a bank. And it can also mean that the lender gets to attach strings to the use or disposal of the property for the life of the loan.

Stretch Those Payables

The simplest way to generate cash on the liability side of the balance sheet is one that everyone who manages a checkbook understands intuitively: Stretch the payables (lines 60 and 61). Or, to put it in plain English, pay bills slower. Bills the organization has accepted as legitimate but not yet paid—accounts payable—are in fact a prime source of cash for most nonprofit corporations. This is why some nonprofits have a reputation for paying their bills slowly. It may be difficult to squeeze A/R or collateralize buildings, but it doesn't take much to postpone paying an invoice or delay awarding a grant.

The trick is to stretch one's payables until just before it begins to cost either money or supplier goodwill. It may be easier than you would think since a surprising number of business managers and bookkeepers often seem to strive to pay all bills practically before sundown on the day they are received. Just as important, stretching the payables should be part of a coordinated, deliberate plan rather than a haphazard game of chance.

Note that our sample nonprofit has already stretched its payables to—or perhaps beyond—the breaking point. At a yearly revenue of $3,500,000, the $779,426 in payables reported here represent a hefty 22 percent of their entire year's budget. Making the reasonable assumptions that the minor share of their budget is in nonpayroll expenses and that none of the reported payables include overdue payroll, we can conclude that a huge portion of this group's nonpayroll spending is piling up in unpaid bills.

Support and Revenue Designated for Future Periods

It is nice money if you can get it. Most nonprofits have enough trouble getting revenue for the current period, let alone for the future (line 62). However, in certain situations, particularly membership organizations, it may be possible to coax some future revenue out of members ("buy a three-year membership today") fairly painlessly. Just be careful not to discount the future revenue too heavily. A dollar in three years is worth 80 or 90 cents today, not 50 cents. Done on a large scale, this kind of shortsightedness could actually hurt cash flows in the future, not help.

Loans from Officers, Directors, Trustees, and Key Employees

First question: Do you really want to be carrying these loans (line 63)? Yes it's a benefit for executives, and yes, it's desirable to support officers and directors in every way possible, but consider the intangible cost. Since the

WHY PROMPT BILL PAYING MAY BE A SIGN OF LAZINESS

Some nonprofits have a reputation for not paying their bills on time, but some have just the opposite problem: They seem to pay bills within minutes of receiving them.

Why do we call it a problem? For two reasons: The obvious one is that cash paid out prematurely robs the organization of a bit of interest-earning power. Admittedly, this is more symbol than substance, unless one is talking about bill-paying systems processing millions of dollars.

The subtle reason is that the practice may be rooted in old-fashioned sloppiness. The truth is, as long as an organization has the money, it is quicker and easier for bookkeepers to pay bills as soon as they come in. But this not only robs the organization of potential earned interest, it robs it of cash flow control. Often, the explanation is that the accounts payable person hasn't learned how to use the bill payment–scheduling function on the accounting software, which will allow him or her to enter the bill for payment, select an appropriate payment date, and set a reminder to send out the check or direct deposit when that day comes.

early 1990s, the media has been growing more and more aware of these types of arrangements and treats them, with some justification, as the non-profit equivalent of insider training. No, it probably isn't possible to call the loans, but not making them to begin with will ultimately save cash, not to mention public relations headaches.

Mortgages and Other Notes Payable

Any long-term debt you assume shows up here (line 64). It may seem strange at first, but activity on line 64 should be completely disconnected from cash flow management unless the terms of a line of credit cause it to be recorded here. Why? Cash flow is by definition a short-term phenomenon that should be met with short-term resources. Incurring long-term debt to take care of cash flow needs means the organization's economics are fundamentally out of sync. Translation: If you find yourself tempted to take on a mortgage to help with cash flow, regard it as a red flag.

Net Assets

Net assets (lines 67a–74) have nothing to do with cash either, except to the extent that this accumulation of yearly surpluses will, if liabilities are held down, be offset by a greater asset base that can eventually be turned into cash if necessary.

How Much Cash Is Enough?

Time now for the classic question: How much cash do we need to keep on hand? To which the only proper response is the equally classic, muddled, and entirely unsatisfying: It depends.

Suppose you are starting a business, nonprofit or for-profit, and have taken care of the cash needs of all start-up costs and investments. The business is expected to do $10,000 per day every day of the year. Suppose further that this is completely a cash business. At the end of the first day, you would be $10,000 richer since no suppliers would have had to have been paid and no employees would have received a paycheck. At the end of the second day you would be nearly $20,000 ahead, minus whatever small cash outlays might have been necessary to buy emergency supplies, put gas in a vehicle, and so on. In fact, it would probably take a week or two before you had to start paying money out in the form of payroll and invoices from suppliers, but by that time you would be way ahead of things from a cash perspective—at least until the economics of your business caught up with you.

Now go in the other direction. Assume your business receives no income at all in cash, and that every dollar of revenue is received only after sending a bill for it. This would mean that you would be carrying the entire operation— paying salaries, occupancy costs, and myriad other expenses—without an ounce of cash until you could translate your work into a bill to be sent out. Even then, you would have to continue in that cashless manner until whoever received the bill paid it (and until that payment cleared the bank). Until that point, you get no cash in the door whatsoever.

This type of cash flow scenario is represented by this graphic:

TOTAL DAYS ELAPSED

30 Days	15 Days
←	→
Work in Process (WIP)	Days in Receivables

Here, it takes 30 days to deliver the services and then bill for them. For the sake of simplicity, we have assumed that it takes no time at all to generate the bill itself; clearly an impossibility in reality, but okay for now. If the nonprofit's typical days in receivables number 15 then the amount of cash needed on hand is at least 45 days' worth of the entity's average expenses. To this number must be added a "cushion" to allow for slippage and unforeseen expenses.

MAKING THE DOLLARS PERFORM TOO

Performing arts groups must meet multiple financial challenges even before the curtain goes up. Usually they have to secure a suitable venue, and often that means building one according to unique specifications. They must invest in associated equipment such as costumes, sets, and organs, and they have to hire and pay performers. Worse, they have to do all that before they can sell a single ticket. This inherently difficult service model is one of the things that subscription ticket series are meant to help correct. Nevertheless, arts organizations have to be creative in other ways as well, especially when it comes to financing their operations.

One ballet group solved their version of this problem with a creative financing plan that had three parts. First, they took out a $1.5M seasonal line of credit. The ballet performance schedule had deep troughs in the cash flow cycle, so this vehicle provided cash to carry them through the lean periods. The line of credit was secured in part by their endowment.

Next they had to make leasehold improvements in their practice space, which they financed through a fixed rate, fully amortized (or "spread out") payment schedule that ended when the lease ended.

But wait, we're not done yet. Because the capital campaign produced pledges over a three-to-five-year period, they added a bridge loan tied to capital campaign receipts. This source revolved as pledges came in over the receipt period. Taken as a whole, these three vehicles represented a sophisticated latticework of financial arrangements that required careful attention. Which may explain why the CEO's favorite phrase was "big art takes big bucks."

The Fail-Safe Source of Cash—Profits

In the end, there is no better source of cash available to the nonprofit corporation than profitability. Simply put, a sustained period of time in which the organization takes in more revenue than it puts out as expenses will take care of most cash flow needs quite nicely. The good thing about cash flow from operations is that it is cheap (no interest charges), readily available, and relatively easy to create. In fact, nonprofits' chronic cash shortage is partly the direct result of an industry managing itself so as to avoid profit.

There are many restrictions on a nonprofit's ability to generate a profit, some imagined and some real. Payers' rules, board of directors' (or management's) reluctance, intense demand for additional services, and simply a desire to use every last dime in the service of mission are just a few of the forces acting to keep profitability down. This means that profitability alone will enhance cash flow only slowly, probably a few percentage points a year at best. Other means will have to be used as well. Still, running a consistent profit is the best foundation for adequate cash flow.

The Cash Flow Projection

Now, turn to the mechanics of cash flow management. A single sheet of paper should do it, from a management perspective anyway. The cash flow projection is the heart of cash flow management, and every nonprofit corporation should use it regularly. It is and must remain strictly an internal report—not the kind of thing even the board of directors needs or should want to see routinely. Someone in the business office needs to produce the projection at least quarterly, and preferably monthly. Then, management should read it.

The cash flow projection is not rocket science. All it displays is cash expected to come in, cash expected to go out, and the difference between the two numbers plus an explanation of how any negative difference will be financed. Exhibit 10.2 is a sample cash flow projection.

The key lines are at the bottom, as ever. The Beginning Balance shows the level of indebtedness with which the organization began the month, probably drawing the financing from something like a line of credit or transfers from nonoperating funds. The Ending Balance shows the impact of that month's cash loss or gain on the source of financing.

Thoughtful Cash Flow Projections. Look at Exhibit 10.2. Here, fund-raising, for example, is much more irregular as a cash source, starting

EXHIBIT 10.2 RELIABLE CASH FLOW PROJECTION

	Jan	Feb	Mar	Apr	May	Jun	Jul	Aug	Sep	Oct	Nov	Dec
Cash in												
Program services	$300,000	$300,000	$300,000	$300,000	$300,000	$200,000	$150,000	$450,000	$400,000	$300,000	$300,000	$300,000
Fund-raising	50,000	50,000	50,000	50,000	50,000	75,000	75,000	75,000	75,000	250,000	25,000	75,000
Miscellaneous	13,333	13,333	13,333	13,333	13,333	13,333	13,333	13,333	13,333	13,333	13,333	13,333
Total in	$363,333	$363,333	$363,333	$363,333	$363,333	$288,333	$238,333	$538,333	$488,333	$563,333	$338,333	$388,333
Cash out												
Salaries	$227,160	$227,160	$340,740	$227,160	$227,160	$340,740	$238,809	$238,809	$358,214	$238,809	$238,809	$358,214
Payroll taxes	22,716	22,716	34,074	22,716	22,716	34,074	23,881	23,881	35,821	23,881	23,881	35,821
Employee benefits	22,240	22,240	22,240	22,240	22,240	22,240	22,240	58,240	22,240	22,240	22,240	22,240
Consultants	0	0	0	0	2,500	0	0	0	5,000	7,500	7,500	7,500
Legal/audit	0	0	0	1,000	2,000	2,000	2,500	2,500	2,500	2,500	0	0
Contracted services	3,000	3,000	3,000	3,000	3,000	3,000	3,000	3,000	3,000	3,000	3,000	3,000
Program supplies	47,000	47,000	47,000	47,000	47,000	47,000	47,000	47,000	23,000	47,000	47,000	47,000
Vehicle expense	1,500	1,500	1,500	1,500	1,500	1,500	1,500	1,500	1,500	1,500	1,500	1,500
Equipment leases	1,600	1,600	1,600	1,600	4,000	1,600	1,600	1,600	1,600	4,000	1,600	1,600
Rent	24,000	24,000	24,000	24,000	24,000	24,000	26,000	26,000	26,000	26,000	26,000	26,000
Utilities	4,500	4,500	4,500	4,500	1,500	1,500	1,500	1,500	1,500	2,500	4,000	4,000
Property insurance	0	0	0	0	0	0	0	6,000	6,000	6,000	6,000	0
Total out	$353,716	$353,716	$478,654	$354,716	$357,616	$477,654	$368,030	$410,030	$486,375	$384,930	$381,530	$506,875
Net inflow (outflow)	$ 9,617	$ 9,617	$(115,321)	$ 8,617	$ 5,717	$(189,321)	$(129,697)	$128,303	$ 1,958	$178,403	$(43,197)	$(118,542)
Beginning balance	10,000	19,617	29,234	(86,087)	(77,470)	(71,753)	(261,074)	(390,771)	(262,468)	(260,510)	(82,107)	(125,304)
Ending balance	19,617	29,234	(86,087)	(77,470)	(71,753)	(261,074)	(390,771)	(262,468)	(260,510)	(82,107)	(125,304)	(243,846)

LAG TIME AFFECTS CASH FLOW

Accounting for lag time is a key aspect to accurate cash flow projection. Suppose a new employee starts work on July 8 at a yearly salary of $60,000 in an organization that pays employees on the 15th and the last day of the month. Their impact on cash outflow as of July 31 is only for that second half of the first payroll of the month, or $1,250 because her July 31 payment is for July 8–July 15, which is half of the regular twice a month payment of $2,500. Moreover, the health insurance charge probably won't show up until August or possibly even September, and other coverages are probably invoiced quarterly. Payroll taxes will not have a cash impact because they're not even due until a few days after the July 31 payroll. One person won't have much impact on cash, but if a whole new department was starting up, the relief on cash outflow would be wonderful. Moral of the story: If you pay twice monthly, start new programs in the second half of the month. It could save you considerable cash outflow in the short term.

with a lower monthly amount and including a whopping big month in October. We can safely assume that some sort of major fund-raiser is expected for the month of September, with the bulk of cash received in October, or, it's an October cash-based, fund-raising activity.

Salaries seem to fluctuate, but look again. This organization obviously pays its employees every two weeks. For two of every three months, there are only two payrolls. Every third month, however, there are actually three payrolls. This quite predictable variation occurs once each quarter, or every 13 weeks. Payroll taxes, being calculated on the basis of monthly payrolls, fluctuate in parallel.

Employee benefits are insulated from this type of variation but have their own quirks. A logical inference here is that a pension plan or some form of insurance requires a big one-year payment in August, probably in advance of a new policy year beginning September 1. Incidentally, many benefits suppliers offer payment plans that will flatten this kind of peak cash drain, although it will probably cost less to finance it yourself.

With planning, consulting expenses are very predictable. Consultants are also paid in arrears. Looks like big consultations are planned for April and August through November. Audit fees are very predictable, and in the exhibits they seem to be blended with legal costs that are more susceptible to yearly variations.

The organization must expect a fall-off in utilization in August, which will translate into a smaller cash outlay when the bills are paid in September.

Service contracts are often considered part of equipment leasing costs. A big payment is due in May and another in November. Usage adjustment charges might behave the same way, depending on how the lease agreement is written.

Winter in most of the country means higher utility bills, as we can see in the November to April period. Sometimes major utility companies will offer ways to stretch payments over a 10- or even 12-month period. This helps the cash flow, but at what cost? The operative question is whether you can "borrow" the money cheaper from yourself (especially through careful cash management) or another source at better rates than what the utility company will offer. *Hint:* Usually you can.

Property insurance gets paid in one big bite or a few smaller ones. The financing decision is the same as for utilities.

While reading a cash flow projection is not likely to cause someone to break into the intellectual equivalent of a sweat, preparing one might. The accompanying disk includes some files that will be helpful in projecting cash flow. The difference between useful cash flow projections and mediocre ones is largely the amount of planning and thought that goes into their preparation. In turn, the nonprofit manager's job is to be able to recognize and demand good projections.

CONCLUSION

Regular cash flow projections ought to be the responsibility of the chief financial person. Use the format in Exhibit 10.2 as a guide, but modify it freely. There is no single correct format.

Many nonprofit financial managers at all sizes of organizations do rudimentary cash flow projections in their heads all the time. The benefit of a formalized, written process is that it puts the information on paper where everybody can see it and act accordingly. What the nonfinancial manager contributes by insisting on a written document is not just getting the job done but communicating the importance of cash management to the organization. Knowing a little about the process adds the ability to distinguish a helpful plan from a mediocre one.

CHAPTER 11

Capital: Why Capital Is Not a Four-Letter Word

For a major wellspring of financial health—or lack of it—look no further than a nonprofit's capital structure. Its degree of liquidity will determine how fast it can move. Its profitability will determine its ability to sustain itself. But as a barometer of financial vitality, and sometimes as an indication of financial sophistication, the decisions a nonprofit makes about how it acquires and deploys its capital are unsurpassed.

Capital refers to the long-term debt and net assets carried by the non-profit. The capital structure of a nonprofit is so important that it will help determine how well the organization carries out its day-to-day business. One reason why this happens is that capital buffers an organization from external ups and downs. For instance, owning a capital asset is usually less expensive in the long term than leasing it. More subtly, the greater control that comes with ownership can prevent such institutionally draining crises as having to move every few years because the landlord raises the rent. These are just two ways that a good capital structure insulates an organization from threats to its stability.

There is a popular cynical observation that "money talks," roughly translated as "greed rules." But what that phrase can also mean is that we talk with money. Every purchase or investment decision is a way of expressing ourselves and our choices. This is why, as noted in Chapter 2, the real bottom line is not revenues minus expenses but rather the ability of the nonprofit to continue to attract money from the outside. As long as a nonprofit can find some way of getting outside capital into the organization, it can usually survive.

A for-profit corporation has three ways of bringing in capital: (1) generating profits, (2) borrowing, or (3) selling a share of ownership. A nonprofit has the first two, since it cannot sell shares. By itself, this prohibition against selling shares—which is an entirely appropriate and necessary part of being granted the special status of tax exemption—radically reduces the chances of the average nonprofit being adequately capitalized. Ensuring that it is well capitalized for its mission requires a conscious act of will.

And a good capital campaign doesn't exactly hurt either. This is the third means of bringing capital into a nonprofit. The capital campaign is the nonprofit world's equivalent of an initial public offering (IPO), during which a for-profit company's stock is first sold to the outside world. It's a grueling, years-long, all-encompassing undertaking for most nonprofits, but the payoff is in the large amount of capital that one brings in for a much smaller cost than would usually be the case.

THE MECHANICS OF CAPITAL FINANCING

Before we get too deeply into a nonprofit's potential sources of capital—a far more critical question than is commonly realized—let's cover the mechanics of capital finance. Exhibit 11.1 tells the initial story of a $100,000 loan at 5 percent interest for 20 years, while Exhibits 11.2 and 11.3 display the same information graphically. At the end of twenty years the loan has been amortized, or paid off in decrements. Monthly payments for each of the 240 months of the loan are a steady $659.96, or a yearly total of $7,919.52.

These amounts stay the same throughout the life of the loan, accounting for the straight line at the top of Exhibit 11.2, but the composition of the payments changes every month. Exhibit 11.1 tracks these changes in dollar terms over the life of the loan. Each payment is composed of a certain amount of principal (a fraction of the original loaned amount) and a certain amount of interest (the cost of borrowing the money). Because the interest on the loan is recomputed after each month's payment on the basis of a slightly smaller principal, the interest payments start out being much higher than the part of the monthly payment that repays the principal. At the end of the first year, for example, $4,911.83 has been paid in interest

EXHIBIT 11.1   AMORTIZATION SCHEDULE

End of Year	Month	Date	Payment	Interest	Principal	Balance
		01-01-20XX				$100,000.00
	1	01-30-20XX	$659.96	$397.26	$262.70	99,737.30
	2	02-28-20XX	659.96	415.57	244.39	99,492.91
	3	03-30-20XX	659.96	414.55	245.41	99,247.50
	4	04-30-20XX	659.96	413.53	246.43	99,001.07
	5	05-30-20XX	659.96	412.50	247.46	98,753.61
	6	06-30-20XX	659.96	411.47	248.49	98,505.12
	7	07-30-20XX	659.96	410.44	249.52	98,255.60
	8	08-30-20XX	659.96	409.40	250.56	98,005.04
	9	09-30-20XX	659.96	408.35	251.61	97,753.43
	10	10-30-20XX	659.96	407.31	252.65	97,500.78
	11	11-30-20XX	659.96	406.25	253.71	97,247.07
	12	12-30-20XX	659.96	405.20	254.76	96,992.31
1	Totals		7,919.52	4,911.83	3,007.69	96,992.31
2	Totals		7,919.52	4,778.26	3,141.26	93,851.05
3	Totals		7,919.52	4,617.57	3,301.95	90,549.10
4	Totals		7,919.52	4,448.65	3,470.87	87,078.23
5	Totals		7,919.52	4,271.06	3,648.46	83,429.77
6	Totals		7,919.52	4,084.38	3,835.14	79,594.63
7	Totals		7,919.52	3,888.19	4,031.33	75,563.30
8	Totals		7,919.52	3,681.94	4,237.58	71,325.72

(Continued)

EXHIBIT 11.1 (CONTINUED)

End of Year	Month	Date	Payment	Interest	Principal	Balance
9	Totals		7,919.52	3,465.14	4,454.38	66,871.34
10	Totals		7,919.52	3,237.23	4,682.29	62,189.05
11	Totals		7,919.52	2,997.67	4,921.85	57,267.20
12	Totals		7,919.52	2,745.85	5,173.67	52,093.53
13	Totals		7,919.52	2,481.19	5,438.33	46,655.20
14	Totals		7,919.52	2,202.95	5,716.57	40,938.63
15	Totals		7,919.52	1,910.45	6,009.07	34,929.56
16	Totals		7,919.52	1,603.01	6,316.51	28,613.05
17	Totals		7,919.52	1,279.85	6,639.67	21,973.38
18	Totals		7,919.52	940.16	6,979.36	14,994.02
19	Totals		7,919.52	583.10	7,336.42	7,657.60
20	Totals		7,865.34	207.74	7,657.60	0.00
	Grand Totals		$158,336.22	$58,336.22	$100,000.00	

Amounts
(Thousands)

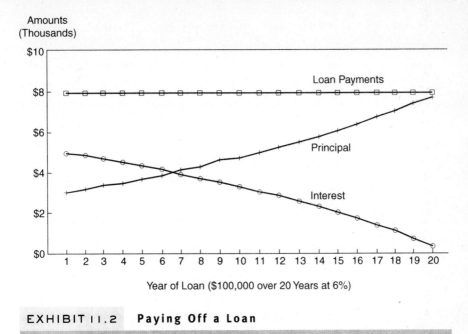

Year of Loan ($100,000 over 20 Years at 6%)

EXHIBIT 11.2   Paying Off a Loan

Amounts
Paid
(Thousands)

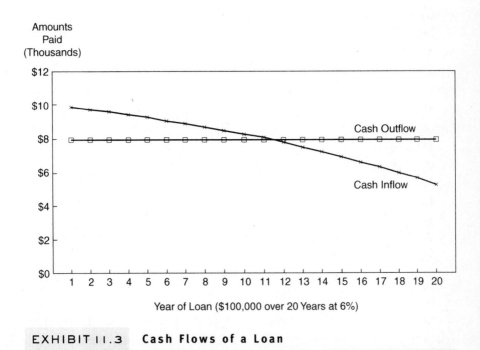

Year of Loan ($100,000 over 20 Years at 6%)

EXHIBIT 11.3   Cash Flows of a Loan

while only \$3,007.69 has been repaid in principal. Thereafter, the two amounts slowly switch relative positions.

The cash flow created by the loan is an entirely different story at the heart of which is the concept of depreciation. A capital asset can be expected to last for more than a single year. Since the lifetime of a capital asset will cross fiscal years, there needs to be a way to express the idea that each year a "piece" of the asset gets used up or "consumed" in the same way that any other tangible item would be consumed in the course of operations. We need a way to show that the true cost of a capital asset is paid in segments over a number of years. This is the role of depreciation.

The simplest way to express this concept of yearly consumption of part of a capital asset is by dividing the asset's acquisition cost by the number of years it can be expected to last (see Box). Known as the *useful life* of the asset, this time period is established for each type of asset (although sometimes funding sources will insist on a specific useful life). For an asset costing \$25,000 with a useful life of five years and no remaining value at that point, the yearly depreciation cost would be \$5,000, or \$416.67 per month. This amount would be charged automatically each month to the cost of the program using the asset.

Exhibit 11.3 shows the very positive effects on cash flow in the early years of the loan. Cash outflow is stable throughout the life of the loan, since it is simply the same payment each month. Note that we consider only financing costs here, not operations-related costs such as maintenance or repair. The cash inflow side, on the other hand, actually starts at a point higher than the outflow and then declines throughout the loan's term to reach a level several thousand dollars per year less than the outflow.

> Banks must put aside—or "reserve"—different amounts of money for different types of loans. This is why banks have an incentive to increase their asset base—it enables them to loan more money while complying with reserve requirements.

The nature of reimbursement for capital costs accounts for the reversal. Assume that all costs associated with the loan itself are fully reimbursed, a good assumption unless the nonprofit has another benevolent source of funding to cover permanent deficiencies. What is actually being reimbursed is not the loan payment itself but rather the depreciation, which we know to be $5,000 per year, plus the actual cost of the interest payments for that year. We also know that depreciation is an expense that does not get paid in cash, so any reimbursement that covers the cost of the service is actually bringing in cash that was not paid out. Therefore, in year one of the loan the actual cash inflow is equal to $5,000 plus $4,912 in interest cost for a total of almost $10,000—this at a time when total cash outflow is only $7,919. By contrast, reimbursement in the final year is the same $5,000 plus a mere $207.74 while the loan payment is the same $7,919.

HOW DEPRECIATION IS CALCULATED

Owing to the powerful effect on cash flow and profitability that depreciation charges can have, there are different ways of calculating it. The method referred to in the text is called *straight-line depreciation* and is used by virtually all nonprofits. There are other methods and accompanying rationalizations for calculating depreciation in different ways. What they all have in common is that for-profit organizations can use them to accelerate depreciation charges. Higher depreciation charges can mean more cash and less profits, which can in turn reduce the tax bill. Methods for calculating depreciation are a perennial hot topic with for-profit corporations and their tax advisors, but have little relevance to most nonprofits.

The pattern sketched here is true for any capital financing, although there are myriad modifications and variations possible. Assuming that depreciation and interest payments are somehow fully covered, cash flows will always go from very favorable in the early years to unfavorable at the end of the loan's term.

HOW ROWDY TEENAGERS CAN SHAPE DEPRECIATION POLICIES

Let us say you are running a program for teenage boys who have all been convicted of a criminal offense that contains the phrase "violence against property." Let us further suppose that you purchase for said program a brand new $5,000 living room set. Normally you would assume the useful life of that living room set to be something like five or ten years. But considering the nature of the population, that living room set could be reduced to toothpick-sized pieces one day and you'd have to "write down" or eliminate the remaining undepreciated cost all at once. So why not accept reality and not even bother trying to amortize the asset? In that case you'd consider the living room set an expense, and charge it all in one year. Expensive? You bet. But at least it's a simpler process, and you've made your accounting fit reality.

THE PRESENT VALUE OF MONEY

To the above virtues of capital finance one must also add the effect of the present value of money. This concept is one of those ideas that practically invites complexity even though it is really quite simple. Everyone knows instinctively that $1,000 today is worth more than $1,000 a year from today. Even if we disregard the effects of inflation as well as the possible risk of waiting a year for the money, the fact is that the sooner we can put money to use for us the sooner it will produce benefits. If nothing else, we can put it into a simple interest-bearing account for a year. For example, if we were to put $952.38 into an account paying 5 percent interest compounded yearly it would be worth $1,000 in one year.

Another way of looking at it is that $952.38 is today's value of $1,000 in one year at 5 percent interest compounded yearly. Given a choice between a guaranteed $952.38 today or a guaranteed $1,000 in one year, we would be indifferent. If, on the other hand, we felt that we could take that same $952.38 today and put it someplace where it would produce 6 percent interest in one year, we would have $1,009.52 instead of $1,000. In finance lingo, the future value of the cash flow is better at the higher interest rate.

This is the kind of thinking that brings structure to capital finance decisions. What is the present value of the projected stream of cash? How much does it change when my assumptions change? What are the alternatives? As might be expected, the same methods of analysis work with purchases as well as with financing. In fact, in any financial setting where regular streams of cash exist, the present value calculation can bring order to what otherwise might seem a jumble of numbers. This same technique can lead to thinking that, taken too far, can betray the mission by focusing exclusively on financial considerations when deciding whether to make an investment.

The actual present value formula? No need for it. Go to the nearest computerized spreadsheet package or buy a simple business calculator and follow the steps laid out in the manual. Or go to the library for a book of tables. Better still, have a staff member do it.

SOURCES OF CAPITAL

Nonprofits actually have a relatively large number of sources of capital. It's just that they aren't always labeled that way, nor do they add up to an especially potent capital structure. One of the most common and yet most unacknowledged sources of short-term capital is accounts payable, or the nonprofit's bills that have not yet been paid.

Think of the term *capital* as "sticky money." Unlike revenue, which is expected to come into the organization and then leave again as expenses, capital stays put. If you are looking for evidence of the capital structure, look on the liability side of the balance sheet. Every entry under liabilities and net assets represents some type of capital. We call it sticky money because capital really represents dollars with strings attached to them.

Each of the liability entries can be traced back to an outside party with some sort of claim to the funds. Accounts payable are dollars rightfully due to vendors and suppliers: but for an accident of timing, those dollars would already be in vendors' and suppliers' hands. Deferred revenue was received from outside parties in anticipation of some sort of service being delivered to them. Were those services not to be delivered, the revenue should be returned. Until then, the vendors have a claim on these dollars. Short-term notes and mortgages clearly are expected to be repaid to the lenders. And nonprofit incorporation regulations effectively require that leftover assets be distributed to similar organizations should the originating nonprofit ever go out of business, so their "owner" can truly be said to be the public at large.

For any organization, capital represents a means to growth. The single most important financial distinction between for-profits and nonprofits is where they get their capital. For-profit businesses have three major choices: profit, borrowing, and selling shares of ownership. Nonprofits don't have the latter option because they cannot have owners. However, nonprofits are perfectly capable of raising money for tangible assets like buildings and equipment (why else do they call it a "capital campaign"?). Note that ordinary donations cannot be expected to supply capital because presumably every donated dollar is earmarked to be spent on providing some sort of service.

The reason why for-profit corporations can grow so much faster and more reliably than nonprofits is because their sources of capital are virtually unlimited. If the real bottom line in any organization is its ability to raise capital from outsiders, for-profits will always have a far better outlook as long as they can interest outsiders in buying ownership shares.

Before we go any further, let's acknowledge a central fact: Money is a commodity. Possession of it gets transferred for profit the same way that any other commodity gets transferred for a profit. This means that the more of it that gets transferred and for a longer period of time, the lower the cost to the recipient. Generally, owners of capital want to transfer it in the largest chunks possible and to be guaranteed to receive interest payments on it for the longest period of time possible.

Perhaps not surprisingly, the market for this commodity resembles the market for many others. We might compare the capital distribution system for nonprofits to the way we buy another familiar commodity, milk. At the lowest end of the retail chain is the half-pint carton of milk. Somewhere in the middle is the equally familiar gallon container of milk, and at the far end of the spectrum are the institutional multigallon containers used by restaurants and food manufacturers.

That half pint of milk is like the loan for a nonprofit's copy machine. It's about the smallest amount of money that a lender will want to lend, so the cost per unit of the commodity is high. The retailer is really selling access, as signaled in the milk world by the fact that the typical vendor of that little carton is a convenience store. In the financial world, loans like these may not even be made by traditional banks but rather by specialty leasing or credit corporations.

Commercial banks are the half gallon and gallon milk vendors. Single transactions may not amount to much, but the overall volume of business is significant and profitable. These customers have a bit longer time horizon, or at least a demand for more of the stuff. Gallon containers fit their budgets, storage capacity, and rate of consumption. The milk retailers gear their operations to large numbers of small transactions.

At the high end of this fanciful spectrum are the bulk consumers of milk and capital. No half pints or even grocery carts full of gallons for these consumers. They buy in bulk, demand and get discounts, and are generally comfortable with purchasing and using massive quantities. They may even understand the milk business as well as their milk suppliers but have chosen for whatever reason to concentrate their business energies elsewhere. The nonprofit finance equivalent to these bulk milk purchasers are institutions that can participate in the bulk money market, better known as the bond market. These institutions are the large and sophisticated borrowers of huge amounts of capital. They build massive physical plants and routinely invest heavily in equipment. They tend to be hospitals and universities, mainly because both of these tax-exempt activities require large-scale use of both buildings and technology.

THE GREAT DIVIDE AMONG NONPROFITS

Perhaps you can now see the Great Divide among nonprofit organizations, or the line between those with regular access to traditional capital markets and those without. The difference is dimly experienced by the latter as a feeling that their colleagues on the other side of the line are *different* from them, although in exactly what way other than sheer size is usually not clear. A big reason for this feeling of differentness is the fact that, in capital finance terms, they *are* different.

One of the cardinal rules of capital finance is that one must never borrow money for the long-term at short-term rates. Lenders of money for short-term needs know that they will be getting it back in the near future and must then find another borrower under market conditions that no one can predict. Naturally, they will charge more just to cover their higher administrative costs and the risk from uncertainty. Nonprofits without access to the capital market may have to violate that cardinal rule, borrowing money for long-term capital investments at rates geared for short-term returns.

MANAGING YOUR ASSETS

Here is a foolhardy attempt to summarize in a box something to which entire careers have been devoted: managing your assets. Once you have enough money to put in investments for a long time (spelled e-n-d-o-w-m-e-n-t), you need to manage those funds. Here are the key steps:

Get a professional to do it. Hire a professional money manager to oversee your investment portfolio (hire more than one if you have a lot of assets—it's called spreading the risk). The board member's brother-in-law who is really good with spreadsheets is not an investment manager.

Determine your investment policy. Broadly, the investment manager will put your assets in three categories: equities, fixed income instruments (bonds), and cash. There are many varieties and gradations of each, but those are the basics. The percentage of the total that you hold in each category is called your asset allocation policy. A common mix is, say, 60 percent equities, 35 percent fixed income, and 5 percent cash. But this can and should change over time, as market conditions change. This is one of the things you hire an investment manager to do.

Decide how much to withdraw. The trick is to withdraw an amount of money for use each year that will be sufficient to allow the portfolio to grow enough to cover inflation and still produce a reasonable rate of return. Remember that your portfolio in most years should produce interest income plus a certain amount of growth in the base. Add these two items together and you have the portfolio's total return. Conventional wisdom in this field suggests that, over time, withdrawing 4–5 percent of a portfolio each year to be spent as operating funds is usually conservative enough to maintain a portfolio of investments indefinitely.

A more likely scenario is that they will have to pay for a middle person to stand between them and the capital markets. This is the role played by the average bank. Because of the economics described earlier, most major capital sources are uninterested and unequipped to loan money to, say, convert a single family house into a small office. Middle persons cost money, so the cost of borrowing that amount of money is higher because it has to be packaged in a smaller amount. The difference may only be a matter of a point or two on the interest rate, but over the long-term that adds up to a lot of money that flows out of the nonprofit for the convenience of borrowing capital.

Borrowing larger amounts of money more directly from the source is preferable, but the problem for most nonprofits is that the economics of this type of capital finance work against them. When capital is sought from banks in small amounts, as it has to be for the majority of nonprofits, the costs of borrowing are higher. The challenge for nonprofits is to constantly try to get as close to the sources of capital as possible. An increasing number of nonprofits are entering the capital markets, but there are still obstacles.

One obstacle is what might be termed historic inertia. Because most nonprofits haven't participated in capital markets, they don't participate now. Except for hospitals and universities, they are frequently not written into enabling legislation for bonding authorities, they are not rated for borrowing by the rating services, and so forth.

A bigger stumbling block is the economics of bonds themselves. A bond is essentially a promise to repay a loan, except that that promise is a written document that can itself be bought and sold. As publicly traded debt instruments, bonds must be highly standardized because bond buyers—often insurance companies and pension funds—cannot afford to spend a lot of time examining all aspects of a bond before purchasing it. This means that bonds have to meet various standards. The cost of meeting those standards such as legal and accounting fees and insurance charges runs into six figures. Even though bonds issued by a tax-exempt entity are themselves exempt from tax on the investors' proceeds and therefore the borrower pays less interest, these fixed costs drive up the overall expense of the borrowing. In effect, this means that no bond offering can be less than a few million dollars, putting bond financing out of the reach of the majority of nonprofits. Farsighted nonprofits will also factor in the possible long-term effects of the tax on unrelated business income: Profits realized by the sale of an asset acquired using debt financing trigger the unrelated business income tax, thereby boosting the overall cost of the financing even more.

FUTURE ACCESS TO CAPITAL MARKETS

There are, however, reasons for hope that more nonprofits will gain access to capital markets in the future (see following Box). One very good reason is the change in laws governing bond issuance. For years, private industrial and housing developers could use government-backed bonds to finance their projects. But many congressional staffers and legislators objected to what they

CAPITAL IDEAS—INNOVATION IN FINANCING FOR NONPROFITS

Some creative thinking can expand nonprofits' access to lower-cost capital. Here are a few promising ideas:

- **Pooled Bond Issue**
  A handful of similar organizations get together to float a single bond. They share issuance costs and proceeds proportionately, and the bond is sold to the public just like any other investment vehicle.

- **Pooled Pension Funds**
  Another idea much discussed but not yet acted on in any widespread way is to pool pension funds from a large number of nonprofit employees for the express purpose of purchasing bonds issued by nonprofits.

- **Private Foundations**
  Private foundations in some parts of the country have innovative borrowing programs.

- **Private Bond Offerings**
  Private bond offerings have always been possible, in which a few private investors get together to purchase a bond floated by a particular organization. This approach has the benefit of being somewhat less expensive and free of many of the restrictions imposed on bonds offered for sale to the public although the issuer has to be of substantial enough size to handle the issue.

- **Program-Related Investments (PRI)**
  Although relatively few do so, private foundations are allowed to make program-related investments in organizations that look much like conventional financing vehicles—loans and loan guarantees, and equity investments, for example. PRIs are an under-utilized but promising avenue.

saw as a funneling of government funds into private hands, and so tax reform legislation in the mid-1980s began to severely restrict that form of bond financing. Massachusetts's ceiling, for instance, dropped from $1.5 billion worth of financing in 1985 to $290 million just five years later.

Intentionally or not, the reforms allowed virtually unlimited financing to continue flowing to charitable organizations. Consequently, quasi-public bond authorities and the associated finance professionals who were squeezed out of industrial and housing bonds suddenly found tax-exempt issues much more attractive. Regulations were rewritten to include other forms of non-profit public charities and the traditional definition of a borrower was liberalized. This shift has begun to eliminate the historic inertia problem.

Simply broadening access does nothing to solve the problem of the underlying economics of bond financing. But even here, there is reason for optimism. Like most other fields, finance has undergone radical transformation in recent years and promises to continue doing so. One director of a bond-issuing agency notes that there are investment banking firms that get 60 percent of their revenue today from financial vehicles that didn't even exist 10 years ago.

The Role of Net Assets

As the nonprofit equivalent of net worth or equity, net assets play a key role in an organization's capital structure. Net assets do not represent money put into the organization but rather the accumulation of yearly surpluses over the history of the corporation. A large net assets amount is not necessarily a goal in itself, but will be the outcome of a prolonged period of profitable management. It should be developed and protected to the maximum extent possible. Grown large enough, it may signal that a nonprofit has the internal resources to reduce its reliance on outside capital.

Strategic Capital Management

Finally, some institutions are responding to their need for additional capital strategically. More and more nonprofits are seriously considering mergers in response to changes in their environment. Access to capital is often one of the driving forces in that decision, although participants usually express it as a need for better facilities, program expansion, and so on, rather than as a financial tactic.

Capital is not a four-letter word. In fact, it underlies much of the way a nonprofit is organized and determines a great deal about its cost effectiveness. Wise managers and board members will pay as much attention to capital structure as they do to profitability. It's the foundation of good financial health, in more ways than one.

CHAPTER 12

Budgeting: Taming the Budget Beast

Budgets are often regarded like instant lottery tickets—expend a bit of effort and the number is magically revealed. This idea leaves you wondering where the numbers came from. The real work in budgeting has nothing to do with the numbers that wind up on the final copy of the final version. By the time the budget amounts are published, it's too late to change much anyway. It's what underlies the numbers that counts. Putting the budget together in the first place is where the hard work gets done.

In budgeting, a single phrase trumps everything else: *It's not in the budget.* More good ideas (and bad ones) have shipwrecked on that simple phrase than on any other. More programs have not started, and more frustration has been generated, from the use of those words than with just about any others in the manager's vocabulary.

This is backward. Budgets are supposed to help managers, not intimidate them. Budgets are intended to be a tool, a means to an end, not a holy grail. It seems so unnecessary, doesn't it? And yet it happens so often that it hardly seems accidental.

There is a lot written about budgets and budgeting processes, and much of it is simply wishful thinking. Budgets, especially program budgets, get built and approved in a variety of ways that don't always adhere to the theories. Any useful budget had to have been constructed from the ground up at some point. Starting with the numbers in the budget therefore begs the most important question of how the numbers got into the budget in the first place. This chapter will try to deal with exactly that question.

Exhibit 12.1 shows a program budget for the Committee to Clean Up Amigosville's (CCUA) municipal recycling program. This is the kind of presentation you would expect to see at a management team meeting or as part of a yearly planning document. What we are going to do is to look underneath it to see how the numbers were composed.

EXHIBIT 12.1   CCUA MUNICIPAL RECYCLING PROGRAM BUDGET

Revenue			
Government contracts/grants	$375,600		
Total in	$375,600		
Expenses			
Salaries	FTE		
Program director	0.5	$37,500	$ 18,750
Promotions specialist	0.3	32,000	10,560
Event coordinator	0.5	30,000	15,000
Drivers	2.5	25,000	62,500
Technicians	2.5	20,000	50,000
Mechanic	0.2	29,000	5,800
Secretarial/clerical	0.5	24,000	12,000
Relief/overtime factor			11,830
Payroll taxes			15,475
Employee benefits			11,000
Other			3,000
Consultants			3,000
Advertising			25,000
Supplies			7,000
Vehicle expense			15,000
Equipment leases			3,500
Depreciation			3,231
Rent			12,000
Utilities			2,000
Property insurance			2,500
General & administrative			86,454
Total expenses			$375,600

PLAYING REVENUES LIKE A SYMPHONY

The top line doesn't get much attention in nonprofit organizations, and for good reason. In the past, most of the action took place in the expense category. That is, since revenues often tend to be predictable, any change in budget structure necessitates a quick trip to the expense category to find some offsetting adjustments.

CCUA's revenue for the municipal recycling program is, well, boring. This program is contractual in nature, meaning that there is a formal and probably legally binding expectation that CCUA will carry out a series of transactions with each municipality that has a definite beginning and a definite end (with probable extensions of the contract).

Usually, the most interesting aspect of revenue portraits is what goes on behind them. In effect, the revenue stream marks what society is willing to put into CCUA, under what terms and conditions, and with what degree of certainty. The real power—or the frustration—of all these different types of revenue streams is the interaction between and among them. The nonprofit manager's role is to learn the differences, appreciate the strengths

WHY ARE NONPROFIT REVENUES RELATIVELY RELIABLE IN THE SHORT TERM?

By definition, a significant portion of nonprofit revenues must come from public sources, typically donations and government contracts. Both sources as a rule have relatively stable financial environments. Private foundations must generally give out 5% of their assets each year, and asset bases tend to change slowly whether they grow or shrink. Private donors of small to medium sized amounts tend to concentrate their giving during certain times of the year, especially near the end of the tax year, so that revenue base tends to be identified months in advance. Governments notoriously prefer stable environments, at least in the short term, for many philosophical and logistical reasons. This offers nonprofits a substantial buffer against abrupt changes in revenue streams. It is also why certain shrewd for-profit executives are interested in the sector as a source of customers because it is effectively recession-resistant—though not, as the 2008 recession proved, recession-proof.

and weaknesses, and then take maximum advantage of each one according to the situation.

Take CCUA, for example. Those 17 municipal recycling contracts it holds are its single largest chunk of revenue. The CCUA business manager might look at that situation and muse in the following way:

> CCUA's strategic planning process told us that recycling is the major way we want to clean up Amigosville, and here we just picked up 17 cost reimbursement recycling contracts fairly easily. Furthermore, it looks like we could add another few dozen without much effort. Generally, the municipalities pay steadily but slowly, which means that each new contract is going to require a month or two worth of cash to cover expenses before reimbursements kick in. Since we're not awash in cash, we need to get better cash flow so that we can offset that cashless month or two that each new contract will entail. Now, if I remember correctly, the AllGreen Foundation offers recycling cash flow grants. . . .

Alternatively, the business manager may decide to carry out some of that expansion into recycling via funding sources that offer better cash flow than municipalities' cost reimbursement methods, *even if those other sources have some other undesirable financial aspect.* In this type of situation, there is potential for financial considerations to unduly influence the way the nonprofit carries out its mission. Frankly, however, it requires an unusually strong financial person (or a weak executive) before this risk becomes a real threat. For most situations, keeping this sort of planning scrupulously connected to mission helps keep the nonprofit viable and effective.

Expenses

Salaries

The first thing you will notice in Exhibit 12.1 about salary expense is that it is measured in FTEs, or full-time equivalents. This is a handy though not universal way of expressing the cost of one person working full time for 52 weeks. (Yes, there is a way to cover vacation time, but hold that thought.) It's a good way to be sure that personnel expenditures are measured uniformly. To calculate the total cost for the year for a particular position, multiply by the FTEs for that position. Note that the total yearly cost is often the only number that actually appears on the budget; ideally, this is because the multiplication described above is done on unpublished worksheets.

Read a budget's details for the stories they tell. Exhibit 12.1 tells us many things just by the personnel complement. A half-time program director in a program of this size may mean that the same full-time employee is responsible for the municipal recycling program half of the time and another program the other half of the time, since responsibility for a program of this size is hard to manage as a part-time employee.

The combination of the promotions specialist and the event coordinator suggests a few themes. For one thing, the municipalities contracting with CCUA obviously believe that part of recycling involves education and that they cannot or will not do it themselves. It may even be voluntary recycling; if it were mandatory, the towns would have other ways of publicizing the message.

The presence of an event coordinator in a relatively small program budget like this implies a lot about the scope of CCUA's effort. Two and a half drivers and the same number of technicians, along with a mechanic who only works one day a week (0.2 FTE times 40 hours per week) can't cover a lot of ground, environmentally speaking. With the number of municipalities represented here (see Part III of the 990), it is highly unlikely that the program handles weekly recycling chores in more than one or two of them. Therefore, a good part of the reason for the contract's existence must be to hold special events. We can imagine that the promotions specialist and the event coordinator and even the program director probably spend a fair amount of time on one-time-only recycling days, fairs, conferences, and the like. The advertising budget is their tool.

Relief/Overtime

Exhibit 12.1 illustrates another aspect of this program and in the process raises a vexing personnel budgeting question. Sooner or later one of the drivers is going to go on vacation or get sick or need a few days off for the funeral of a close relative. If this were the type of position that involved, say, long-range planning or reconciling checking accounts, no problem—the work could wait a few days. But in a municipal recycling program, if there is no driver, there is no recycling. And if there is no recycling on a day when it was supposed to occur, there will be a bunch of angry homeowners.

Municipalities don't like angry homeowners, so the program must go on even if the driver cannot.

This is the purpose of the relief/overtime line item. On a day when a driver calls in sick, the program director calls the backup driver he was smart enough to recruit for such an eventuality and pays for the backup out of the relief/overtime line. This line also covers other necessary overtime payments. Before getting into exactly how it does that, however, it is necessary to make a brief digression into the world of labor laws. Over 70 years ago, Congress passed and the President signed the Fair Labor Standards Act (FLSA). One of the things the FLSA and its later amendments did was to stipulate that workers who put in more than 40 hours per week of work must get paid overtime, or 1.5 times a basic hour's pay, for the 41st hour onward. This provision was intended as a penalty to the employer and an incentive to avoid the sweatshop environment of the early industrial period in our country. At the same time, the FLSA recognized that for some occupations it was impractical or undesirable to adhere to such a standard. Professionals, administrators, and certain types of salespeople are good examples of this group; they are known as exempt employees.

Everyone without a good reason for being exempt from the requirements of the FLSA ("good" being defined by FLSA itself) is considered a nonexempt employee, and the provisions of the FLSA apply fully. Nonprofit corporations are *not* exempt merely because of their tax status. Exemptions are decided only on the basis of individual employees or classes of employees. In CCUA's municipal recycling program, the drivers, technicians, and mechanic are nonexempt employees, and therefore any work time greater than 40 hours must be compensated at 1.5 times their normal hourly rate. The secretary/clerk may very well be considered nonexempt too, but it is probably a safe bet that the secretary/clerk will not actually incur overtime since it should be possible to share any extraordinary workload with other CCUA secretaries or clerks.

With this as background, it is possible to dig deeper into the recycling budget to see how its creators envision using relief or overtime funds. A quick calculation ($11,830/($62,500 + $50,000 + $5,800)) suggests that they used a flat 10 percent as the factor for relief and overtime. To budget veterans, 10 percent of anything has the smell of a conventional guess, so let's see what it really buys.

Assuming that the relief factor was calculated with the expectation that it would apply equally to all three positions, and in view of the fact that the average salary for the three positions (see the Per FTE column) is $11.86 per hour ($25,000 + $20,000 + $29,000/52 weeks/120 hours per week), the line as funded will purchase 997 hours of substitute labor at straight time.

Most employers give employees vacation time, sick time, and holidays as paid time off. In the case of holidays, recycling crews are not going to work since the municipality itself is usually considered closed except for essential services. That means that we don't need to cover holidays via the relief/overtime budget. If sick time is earned at a rate of, say, one day per month—and if there is some sort of reasonable cap on the amount of sick time employees can accumulate, as there really should be—then the heaviest call on the relief budget will be for no more than 12 days out of a possible 250 days per year, or about 5 percent.

Our 10 percent relief budget looks healthy at this point. Although that provision for accumulating sick time could be a concern depending on where the cap is set, one could still expect no more than a single employee to hit the cap in any one year, which gives CCUA some good protection. Plus, people working in these types of positions tend not to stay long enough to develop budgetbusting levels of sick time anyhow. Also in CCUA's favor is that individuals working as part of a two-person team typically are less motivated to call in sick frivolously and put extra burden on a partner they will have to face upon returning to work.

Finally, if we assume that the mechanic, only a 0.2 FTE employee, is replaceable in some other way (another mechanic from the organization, for instance, or a cooperative local repair shop), then the relief pool grows higher.

On the other hand, overtime will drive things in a completely different direction. Remember that overtime pay must be 150 percent of the normal hourly rate. Under these terms, the maximum time available from the relief/overtime line would have to be calculated at 1.5 times the average $11.86 salary described earlier, or $17.79 per hour. At this higher hourly rate, the maximum hours available from the budget as overtime with no spending whatsoever on straight time relief is a mere 664 hours.

A minor digression from a digression. For many employers, especially nonprofit organizations, it is popular to give overtime as time off. Doing so properly, unfortunately, is difficult. First of all, the time off has to be calculated according to the same 1.5 multiple, so an hour of overtime must be compensated with an hour and a half of time off. Second, payment must be made or time off taken in the same pay period. These strictures make time off in lieu of pay problematic, to say the least.

This line can get hit from two different directions. We have no way of knowing what mix of relief and overtime pay CCUA is expecting to use with this small amount, but given what we know about the program, it is fair to surmise that they will tend toward straight time replacement costs and try to keep overtime under strict control. This is a typical strategy for most nonprofits and, for that matter, for most small businesses.

What we have just done is to build the relief/overtime line item from scratch. In practice, most organizations will quickly develop rules of thumb for budget planning, such as the 10 percent factor used here. Some rough planning indices may even be available from trade associations and the like in industries where relief or overtime are major budget issues. The idea is to use whatever legitimate shortcuts are available, but continually subject them to tests of usefulness and accuracy.

Payroll Taxes

No good deed goes untaxed, and the act of giving people jobs is no exception. Even tax-exempt organizations must pay when it comes to payroll taxes, though there is a break or two to be had. The first and foremost payroll tax is the Federal Insurance Contributions Act (FICA), better known as Social Security. This one has grown more complicated in recent years, but in essence the employer pays a flat percentage (7.65 percent) of the first $100,000 or so in wages, known as the Social Security Wage Base. The employee kicks in the same. The little twist is that of the 7.65%, 1.45% goes toward funding Medicare and that part is not capped. Years ago, large numbers of nonprofits were allowed to opt out of the system, but that changed in 1984 and now virtually all organizations must participate.

Then there's unemployment insurance. While the federal government demands an unemployment tax from proprietary corporations, public charities are exempt. States have their own unemployment tax systems, however, and, although it will differ from state to state, the thrust of it will be a percentage tax on payroll. States will allow nonprofit public charities to get out of the unemployment insurance system, but in return the agency must agree to pay claims as they come due. It's called self-insurance and is a good way to save money as long as one's payments are less than what would have been paid using the conventional, or "insured," method.

Another tax on payroll is for yet another social insurance program. Like unemployment, the Worker's Compensation system is administered by each state. It's hard to generalize about individual states' methods but for these purposes we don't have to. Worker's Compensation insurance will show up as a bite out of payroll paid for by the employer.

There may be other taxes, especially city taxes, in various localities. Good budgets take these into account. Again, program budgeters usually don't have to blaze financial management trails, so the best method of budgeting for payroll taxes is to use the same organization-wide percentage that other programs have historically spent.

Independent Contractors versus Employees

One popular way of escaping payroll taxes is to pay individuals as independent contractors rather than salaried or wage-earning employees. The advantage of this strategy is that the employer doesn't have to pay payroll taxes or report anything very complicated to the Internal Revenue Service (IRS) since the employee does it all. The disadvantage is that improperly characterizing employees as independent contractors can get an organization into—this is a technical term—a whole bunch of trouble.

It is simply not possible to make sweeping pronouncements that will be valid in every case. There are, however, some guidelines employers can use. Generally speaking, independent contractors or consultants arrange with an employer to do certain work according to their own methods and without being subject to the control of others. The employer's *right* to control the details and means of an individual's work is a key determinant here; whether the employer actually exercises that right is irrelevant. In a true contractor relationship, the employer controls only *what* gets done. *How* it gets done is up to the contractor.

As you might imagine, issues of control are at the heart of the independent contractor versus employee issue. And you can tell the IRS really doesn't want any messin' around with the rules. They put it clearly:

"If you have an employer-employee relationship, it makes no difference how it is labeled. The substance of the relationship, not the label, governs the worker's status. Nor does it matter whether the individual is employed full time or part time."

Note: all IRS quotes in this section are from the very handy though unexcitedly named Publication 15A.

The IRS goes on to note that people such as lawyers and contractors who represent a specific trade and offer their services to the general public usually are not employees, but whether they are considered independent contractors depends entirely on the facts in each case. What the IRS is interested in is evidence of the degree of control and the degree of independence. They say that facts about these things fall into three categories: behavioral control; financial control; and the relationship of the parties.

Behavioral control relates to how the individual does the job assigned to them. This includes things like the type of instructions the business gives to the worker about how to do the work. These would be directions such as:

- "When and where to do the work.
- What tools or equipment to use.
- What workers to hire or to assist with the work.
- Where to purchase supplies and services.
- What work must be performed by a specified individual.
- What order or sequence to follow."

Behavioral control also includes things such as training that the business gives the worker.

Financial control is tipped off by things like the degree of investment the worker has in their business, how the worker is paid, whether and how the worker markets his or her services on the open market, the extent of the worker's unreimbursed business expenses (contractors are much more likely to have these), and whether the worker can earn a profit or suffer a loss.

Finally, the IRS looks at the nature of the business relationship. Facts that mean something to the IRS here include whether written contracts are involved, if the business supplies the worker with employee-like benefits, the permanency of the relationship (an indefinite relationship is a tip-off of employee status), and the degree to which the individual's services are a key part of the company's business.

Why is this an important question? Enterprising—may we call them maniacally frugal?—employers are always looking for a way to lessen their costs, and the possibility of unloading large numbers of employees' person-nel-related tasks is quite attractive. Usually it's not that easy. Both the IRS and the Department of Labor, as enforcers of FLSA, have the right to impose stiff penalties on employers who are not in compliance. Being sure that your nonprofit meets all of the guidelines is not only good budgeting, it's good business too.

Benefits

Of all the areas in the typical budget, employee benefits have changed the most in recent years. Typically, the largest single benefit cost is health insurance, and in small nonprofits as well as in comparable small businesses, health insurance can be so expensive that it eats up almost all of the benefits budget.

Various insurance coverages tend to rank next in frequency of offering. Life insurance is a big one, not necessarily because it's desired by large numbers of employees but because it tends to be among the least expensive benefits and because in some cases insurance companies bundle life insurance with other types of coverage to make an overall program more economically feasible for them. Short- and long-term disability insurance coverage is also popular, as is dental insurance. Pension plans are also very popular, and growing more so with the aging of the nonprofit baby boomer generation.

Incidentally, one method for coping with the high cost of benefits starts with the IRS. Section 125 plans, so named for their location in the code, allow employers a range of money-saving alternatives. At the low end of the spectrum is what is variously called a premium conversion or salary reduction plan, in which the dollars previously removed from an employee's paycheck to pay part of the health insurance premium get removed *before* taxes instead. This action has the effect of increasing employee's take-home pay since they no longer pay FICA on the money that goes to their premium. It saves FICA payments for the employer too, which makes it a win–win situation for everyone but the federal government.

Next along the spectrum are flexible spending accounts (FSAs), in which the employee sets aside an individually tailored portion of the monthly paycheck, also pretax, to be "deposited" in a "spending account" for use with health expenses or dependent care needs. At the high end is the more familiar idea of cafeteria plans, in which employees get all of the preceding advantages plus the choice of taking some or all of them in the cash equivalent.

Some friendly advice—the area of benefits planning is extraordinarily complex. These descriptions don't even begin to touch on the subtleties of these arrangements, and the details tend to change regularly anyway. It's best to consult a professional before making serious moves in this part of the budget. Fortunately, it's also worth it.

The budget category of fringe benefits is as notable for what it does *not* include as what it does include. Most people assume that this is the budget category that encompasses tuition assistance, time off, and the office picnic. For different reasons in each case, it does not. The federal government applies certain guidelines to fringe benefits that are actually fairly restrictive. Tuition assistance, for instance, is not considered a fringe benefit but an operational expense. Time off gets handled as described in the personnel budgeting section, and the office picnic has to be covered via a line item that might read "Seasonal Personnel Development" or perhaps "Office Communications Expense," total candor sometimes being a handicap in these matters.

As with payroll taxes, budgeting for fringe benefits can be most easily accomplished in an organization with a track record simply by referring to the past. For planning purposes, a standard percentage of salaries and wages should be sufficient, although it should be noted that recently the cost of fringe benefits has gone up more both relatively and in absolute terms than the cost of payroll taxes.

Other Direct Expenses

All other direct expenses (lines "Other" through "Property Insurance") will be different each year for each program. Perhaps the most significant commentary about the rest of the direct expenses is not *what* they are but *that* they are. At a minimum, it's the responsibility of budgeters to capture all of the costs associated with a program, and the place to deposit them is after personnel costs and before general and administrative costs.

Notice that these direct costs show up here, meaning that they can easily and directly be attributed to program services. They are, in a sense, the donut; indirect costs—or general and administrative costs—are the hole.

And the shape and size of that hole is the single biggest debating point in nonprofit financial management.

INDIRECT (GENERAL AND ADMINISTRATIVE) COSTS

In any operation, there are costs that are not the direct and exclusive responsibility of any one program or service division. The CEO's salary, for instance, pays for a level of effort that cannot be attributed to a specific program because it was expended on behalf of the nonprofit as a whole. Payroll processing costs from an outside payroll service are another good example of an expense not attributable to direct service.

Theoretically, a huge accounting system and large amounts of staff time and patience could make indirect costs disappear. Everything would be charged directly to program services. Every 10 minutes the CEO spent in a meeting, every pencil the bookkeeper picked up to scribble an accounting note, every kilowatt that flowed into the organization's headquarters would be tracked and properly allocated to a specific service.

But does this really matter? Not only do we not need that level of detail to manage operations, the compromises and estimates that the whole scheme would entail would make any output misleading and possibly dangerously unreliable.

Now go in the other direction. Striving for the maximum degree of simplicity and convenience, one might forget about dividing up (allocating) most expenses and instead throw them into a big pool called *indirect costs*. Then, to get each different service to carry its own weight, figure out what portion of that pool should be assigned to each individual service or program. This would be a whole lot simpler than painstakingly coding each bill according to which service should pay it.

These are extremes. But they indicate the two poles between which nonprofit budgeting for indirect costs must play. Being reasonable types, we might be inclined to split the difference and attempt to find the elusive happy medium. Mathematically and accounting-wise this strategy may be perfectly acceptable, but it fails because it ignores human nature.

No one likes administrative costs, especially people who give money to nonprofit organizations that are expected to do good things with that money. To the average donor, money for administration buys paperwork and photocopies of paperwork, not active problem solving and services in support of the mission. Oversimplifying only slightly, a low indirect cost rate signals responsible administration to the average observer, while a high rate suggests waste. The new crop of charity watchers has intensified this predisposition with its emphasis on administrative costs as a part of its rating formula.

Still, what are administrative costs? In the absence of funding sources' mandatory definitions, administrative costs are largely what you make them. This means that they are determined by a combination of accounting judgments and the capacity of administrative systems.

One final note on administrative cost behavior. A certain level of administrative cost is inevitable. One needs a central office and a financial operation of some size, and there are many other expenses that cannot easily be charged directly to programs but that are necessary regardless of how much direct service is provided. As a result, small nonprofits usually have the highest percentage of administrative expenses. Conversely, as a nonprofit grows, it often can add many more programs with only a modest increase in administrative cost. The secret is knowing that this dynamic exists, and how to manage it.

In our experience, most nonprofit executives are sincerely cost conscious when it comes to administrative expenses. They try to control administrative expense, and if they can't it's probably because they can't control other expenses either. In the end, the governing force in reporting nonprofit administrative expenses is the environment in which the organization operates. If the environment signals through formal or informal means that it wants administrative expense reporting handled in a certain way, over time that is exactly what will happen.

Conclusion

In most settings, budgets and budgeting are overly feared exercises. With the proper knowledge they can be used as the management aids they are intended to be. Budgets can surely be beasts, but only when their human handlers demand it.

CHAPTER 13

Indirect Costs
and Other Despised Items

A famous professional athlete's commercial advertised a fund-raiser for his charitable organization with the assurance that "all money raised will go to direct services, and none to administration." This well-meaning pledge neatly summarizes the prevailing attitude toward administrative—or *indirect*—costs. First, it says pretty plainly that administrative costs are unseemly and should be avoided. This is the dominant attitude toward nonprofits' indirect costs among the general public, most board members, and many nonprofit managers themselves.

This is a laudable sentiment. Who wants to pay for costs not closely associated with direct service delivery? It's hard to see how managers' lavish offices, company-paid cars, and multiple perks could help deliver better museum exhibits, more health care for kids, or superior graduate school courses. Lately the backlash against executive compensation has gained new life with the Wall Street meltdown of 2008.

The problem with the sentiment is not its general direction but with the fact that it is so completely naive. Administrative costs are an inescapable part of providing services, and no amount of well-meaning huffing will change that fact. Pretending that administrative costs can be wished away is either self-delusional or hopelessly out of touch with reality.

The second problem is that the athlete's pledge was selfish. Even if it were somehow true that his fund-raising follow-up really could ensure that not a single dime of the proceeds went to administrative costs—a dubious proposition—all he was really doing was playing a cost-shifting shell game. Someone somewhere along the line was going to have to pay for that overhead, and if he managed to avoid paying for his share it only meant that everyone else giving money to the organization was going to have to pay more than their fair share in administrative costs.

STILL, IT'S LOW THAT COUNTS

Having said all that, we must acknowledge the inescapable reality that a low overhead rate in a nonprofit carries huge symbolic value. The universal litmus test for casual observers is simple: Low overhead means a responsible organization, high overhead means a spendthrift group not worthy of any more money. So nonprofit managers have no choice but to keep their overhead rates as low as possible. To do that, they must master the intricacies of overhead calculations.

First, some definitions. Direct charges are those expenses that can be easily linked to specific programs and services. Food for preschool students is a good example of a direct cost. So is the expense of the preschool teachers' salaries.

By contrast, indirect costs are those expenses that, while necessary, cannot be reasonably tied to specific programs and services. The preschool's director and the cost of the payroll service are classic indirect expenses. Indirect costs are also known as administrative costs, general and administrative expenses, and indirect charges, among other terms.

There is a bit of a where-do-we-draw-the-line question here. While food and teachers' salaries are clearly direct expenses, what about copy paper? Technically, the answer here is that the paper and other supplies used by and for direct service employees such as teachers are direct costs, while those used by the CEO or for administrative purposes are indirect.

No problem. All we need to do is give everyone a coded copy machine key that automatically attributes any copies they make to their own department. But what about the cost of the toner cartridge, that pricey Star Wars piece of plastic and metal that always runs low just before you need to make 25 copies of an urgent 75-page report? No problem here, either. Just calculate the total number of direct copies and the total number of indirect, take the percentages and charge the applicable percentage of the toner cartridge cost to direct and indirect charges. But what about the ink supply? It's a color copier, and the direct service people are always making color copies, which takes more of the most costly kind of ink. Okay, we'll fix that by calculating the number of color copies produced by direct and indirect users. Then we'll multiply the cost of the colored ink by the total percentages of direct and indirect users. Then we'll . . .

You can see where this is going. Theoretically, it is possible to turn every indirect cost into a direct cost just by keeping track of a number of extra variables. But this process of endless reductionism reaches an absurd level quickly. Sure it may be possible to turn everything into a direct cost, but at what expense? The hassle factor associated with this potentially endless process says we need to find a different way of calculating and charging indirect costs.

This is the point of the indirect cost rate. The idea is to come up with a reliable way of attributing—or allocating—indirect costs to direct service efforts. That way, each program or service can be assured that it will be asked to carry its fair share of the administrative burden. Budget makers usually have some type of indirect cost allocation policy to guide them.

But the key question is how that allocation is derived. As it happens, there are many ways of getting there. Here are a few of the most common.

Percentage of Personnel

The simplest and perhaps most common method of allocating indirect costs is to figure out the percentage of total personnel costs for which each individual program is responsible and then apply it to the total of all indirect costs. This is Math 101 stuff—if a program uses 40 percent of all personnel, it gets charged 40 percent of the total indirect costs. The argument here is that, since personnel tend to be the biggest high-maintenance item in any budget, indirect or administrative costs will probably flow proportionately to heavy concentrations of personnel.

Percentage of Expenses

Then there is another simple formula, which we will call the percentage of expenses formula. You get this one by calculating the total percentage of spending on personnel *and* other direct expenses that each program incurs, then multiplying it by the total of all indirect costs. If my program is responsible for 27 percent of all expenses then my share of the indirect cost is

27 percent. This one carries the percentage-of-personnel formula a step further by assuming that personnel are just one indicator of spending on indirect items, and that the true measure of indirect effort is a combination of personnel and other direct costs.

The Federal Method

For frequent flyers on the federal dollar, the folks in Washington have a special program. Recognizing that it was getting boring to set up an indirect rate for every contract or grant with the federal government, the federal government many years ago established a policy of setting up a single overhead rate that would apply to all federal government–related business. Guidance on the acceptable ways of doing this can be found in Office of Management and Budget Circular A-122 (OMB A-122) "Cost Principles for Nonprofit Organizations."

SECRET OF THE INDIRECT COST GAME

What these methods all share is that they represent a uniform, predictable method for calculating overhead costs. In fact, it's the uniform and rational application of the method that is as important as the results themselves, because otherwise the allocation of indirect costs becomes an exercise in arbitrariness. A sure sign of trouble is when the chief financial person starts to apply different standards for overhead charges to different programs—retroactively. This practice amounts to changing the rules of the game after it's been played.

Speaking of games, the whole area of indirect costs is a treasure trove of gamesmanship. And even when games aren't being played, the mechanics of overhead calculations can produce some intriguing results. Thus, we enter the funhouse mirror world of indirect cost reporting.

Recently, we had conversations with two different nonprofit managers, each of whom was quite pleased that their organizations routinely post administrative costs of close to 8 percent. "We try to put the money into direct care," said one.

A laudable sentiment, to be sure. On the other hand, is there any nonprofit manager out there whose organization tries to spend money on overhead expenses instead of direct service? Like most such assertions, this one was as much an expression of philosophy as a statement of fact. From what we knew of both agencies, they certainly did not overspend on administrative costs. On the other hand, they were not cold-water-bath-rooms-60-watt-bulbs-and-re-use-the-teabag-types either.

Ironically, just a few miles away from where one of the CEOs sat was a major research-intensive university that we happen to know carries a routine overhead rate of over 100 percent. And while we have never asked, we suspect that that organization would also say it likes to keep its overhead low and put most of its funds directly into education.

How can one explain this seeming paradox? Is it really true that two nonprofits can have such dramatically different overhead rates? Who's mistaken here?

Defining and Calculating Indirect Costs

The puzzling answer is that there is no mistake. They are both right, each in their own way. For its part, the vast majority of the university's buildings are relatively no more opulent than those of the smaller nonprofit. And although the university does generally have a much larger overhead structure, it's certainly not 12.5 times larger, as its 100 percent overhead rate would suggest. So why are they both right?

The answer lies in how you define and then calculate indirect costs. Exhibit 13.1 shows a highly simplified nonprofit organization budget based

EXHIBIT 13.1   DIRECT COSTS

Item	Dollars
CEO	$ 60,000
Program managers (2)	80,000
Administrative assistant (1)	25,000
Direct service staff	200,000
Payroll taxes & benefits (22% of salaries)	80,300
Direct supplies	40,000
Program rent	10,000
Administrative rent	5,000
Vehicle costs	5,000
Miscellaneous	2,000
Total	$507,300

on two programs and various related expenses. What is the entity's indirect cost rate? If you said 10 percent, you would be right. If you said 71 percent, you would also be right. And if you gave a variety of other percentages, you would probably be right as well, because it all depends on how you define indirect costs.

Here's how we get those two very different results. In Exhibit 13.2, we try to make every conceivable expense a direct charge. So we argue that the CEO, normally an indirect cost, spends half of her time supervising the two program directors. The administrative assistant is said to spend a third of her time dealing with indirect matters, and we accept the full charge for rental of the administrative space.

Formula: Indirect costs are drawn from the shaded areas. Based on this example, that means:

- Fifty percent of the CEO's time plus 22 percent for taxes and benefits for a total of $36,600

- Thirty-three percent of the administrative assistant's time plus 22 percent for taxes and benefits for a total of $10,065

- Five thousand dollars for administrative rent

This produces a total indirect cost of $51,665. This indirect cost as a percentage of total cost creates an indirect rate of 10 percent.

EXHIBIT 13.2   10%—AGGRESSIVE COMPUTATION OF INDIRECT COSTS

Item	Dollars
CEO	$ 60,000
Program managers (2)	80,000
Administrative assistant (1)	25,000
Direct service staff	200,000
Payroll taxes & benefits (22% of salaries)	80,300
Direct supplies	40,000
Program rent	10,000
Administrative rent	5,000
Vehicle costs	5,000
Miscellaneous	2,000
Total	$507,300

In Exhibit 13.3, we define indirect expenses extremely broadly. This is what happens in federal funding (like what our university gets), where recipient organizations must charge a federal overhead rate based on a specific formula. It's also related to why the Pentagon used to be accused of things like buying $80 screwdrivers ($6.00 for the screwdriver and a $74.00 automatic overhead charge on every order). In this computation, we express the rate as a percentage of direct costs, not on the total budget as in the first example, which drives the rate even higher.

Formula: Indirect costs are again drawn from the shaded areas. Indirect costs are:

- One hundred percent of the time of all staff other than direct service staff plus 22 percent for taxes and benefits for a total of $201,300

- One hundred percent of administrative rent and vehicle costs total $10,000

This totals $211,300, making the indirect rate 71 percent. Remember, unlike in the previous example, we are defining indirect cost as a percentage of direct cost, not total budget. Direct cost is $296,000, so $211,300/296,000 is 71 percent.

EXHIBIT 13.3   71%—BROAD COMPUTATION OF INDIRECT COST

Item	Dollars
CEO	$ 60,000
Program managers (2)	80,000
Administrative assistant (1)	25,000
Direct service staff	200,000
Payroll taxes & benefits (22% of salaries)	80,300
Direct supplies	40,000
Program rent	10,000
Administrative rent	5,000
Vehicle costs	5,000
Miscellaneous	2,000
Total	$507,300

Why It Matters

As we noted earlier, the general public believes that indirect costs in a non-profit are inherently bad and should be minimized or eliminated altogether, and we have to go along or risk losing funding or credibility. So we attempt to creatively define indirect costs out of existence.

But the real problem is that by claiming our indirect rates are rock-bottom-low, we are subtly devaluing the work of management and mis-leading ourselves if we take our press releases too seriously. That will be an even bigger problem in the future because the demands of the external environment are forcing the cost of management up, not down. Greater use of technology, the need to do more fund-raising, and the overall cost of doing business all drive indirect costs up. Those who truly believe they can get away with less and less spending in this area are simply being shortsighted.

Yet the tension will continue. The average donor, empowered with more and more freely available information about nonprofit recipients, will demand low indirect costs as a condition of philanthropy. Media out-lets are becoming savvier about the implied cost–benefit ratio of indirect costs to direct costs.

The pressure to report low indirect costs will not go away. Considering the relative lack of other structural pressures on nonprofits, this may very well be healthy for the sector overall. But that doesn't mean individual nonprofit managers should take their own press releases too literally. They must find a way to honestly report competitively low indirect costs even as they pay more and more attention to management matters. That can be our little secret.

14

Pricing: How Much *Should* It Cost?

In the end, price is nothing more than a barrier to service, and the art of pricing is deciding how high or low to set that barrier. Other factors can be barriers too, such as geography, cultural considerations, and political realities. But few will doubt that pricing is usually the last and most carefully attended hurdle to clear for those desiring a particular service.

What drives consumers to seek a specific service is the value they expect from it. Museums offer the chance to explore a different culture, social clubs the opportunity to relax with others who have similar interests and tastes, and schools the potential of broadened intellectual experience and possibly higher earning power. Each of these types of programs carries an explicit price that a potential consumer must evaluate before deciding to utilize it. These evaluations range from relatively long and considered deliberations about school enrollment to seconds when it comes to emergency services.

In each case, the underlying dynamic is the same: Pricing decisions are merely the arena for a systematic public dialogue about the value of a service. The nonprofit manager's challenge is to step out from being a bystander in this process and to influence it constructively and proactively.

To do so, it is necessary to understand how nonprofit pricing works. One way to understand the pricing process is along the following continuum:

← ——————————————————————→

Commodity   Specialty

Services whose essential nature place them toward the commodity end of this continuum have a dime-a-dozen quality about them. They are plentiful, more or less standardized in the eye of the consumer, and easily accessed. Day care centers and home health services are examples of commodity services. The combination of regulatory demands, economics, and the nature of the service itself make one version tend to resemble most others.

This is painful for nonprofit managers to consider. It is extremely difficult for someone deeply involved in the actual delivery of a service to regard it as anything other than a uniquely and intensely crafted experience. The fact that there may be thousands of other such experiences appears to negate the individuality of the effort. In reality, however, the consumer may not be able to tell the difference between versions of the service or may regard any differences as unimportant. Either way, choices tend to be made on the basis of something other than perceived value. That other basis is usually price.

This is why services near the commodity end of the continuum cannot raise their price easily. Having no perceived uniqueness in the consumer's mind, they can and will be replaced over time by consumers making choices based solely on price. Here, the consumer is very strong, and the average price will tend to rise only as far as the consumer(s) is willing to let it.

Not so at the high end. A whole different set of factors allows these nonprofits to set their own prices, or more accurately, to govern the spending that will result in higher prices. Add formidable barriers to entry such as major capital investments, and you have a prescription for high prices. On this side of the continuum, the consumer is a lot less powerful. The higher perceived value means he or she *must* have it, while the barriers to entry dampen the supply. The result is much more control for the providers of the service.

Two other factors have historically combined to keep nonprofit prices down. First, decision makers in nonprofit organizations tend to be professionals, and professionals need people identified as service recipients in order to perform professionally. Reimbursement considerations aside, physicians must have patients, teachers must have students, and curators need museum-goers. As professionals, their interests are served by lowering prices as much as possible. This is why the most bitter opposition to a nonprofit corporation's price hike often comes from inside the organization itself.

The second downward force on nonprofit pricing has been the typical means of setting the prices. Since most people used to believe—erroneously—that being a nonprofit organization meant making no profit, price in the nonprofit sector came to be equated with cost. Determine the cost of the service, and you have determined the price. The added economic benefit of tax exemption only made the overall economic bargain irresistible. This type of thinking led naturally to what is called *retrospective pricing*, or pricing that is based on historic spending. For a long time retrospective pricing was common in the health care system; let us know what it cost you to provide the service, said the payers, and we'll pay you a future rate derived directly from that historic record. For service providers in a retrospective system, the central beauty is that it is essentially risk-free, a state of affairs more or less happily accepted in return for the inherent aggravations of the daily operations of such a system. Besides, most of the really tedious and aggravating work gets done by outside advisors anyway, and the smart organizations will hire a former government pricing specialist to deal with his old colleagues.

Today, the trend in any field where government or some form of management specialists are primary payers is toward prospective pricing. Prospective pricing systems are most well-developed in the health and social service field, but all share the same unifying theme; they set the price of a given service *before* it's delivered, and do not look to recoup excess payments or supplement losses after the fact. The move toward prospective pricing is the result of a complex set of economic, social, and political variables interacting to produce certain pricing structures as a logical result. Mostly, prospective pricing is disguised under pseudonyms. It's better known as health maintenance organizations, diagnosis-related groups, capitation payments, or class (group) rates.

In all of these methodologies, prices are predetermined. To be effective in the long term, the prices must have at least some relationship to cost, at least the aggregate cost incurred by the industry to produce the required services. But they need not have any direct relationship to the cost structure of any one provider of service. The power of prospectively determined prices is that they tend to drive everyone toward the same average, unless an individual organization can find the means to supplement the basic service.

The effect of this change is to shift risk from the consumer to the provider. Most obvious of the risks is the chance that someone will have guessed wrong about the proper level of pricing. This possibility puts pressure on the provider to monitor costs and pay careful attention to service management, which is exactly what the payers wanted in the first place.

More subtly, the shift to prospective pricing puts far greater pressure on the service provider's management systems. Surviving in a prospective system requires tighter and more efficient management control systems that operate with full knowledge of industry trends. Even more subtle, retrospective payers and their providers must engage each other individually. Typically, they develop a bond. It may be an ambiguous bond, and it may even be rooted in mutual dislike or misunderstanding, but it's a bond nevertheless. Payers in a prospective system tend to have less individual interaction regarding providers more like commodities, while making policy changes that affect whole categories of organizations. Consequently, the class payer can be less of an advocate in certain circumstances.

PRICING METHODOLOGIES

As summarized in Exhibit 14.1, there are many different names and descriptive phrases applicable to payment arrangements, and they vary by locality and area of service. More important, they carry different types of risks and rewards. These types of revenue agreements are discussed next with no particular importance attached to the order.

Fee for Service

The most basic of reimbursement types, fee for service is an exchange of service for money. The price is agreed to beforehand, although exactly who determines the price will vary. When government is a substantial purchaser, it tends to insist on setting the price. When government is a minority or nonexistent purchaser, market pricing will typically dominate. There is no real or implied promise to go beyond a single transaction, nor is there any guarantee of a certain level of service utilization. Fee-for-service revenue comes with the fewest strings attached about how it can be spent, and it offers an excellent possibility of profit. Most consumer services, from manicures to shoe shines, are fee for service. In the nonprofit sector, it tends to be most heavily used in health care.

EXHIBIT 14.1   PRICING STRATEGIES

Type of Payment	Typical Example	Nature of Risk	Possibility of Profit	Comments
Fee for service	College tuition, Medicaid (varies by state)	Overestimate market, lose control of costs	Excellent	The classic way toward financial well-being
Cost-based reimbursement	State or local government contracts	Lose money when actual spending varies from signed budget	None	Requires excellent planning, superb monitoring; good for new or unpredictable services
Unit reimbursement	Same as above	Postcontract audits; political fallout from changed plans	Good	Needs good purchasing systems in place to support purchaser and provider
Class rates	Same as above	Costs higher than most peers would cause losses	Good	Best for average cost, average quality nonprofits, or those with relatively lower costs
Fixed price or project-based	Federal contracts	Underestimate true project costs	Good	Good for start-ups willing to risk a loss or for market leaders good at gauging and carrying out projects
Voucher	Experimental	Marketing failure	Good	Still an experimental approach, but has the potential to become popular in the future; watch carefully
Standard pricing	Open market	Same as above	Excellent	Most appealing to entrepreneurial managers; requires staying power

Cost-Based Reimbursement

The governing principle of cost reimbursement might be called "Give a Receipt and Get Some Green." Costs are reimbursed only when it can be proved that the money was spent, and then only within the restrictions of a previously approved budget. One of the obvious advantages of this method is that it is quite simple in concept and narrowly focused. It is also completely divorced from utilization, which makes it an ideal reimbursement method in start-up situations or when it is not possible to quantify the services (consultation and education, for example) in any meaningful way.

Cost-based reimbursement can be rigid and unforgiving, especially when you've lost the receipt. Also, it leaves the purchaser inherently in arrears to the provider, who has to come up with a way to support the cash flow until the bill has been rendered, considered, and paid. Cost reimbursement leaves no room for profit and, depending on how it is administered, it can leave lots of room for loss. It must occur in the context of a contract or other official relationship since it involves careful and sustained bookkeeping.

Unit Reimbursement

An alternative to the sharp edges of cost reimbursement is a unit-based reimbursement system. Yearly costs are broken into small pieces based on the natural form of measurement for the service (an hour of counseling, a single day in a hospital, one laboratory test). The nonprofit then delivers one unit of that service and gets paid the predetermined value of the unit. Note that the emphasis is on results—services delivered—not on the actual cost to deliver that unit of service.

Unit reimbursement is very similar to fee-for-service reimbursement, except that a unit of service reimbursement agreement is usually part of a long-term contract. As a result, the nonprofit has some level of guarantee that it will have many such transactions; therefore, the unit method of reimbursement becomes significant mainly as a planning tool.

Class Rates

The way the price of the unit of service is determined can also have something to say about how the revenue stream gets treated. When some third party—often a government entity or third-party payer—decides it will pay the same price for a unit of service regardless of who delivers it, where, or when, they are structuring what is often known as a class rate.

Class rates are best used when the service being delivered is commodity-like and relatively small, such as an hour of counseling or a day in a program. They free the payer from the minutiae of setting individualized rates and allow the payer to exercise control over operations by managing cost and utilization information. Association membership dues are frequently class rates, as in "members with 1 to 50 employees pay $X per year, those with 51 to 100 pay $Y."

Often, class rates are set at the median or the mean of the class, which pressures high-priced nonprofits to cut costs and come closer to the average cost of all participants. And that is precisely the point.

Fixed Price or Project-Based

Although they are more common in the for-profit world of professional services, fixed price revenue arrangements are also possible. Typically, this type of payment accompanies a distinct project with definable outputs—say, a report written or a playground constructed. This methodology puts the risk of budget overruns completely on the nonprofit and thereby benefits the payer. It can also favor the well-run and tightly controlled nonprofit.

Vouchers

A potentially powerful development in government-funded programs is the use of vouchers as a purchasing strategy. Typically, vouchering systems either pay a service provider directly on behalf of an eligible client, reimburse consumers for expenses they incur in utilizing a provider, or take the form of cash assistance. Considering that dwindling government resources and consumer empowerment represent independently compelling agendas, vouchers may be the surprise payment mechanism of the future. States such as New York, Pennsylvania, Minnesota, Maine, Kansas, and Idaho have all experimented with some sort of vouchering system.

Consumer-Directed Funding

Another candidate for Most Popular Payment System of the Future is consumer-directed funding. Most popular in traditional government-supported social service programs such as disability services, consumer-directed funding attempts to place the opportunity and the responsibility for decision-making in the hands of the consumer, thereby essentially mimicking the dynamics of the consumer marketplace.

Consumer-directed funding really does two important things quietly. First, it threatens to render useless much of the decision-making systems (and peoples' jobs) already in place that usually characterize government-sponsored programs. Perhaps more important, it also would eventually create a marketplace that would look like a traditional consumer market, with suppliers of services concentrating on marketing, assembling referral systems, and building large scale operations.

Standard or Market Pricing

Most pleasing of all, from a revenue point of view, are the opportunities when the nonprofit can price with regard to the market without considering the binding opinions of third parties. These days it's a rare luxury, although when YMCAs set health club membership prices they can sometimes price according to what the local market will bear rather than what the service actually costs.

Market pricing is good when it's possible—and when it doesn't impede the tax-exempt mission. Often, when there exists a genuine market for a service partly filled by for-profits, a nonprofit will have lower costs and can therefore price at or below prevailing rates. This leads to rumblings about unfair competition, a charge made from time to time by for-profit companies. For a number of reasons, however, nonprofits and for-profits do not typically compete head-to-head, so the unfair competition concern will probably be confined to only one or two segments of the market.

Going the Other Way—Contractual Adjustments and Subsidies

It is important to note that all of the above forms of revenue methods except for fee for service presume the existence of a large institution on the paying end. Increasingly in every field where nonprofits are active, those payers are beginning to throw their economic weight around by demanding discounts and preferential treatment.

A common form of discount is what is euphemistically called a *contractual adjustment*, which is to say an agreement to slice a certain percentage off each bill. In effect, contractual adjustments are merely disguised cost shifting; a consumer responsible for 60 percent of your revenue who demands a contractual adjustment to 50 percent is paying five-sixths of its share, or 83 percent, while the remaining 40 percent of the purchasers must carry the other half of the load, or 125 percent of their fair share. Is this fair? The question could be debated endlessly, but it doesn't matter—it's real.

Finally, nonprofit organizations often choose to subsidize consumers. This subsidy will take the form of sliding fee scales; discounts for children, the elderly, the handicapped, or other groups; or outright grants. Subsidy pricing is nothing more than cost shifting in which one party adds a bit to the full price in order to offset the lower price that another party receives. If the market will not support such premium pricing, then outside revenue sources must make up the difference. Managers need to recognize that subsidy pricing requires them to play a mediator role in a small-scale resource redistribution effort.

PRICING STRATEGIES

We have put all of these considerations together in Exhibit 14.2, which shows the varying pricing strategies typically used by major types of nonprofits. The vertical axis shows the value of each type of organization's services as typically perceived by *the public in general*, as opposed to consumers or providers of the service. The horizontal axis shows the degree to which providers of the service need to invest in a substantial amount of assets in order to provide the service.

These two axes were chosen because perceived value is an essential—perhaps *the* essential—ingredient in determining how much people are willing to pay for any service. Equally important in determining nonprofit pricing is the amount of tangible assets one must have to enter or stay in the business.

This is important for three reasons. First, the higher costs associated with obtaining and using the assets—buildings in the case of all high-capital entries on the map, as well as sophisticated technology in many of them—boosts prices. More pertinent, however, is the fact that the need for capital assets serves as a very effective barrier to possible new entrants. Not only will established providers in a capital-intensive field tend to have lower operational costs associated with their asset base, but the very structure of the tax-exempt corporation works against new entrants. Remember, nonprofit corporations cannot have shareholders. Therefore,

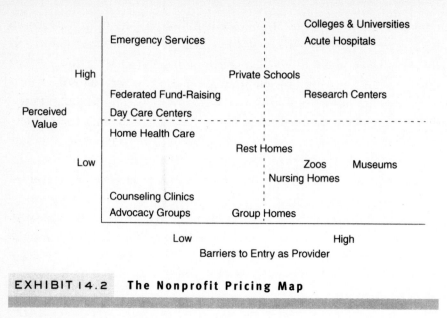

EXHIBIT 14.2   The Nonprofit Pricing Map

there is no possibility of selling shares to new shareholders to raise capital for investing in assets. New entries, then, must find other sources of funding willing to make grants for capital acquisition, and these are the most difficult funding sources to find. Add to that the fact that most proven funding sources are unlikely to support the entry of new groups in favor of the established panel of recipients, and the odds against new entrants' success are very high.

Hospitals solved this type of problem in the 1950s with federal Hill-Burton funding, and colleges and universities have had substantial federal scientific grant programs that served the same purpose. Both types of funding allowed significant investment in capital assets at a critical period for many of today's most powerful and prestigious institutions. At the moment, they are also gone, dwindling, or threatened.

A third aspect of the logic of nonprofit pricing is rooted in competition or, more accurately, the lack of it. Without federal funding and with substantial growth in for-profit providers in some of the high capital areas, the panel of nonprofit providers in the capital-intensive end is effectively closed. How many universities do you recall getting started recently? As a result, existing players are that much more likely to be able to get the prices they charge.

A final characteristic of the nonprofit pricing topography in general is that groups with low capital needs tend to exist for the use of a relatively small segment of the population at a time of acute need, while those on the high end of the capital need spectrum touch large numbers of people. Further, those on the low capital end often deal more with lower income populations, while middle-class clientele either use one of the right-side providers today or expect that they will have to do so eventually.

How to Price

So how does a nonprofit provider of any kind of service go about pricing? For a specific organization, the objective is to move northward on the map. That is, specific organizations should strive to create a public perception of high value, allowing them to charge a higher price, at least to their nongovernmental payers. A day care center affiliated with a prestigious university may be able to charge more than a nonaffiliated peer. A museum with an especially timely exhibit might be able to charge separately for that admission.

At the same time, single nonprofit organizations generally should refrain from moving eastward on the map without uniquely strong protection in the form of patents, geography, or some other such buffers, simply because it is very hard (not to mention ethically questionable) for a single organization to so dominate its market that it effectively bars others from entry. This type of barrier to entry is usually related to capital structure, and it is extremely difficult to move far in this direction alone before losing ground to one's peers who have chosen not to take on greater capital responsibilities.

Over time, the only way to improve pricing flexibility is to move northeastward *as an industry*. Simultaneous movement on both axes gives improved capitalization with the protection of higher public perception to drive service demand. Unfortunately, this strategy demands success at two of the very things that nonprofit organizations as a whole have not been good at in the past: acting in concert and self-policing.

Acting in concert means giving up a bit of autonomy in return for advancement of the field. For a variety of reasons, the normal mode of operation for nonprofits has been much more of an independent style. That kind of genteel anarchy may benefit individual players, but it does nothing for

PRICING YOUR SERVICES AS A CONSULTANT

One hundred dollars per hour. Sounds like a pretty good rate for a consultant, doesn't it? But let's break that down a bit. Most consultants must not only deliver billable services, they have to market themselves too. Plus, there's lots of downtime as well, such as vacations, sick time, dealing-with-the-bank time, and I-just-don't-feel-like-working-today time. And, unlike salaried employees, this downtime comes right out of their pockets—or, more accurately, it prevents money from coming into their pockets.

A reasonable estimate for professional services is that a mid-to-high-level professional will be billable 60 percent of the time. Our $100 per hour consultant could therefore make $120,000 per year, or $100 for 1,200 hours of billable time. But that's gross income. Take away nearly 16 percent for taxes owed to Uncle Sam as a self-employed person, plus some percentage for state and local taxes. Reduce that amount by health insurance, too, and maybe some life insurance (which are both more expensive to buy as an individual than as part of a group).

Oh yes, you will probably need to rent an office and print marketing stuff. Subtract the plane ticket and the three-day hotel bill for that professional conference you attended; no client will reimburse you for any of that. Every telephone call you make is an overhead expense, so deduct it from your gross income. That temporary assistant you hired for a week to handle report production? Subtract that too. And we haven't even gotten to the money you want to set aside for a new house, retirement, or your kids' college education, let alone groceries and the mortgage. Suddenly that $120,000 doesn't look so big anymore.

Begin your letter as follows:

To my valued clients—Effective immediately, my new rate will be $150 per hour.

the whole. Trade groups, professional societies, and nonprofit leaders themselves are the only ones who can boost public perception of value.

Lastly, nonprofits must do a better job of policing themselves. There are rarely any systematic mechanisms in place to ensure that subpar performers will exit the field. Consequently, the public is justified in evaluating a given field at its lowest common denominator. Take child care, for example. Were the average parent to feel that there are solid quality-ensuring systems in place such as meaningful licensing, employee selection, worker training, and strict disciplinary codes, he or she would feel somewhat less ambivalent than they typically do now about leaving a child in a professional day care center, and this greater assurance would be reflected in the price.

Critics will say that such an effort is unrealistic since it would involve working with proprietary day care centers as well as nonprofit organizations, and that in any case it would be more expensive than the average family is willing to pay. That is exactly the point: Nonprofits and for-profits must work together to raise the perception of value for both, or else they will fail working apart. And as to price, in most cities, it currently costs more to house a dog for a day in a kennel than it costs to keep a child in day care. There's plenty of room for upside price flexibility.

CHAPTER 15

Profit: Why and How Much?

A chapter on profitability in nonprofit organizations may seem quixotic, but only because there is an unspoken understanding that we never discuss the subject in public. It doesn't help that the term *nonprofit* seems to settle the question before it's even raised. The result: Those connected with nonprofit organizations—consumers, funders, regulators, and even some managers—have no vocabulary and no common understanding about this financial need that practically cries out for careful attention and management.

This is unfortunate. Profit is part of any organization's economics. The question of who shares in the profit, which is what distinguishes nonprofit organizations from for-profit ones, is really only the last and most uninteresting aspect. Much more important is how it is generated, why, and for what it is used. The lack of frank attention to the subject is what causes us to possess such little collective knowledge of it. The purpose of this chapter is to explain why nonprofit organizations can and would want to earn a profit each year and to suggest ways of making one.

PROFIT DEFINED

First, let's define profit. For our purposes, we will consider profit to be an excess of revenue over expenses during any given fiscal period. As shown earlier, profit will land on the balance sheet as an increase in a nonprofit's net assets, offset by an increase in some asset or mix of assets. This dynamic is extremely significant in appreciating the role profit can play in a nonprofit. Remember for a moment that the balance sheet really sketches the financial boundaries of the organization. The larger these boundaries, the larger the organization. Besides profit, there are only two ways to grow the balance sheet. One way is to borrow long-term funding (such as a mortgage) which pushes up the long-term debt line on the liability side of the balance sheet and the cash or building/equipment line on the asset side. The other way to boost the financial dimensions of *any* type of corporation is to get an outsider to give money directly to it. In the proprietary world, this kind of money is given with the quid pro quo of ownership. Whether the money is given in identical small increments by the general public (stocks) or as an individual pumping a large chunk of funds into the organization doesn't matter. Either way, the source of the funds gets a piece of the corporation in return.

Since nonprofit organizations cannot have individual shareholders, this method of raising funds is off limits. The nonprofit counterpart is grants. The only way to get money into a nonprofit corporation with no explicit expectation of the kind of financial return obtainable from borrowing is through fund-raising. A philanthropic term for that strategy is the *capital campaign,* designed to raise a set amount of money—or capital—in a fixed period of time, usually to be used to acquire an asset. In a way, the capital campaign is the equivalent of a stock offering of a for-profit company. A major, orchestrated attempt to sell all or part of the organization to the general public. The difference is that major donors, unlike major stockholders, can get no promise of control or direct economic value in exchange for their money. Any benefits they do receive, such as public recognition, may in fact have value, but it is incidental to the transaction.

These simple facts create a serious structural blockage to adequate capitalization in a nonprofit corporation. If selling shares in the entity is forbidden and if a capital campaign is unrealistic, as it is for many nonprofits, there will be extra pressure on the two remaining ways of bringing in capital—borrowing and profits.

USES OF PROFIT

Internally generated profits are the major capital source under the routine control of the nonprofit manager. There is no practical alternative. This puts enormous pressure on the organization's internal management controls to produce a surplus on a regular basis, while simultaneously negotiating the kind of political crosscurrents around the profitability issue that will be covered later in this chapter. The pivotal question is how much profit is "enough."

Fortunately, that question now becomes easier to answer. The question of how much profit is enough is intimately linked to the uses to which that profit will be put. To no one's surprise, the uses of profit in a nonprofit corporation are exactly the same as those in a proprietary organization, save for the transfer of wealth to the owner.

First, an explanatory note: The following material—and the formulas themselves—are intended as planning guides rather than as inviolable rules. Their ultimate purpose is to stimulate careful consideration of the uses of profit in nonprofit corporations. Since the uses of profit are unrelated to each other, it is possible to plan for more than one during the same budget period. In that case, the percentages suggested should be regarded as building blocks of the eventual projected profit margin. In any event, these constructs can operate as guiding frameworks for planning and evaluating profitability.

Profit for Stability

Stability is probably the most common and easily understood use for profits in a nonprofit. For a corporation with adequate and reliable funding and good systems, stability created by profitability can mean the ability to concentrate on mission without energy-draining fiscal distractions. A year or two of solid profitability for a nonprofit in crisis can mean that meeting the payroll will become a routine possibility instead of a weekly crisis.

Stability is the holy grail of nonprofit management. It is the desirable financial characteristic most often referred to by nonprofit employees, boards of directors, and management itself. It is also harder to achieve in a nonprofit setting than in a for-profit one, if for no other reason than that the nonprofit's financial bull's-eye is smaller. Miss the target profit goal in a proprietary entity and you might still breakeven. Miss breakeven in a nonprofit and you inescapably lose money.

As an operating guide, the notion of stability is a fuzzy thing. Probe deeply enough and you are likely to get numerous indicators of a state of financial stability. Still, there are probably a few shared themes. Stability is the absence of unpleasant surprises. For those working in an organization, the chief unpleasant surprise is certainly a missed paycheck. Another unpleasant surprise is the overall crunch caused by a large unexpected expense, even if it does not cause a missed payroll. Beyond these, the problems typically encountered in the ordinary course of events ought to be able to be handled by an organization with an ordinarily balanced state of financial health. (See Chapter 6 on diagnostic tools for some insights into what this might look like. *Caution:* It will be different for different organizations.)

If stability for the majority of people in a nonprofit essentially means no missed payrolls and no general feeling of financial pressure, then stability for practicing managers translates into keeping enough cash on hand. Equipped with this insight, we can build a serviceable answer to the question, "How much profit is enough to maintain stability?"

What follows is intended only as a rough planning guide, not a precise formula for action. But first we need to make a few assumptions:

- The rest of the organization is in a more or less steady state, even if that state is not entirely satisfactory to its managers. Therefore, what we will be calculating is an amount over and above existing levels of liquidity.

- The funds generated for stability will go directly to cash and not be diverted to other expenses, such as covering an increase in accounts receivable, or to purchase a building. If this does happen, of course, the cash needed to cover these activities must be generated independently from our profit-for-stability calculation.

- These are one-year estimates only; at some point, the desirable level of cash will have been produced, and when it exists there will be no more need to generate profits solely to achieve stability.

- To cover possible inflation, add a projected inflation percentage to these numbers. For example, historic inflation rates are frequently cited as being in the 2.5–3.0 point range per year.

The formula for profit-for-stability is:

$$P/E \times A$$

Where P = Total annual personnel costs, including payroll taxes and
fringe benefits
E = Total annual expenses

A = Amount of one payroll period expressed as a percentage of annual payroll (Assumes one payroll period beyond the current one is sufficient to be ahead; double it if two payroll periods are desirable instead.)

As an example, suppose an organization spends $7.5 million of its $10 million total budget on personnel-related expenses and wants to be one week ahead of its weekly payroll. Its formula for profit-for-stability would be:

$$\frac{7,500,000}{10,000,000} \times .019 = 1.4\% \text{ Profit margin}$$

Again, it is important to stress that this number is for rough planning purposes only, and that in order for it to adequately bolster the cash position, all other sources and uses of cash must cancel each other out for the period.

Profit for Personnel Bonuses

Another use for profit in a nonprofit is as bonuses for staff. Yes, nonprofits can and do give bonuses. In fact, American employers of all kinds often use some form of incentive-based compensation in lieu of all or part of the yearly merit increase. If anything, nonprofit employers have been a bit slow to adopt the practice.

Economic realities are subtly beginning to change the use of bonuses. Whereas previously a bonus was regarded as something of a human resource management tool—a reward for good work—now it is often used as a means of giving raises that do not automatically carry into the next year. Consequently, its nature has begun to change from motivational to fiscal. To the extent that this trend takes away some of the emotional context of bonuses, it will make managers' jobs less complicated. The bonus will simply become something akin to deferred compensation with no implied judgment about performance.

The way profit is used for bonuses in nonprofits usually involves budgeting on the basis of unchanged or minimally changed salaries and wages from the previous year. Then, approximately nine or ten months into the fiscal year, the CEO and business manager (or their equivalent departments) take stock of the financial situation and decide whether they can afford to give bonuses this year. If they decide to give bonuses, it will typically be done at the end of the fiscal year and be labeled "one-time wage adjustment" or some other innocuous sounding phrase—anything but the term *bonus.*

There is nothing illegal about this practice, although the bookkeeping and linguistic contortions managers often go through do raise the aura of ethical concerns for some. In part, this is due to the now-quaint notion that those who work in a nonprofit organization of any kind must be motivated by the pleasures of the work itself and not by money. At the same time, there is an underlying legal issue related to incentive-based compensation in a tax-exempt sphere that deserves a full explanation.

The legal issue in question is the doctrine of *private inurement,* which is strictly prohibited by federal law. Private inurement at its simplest means that the owners of an organization export all or part of the profits of that organization into their own coffers. In the case of publicly held corporations, this occurs when stockholders vote themselves a dividend. It is not only legal, it is the very reason for the for-profit company's existence.

There is no direct parallel in nonprofit corporations because it simply is not allowed; wealth or profits created by a nonprofit must stay in the organization and not flow into private owners' pockets. Since nonprofits cannot have stockholders, there is no distribution mechanism in place to get wealth out of the organization into private hands. However, there is an extremely common mechanism for drawing certain funds from a nonprofit and putting them into private hands. It is called the payroll, and this is why the most typical form of private inurement in a nonprofit setting is excessive or unreasonable compensation to an insider who has at least some control over the payment of that benefit (i.e., director, officer, trustee, substantial benefactor, family member, key staff person).

The role of compensation as a potential fiscal sluiceway out of the nonprofit corporation is what worries authorities. Still, as Bruce Hopkins points out with a quote from the U.S. Tax Court, "[t]he law places no duty on individuals operating charitable organizations to donate their services; they are entitled to reasonable compensation for their services." Consequently, painting any given compensation arrangement with an insider as a form of private inurement is an intrinsically tricky business. Several years ago, the federal government came up with the notion of intermediate sanctions as a way to deal with organizations that pay excessive compensation. As the name implies, this is a penalty intended to be somewhere between revocation of exempt status and a good tongue lashing from an Internal Revenue Service

(IRS) agent. Intermediate sanctions have now begun to acquire the necessary enforcement infrastructure and are beginning to become bona fide
enforcement tools in the sector.

Each case of alleged private inurement is decided individually, and there
are enough subtle nuances in the decisions that have been rendered to
make most knowledgeable attorneys balk at the idea of declaring a particular arrangement acceptable or not without a court test.

The upshot of all this is that it leaves nonprofit boards and managers a
great deal of latitude in determining incentive-based compensation (although the new IRS Form 990 specifically requires extensive disclosures
in this area, including whether the board had a method for setting compensation levels where it did). One thing that is certain is that they have far
more discretion than most believe. For example, a commission-based system alone is not considered evidence of private inurement. Paying bonuses,
in other words, does not endanger a nonprofit's tax-exempt status. Funding
sources may not like it, but that is a different issue. In practice, we can reasonably expect more and more nonprofits to adopt incentive-based compensation in the coming years as economic conditions virtually demand it.

Happily then, it is permissible to use profit for staff bonuses as long as the
program is properly structured. Having said this, we are once again left
with the question of how much. The question is answerable only in the
aggregate since what we can create is a bonus pool for distribution according to some specially constructed formulas. This time the calculation is a
bit simpler than profit for stability. Profit for bonuses is:

$$\frac{S}{E} \times B$$

Where S = Total annual salaries paid to employees eligible for bonus
       E = Total annual expenses
       B = Amount of average bonus, expressed as a percentage

For example, if a nonprofit with total salaries of $600,000 and total an-
nual expenses of $1,000,000 sought a bonus pool of 3 percent of the actual
margin, they should plan for $18,000, as follows:

$$\frac{\$600,000}{\$1,000,000} \times 0.03 = 0.6 \times 0.03$$

$$= 1.8\% \times \$1,000,000$$
$$= \$18,000$$

This means a profit margin of at least 2 percent. It seems only fair to use profits for personnel bonuses since it is spending on personnel that usually yields the greatest savings, as explained later. These calculations are useful as a guide to planning for profits, or as an after-the-fact guide to using profits created.

Profit for Innovation

Using profits for innovation or research and development is a new concept for some nonprofits because there is usually no incentive for a nonprofit to innovate. Unlike a for-profit company for whom any kind of innovation can translate into increased market share, which can translate into turbo-charged profits, the nonprofit's only motivation for being innovative derives from intangibles such as desire, dedication, or an individual's sheer ego gratification.

Never underestimate the importance of the latter motivation. Some of the most influential and entrepreneurial nonprofits in the country have been built through the force of a single individual's will. A subset of this kind of drive—and a far more common kind than one might imagine—is the will to create a nonprofit organization for ideological reasons. Whole organizations, even entire nonprofit industries, have been created in order to further agendas as diverse as enhancing nonprofits' use of technology, specific religious beliefs, and environment-centered activities.

The larger context is one of values. Starting with some nonprofits' historic roots in religious action, a great many nonprofit organizations have been unique value systems engaged to accomplish a specific purpose. In effect, the currency of a nonprofit organization is not money, but values. This is one of the reasons why the output of many nonprofits is so hard to quantify. Output is a secondary consideration. To varying degrees of explicitness, conflict in a nonprofit will involve the evolution of the value system.

In truth, much of the innovative thinking goes on before the nonprofit entity is even established. Paradoxically, it is precisely when a nonprofit organization is innovative that it has the best chance of advancing its own values. Proponents of community-based mental health services conceived of treatment in the least restrictive environment possible, thereby helping to revolutionize an entire system of care. Community economic development agencies typically feel a passionate commitment to giving poor people greater power over their own housing and employment decisions.

In the twenty-first century, the pressure will be on nonprofits to innovate. Until the 1990s, nonprofits generally had been buffered from the effects of innovation typical of industry because it normally occurred in areas of technology or middle management, neither of which most nonprofit organizations use in abundance. However, in the future, the pressure to innovate will come to direct services (in some areas, it already has), and the intelligent nonprofit will be prepared.

A planned profit to support innovation is difficult to calculate for many reasons, including the fact that it may be a bit arbitrary to draw a line around a certain group of expenses and pronounce them innovation expenses. To the extent that an innovation effort requires new and easily identifiable expenses—like salaries or the purchase of equipment—its formula would look like this:

$$\frac{I}{CE}$$

Where $I =$ Amount of cash required yearly for innovation purposes

$CE =$ Yearly cash expenses

So if a nonprofit needed an annual cash outlay of $80,000 for, say, salaries and direct expenses related to a new way it was developing to secure financing for low-income homebuyers, and its annual cash expenses were $4,000,000, it would need to set aside at least 2 percent of its annual budget as profit.

And don't forget to tack on an estimate of the effects of inflation while you're polishing off the calculation.

Profit for Growth

Finally, profit can play a supporting role in what we will call growth. In some ways, this is a catch-all category composed of the elements defined above, but in a much broader sense, growth in a financial context means growth in revenues and probably in the accompanying balance sheet, although it will come in different ways. For example, growth in some fields necessitates carrying more accounts receivable. At the least, growth in any field means having enough cash available to seize opportunities or cushion unexpected losses. Generating profits can help tremendously.

Due to the wide-open nature of financial growth and what it could mean to any given organization, there really is no formula available to assist with planning. Since growth can take an infinite variety of forms and dimensions, there is no alternative but to look at each situation individually and make an estimate of what is necessary in order to translate it into a profit planning percentage.

A final word of clarification for those of you who object to defining growth exclusively in financial terms—you're right. Growth in a nonprofit whose mission is to serve the public means something fundamentally different than growth in a proprietary company. Many advocacy-oriented nonprofits have achieved significant gains on behalf of public causes with a total number of staff members that could have easily fit inside the average living room and still have lots of room left over.

Still, for many if not most organizations, growth in the ability to accomplish a mission usually entails growth in a financial sense, too. In fact, for many types of public service, the two are inseparable. Growth in the financial dimension should be seen not as a byproduct but as the necessary precondition to growth in mission.

PROFIT—HOW TO GET IT

Nowhere in nonprofit management matters is there a starker division between what is financially desirable and what is politically possible than in the question of how to generate profits. For all our talk otherwise, we as a society show a curious ambivalence about profits in the for-profit world. Rarely does a proprietary concern deal explicitly with something called profit. Instead, profit gets taken out of an entity in the form of high salaries, or it is buried in a mixed category loosely called "overhead," or owners receive "distributions."

We see the same aversion to the idea of profit in the nonprofit sector, except that it is magnified many times over and sometimes generates downright hostility. The unspoken message is that a dollar of profit in a nonprofit means a dollar less of services provided. To make matters more complicated, this is true in extreme cases. Then again, it is the extreme cases that the IRS has the power to discipline, leaving the ordinary non-profit and its management at the mercy of conventional thinking.

What can correct for this tendency is the practical nonprofit executive's or board's realization that constant losses drain the organization instead of ennobling it. Those who understand this contradiction then enter into a kind of schizoid existence in which they must appear to support the conventional thinking with the one hand while with the other they frantically attempt to create profits. Or, to be more precise, they attempt to create situations in which profits can seem to arise, unbidden and unexpected.

This forced serendipity has strange effects. It requires managers to pretend that they are interested in keeping the original budget on track when what they really want to do is shave a bit from it. Those unaware of the riddle see management making apparently senseless decisions and holding back on perfectly reasonable and already justified expenditures.

The unacknowledged game has two major negative impacts on nonprofit organizations. First, lack of profitability means putting the corporation on an endlessly regressive spiral, always looking to cut back and forego rather than to build. The fact that nonprofit groups of all kinds tend to have fixed revenues—either by funding source design or by management's failure to value growth—compounds the inherent need to look to spending reductions for profit. Second, employees are affected. When managers must look for reductions in expenses to create profit, certain spending is exempt. For instance, some occupancy costs, especially leases or mortgages, are inescapable. Other expenses may be flexible within only narrow limits. At any rate, these costs of doing business pale in comparison to the largest and most flexible source of savings of them all—spending on personnel. Most nonprofit organizations spend 60 percent to 80 percent of their budgets on personnel, so it is inevitable that personnel spending gets a lot of attention when the search is on for savings.

Because of this, nonprofit staff often feel under siege and vulnerable. Even if the ultimate use for some of the savings is bonuses, the process of culling the money to fund bonuses from the personnel budget can be a brutal one. Frequently, it requires future staff to give up resources equivalent to present day staff's bonuses. Techniques for causing this shift range from deliberately delaying replacement of departing staff to not hiring for a planned position at all. Still, if everyone understands the reasons for personnel decisions like these, it lays the groundwork for success.

WHAT CAN BE DONE

For-profit corporations do not need to think twice about the role of profit in their organizations; nonprofit organizations do. Since the resources of a nonprofit corporation cannot be transferred into private hands except through the conventional (and more regulated) means of salary and benefits, the question of profit planning becomes one of timing and balance. The nonprofit executive is forever balancing the short-term demands of personnel and suppliers against the long-term financial needs of the entity. Because the resources must remain in the organization no matter what, the debate is over where they will be used.

There is perhaps no better way to prepare for a given level of profit than an informed, organization-wide discussion of the issue. Not that all employees need to become amateur financial managers. Instead, there needs to be widespread understanding and acceptance of the need for profit as an integral part of nonprofit corporate financial health. There need not be great tension around fiscal decisions regarding profit if the realities of nonprofit finance are understood by all key players.

CHAPTER 16

To Raise More Money, Think Cows

Many people think that the secret to successful fund-raising can be found in charity balls, with men in tuxedos and their trophy wives in strapless gowns. Wrong. The real secret to successful fund-raising can be found on the farm; the dairy farm.

We usually think of fund-raising in a very nonprofit-centered way. The unspoken message goes something like this: *Since we're doing such good work you should give us money.* It's puffed up with lots of words and bright smiles, of course, but underneath it all that's what we are really saying.

The problem with this approach is that it only gets half of the equation right. Yes, we are doing good work. That should be a given, because it's how the emotional connection gets made with donors. The Internal Revenue Service (IRS) itself uses this connection as part of its test for the acceptability of tax-favored treatment for certain gifts. They call it *donative intent,* which must be present or else the whole gift might be seen as a shameless tax dodge.

Some development people stop right there. This is unfortunate, because the real power comes from linking donative intent with smart financial decisions. That's where the cows come in.

In economic terms, cows are fairly unique. Not only do they produce value during their lifetimes (milk), they produce it upon their death (beef). So a single cow has two inherent sources of value. If you think of donors' financial assets as being like cows, it will help you to understand how you can manage this dual value to everyone's advantage.

DONATIONS

Donations are the low-hanging fruit of fund-raising, and everyone under-stands how they work. Donors keep their milk-producing cow during their lifetime, making a gift of some of the milk as they wish. The financial benefit to the donor, of course, is that he or she gets to deduct the donation from their taxes. The recipient organization gets the immediate—or present—value of the donation.

BEQUESTS—COW TO CHARITY

Bequests are just like donations, with two exceptions. First, they happen only after the donor's death, which dampens the joy of giving. Second, they benefit the donor by removing the value of the donation from the donor's taxable estate. The benefit can be substantial, since high-net-worth individuals can pay a high percentage of their estate in inheritance taxes. In this case, the value of removing the cow from the estate is likely to be more than the deductible value of a regular donation of the milk in any given year.

CHARITABLE REMAINDER TRUSTS—MILK TO BENEFICIARIES, COW TO CHARITY

For all other planned giving vehicles, the cow and her milk get treated separately. The most common approach is the *charitable remainder trust.* The first item of note here is that word *trust,* because it indicates that the donated asset is irrevocably placed outside of the purview of the donor's estate ("asset" generally means a chunk of cash, stocks, etc., with income-producing potential). As with bequests, this removes the asset from the estate's taxable

TAX DEDUCTION VERSUS TAX CREDIT

Tax credits are the most powerful way to reduce taxes, because they allow taxpayers to subtract a dollar of taxes they would otherwise owe for every dollar of tax credits they have. Tax deductions, on the other hand, only reduce the total amount of income against which the tax-payers' tax rate is applied.

base, thereby avoiding the estate tax. It's called a charitable remainder trust because the charity gets the remainder, or what's left of the original donated asset after the trust beneficiaries get up to 20 years worth of income.

There are two ways of getting the milk to the beneficiaries, and this defines the two types of charitable remainder trusts.

Charitable Remainder Annuity Trusts—The Same Amount of Income Each Year

To ensure that the beneficiaries get a fixed amount of income—"milk"—each year, donors will set up a charitable remainder annuity trust (regrettably known by the acronym CRAT). In this arrangement, the donor stipulates a certain amount that the trust will pay the beneficiary each year, with a minimum payout of 5 percent. The catch is that the payment is fixed and inviolate—if there is not enough interest income in any given year to cover the payment, the trust must make up the difference from the principal or leftover earnings from prior years.

Charitable Remainder Unitrusts—The Same Percentage of Trust Assets as Income Each Year

To ensure that trust assets are protected, donors can decide to give beneficiaries the same percentage of trust assets each year, an amount which will fluctuate with the current value of the assets. Again, the minimum payout is 5 percent, though the donor can stipulate that the distribution cannot exceed total income. These vehicles have the advantage of allowing

GETTING THAT DEDUCTION

One of the reasons why donors use a trust is because it allows them to take a tax deduction for the value of their donation while still retaining some control over how the cow and her milk will be used. The value of the deduction is highly individualized and subject to arcane tax laws, of course, but the idea is always to get the asset off the donor's books and into a trust in order to take the deduction and remove the asset permanently from the estate's future taxable base.

BENEFICIARIES?

Trust beneficiaries can be any lucky soul the donor decides to favor, including the donor himself/herself. Prime candidates are spouses, children, caretakers, financial book authors, and . . . well, the list could be endless. But remember, in a remainder trust it's the charity that ultimately benefits.

beneficiaries to benefit from the appreciation in the trust's assets, which helps outweigh their even more regrettable acronym of CRUT.

Charitable Lead Trusts in Which the Charity Gets the Milk, Beneficiaries the Cow

Flip a CRUT or a CRAT, and you get a trust where the charity benefits every year, while the beneficiary benefits only at termination. Lead trusts can be structured as annuity or unitrusts, but the minimum payout and 20-year lifetime rules don't apply. One catch is that the donor cannot take an income tax deduction upon creating the trust. The donor either gets a gift tax deduction if the lead trust is created when they are alive, or an estate tax deduction if the trust is created upon their death.

In another type of lead trust, the donor holds on to some control over the assets. This allows for a tax deduction upon trust creation equal to the present value of the income interest gifted to the charity, but the donor must pay taxes on the amounts paid to the charity each year.

If this information all makes sense to you, it may be time to consider becoming a tax lawyer. For the rest of us, it's time to move on to other types of planned giving vehicles.

POOLED INCOME FUNDS—DONORS PUT THEIR COWS IN A HERD, KEEP RIGHTS TO MILK

Okay, the cow thing is wearing thin. This will be the last one. In a pooled income fund, donors gift a future interest in an asset while retaining their ability to receive income from it. If this sounds like a charitable remainder

THE LONG, SLOW-W-W-W DEATH OF THE DEATH TAX. MAYBE.

In 2001, President Bush signed an historic tax-reduction bill which also began phasing out the estate tax, which Republicans had taken to calling "the death tax." After much wrangling, Congress and the president agreed on a plan to gradually increase the level at which the estate tax would apply, from $675,000 when the bill was signed to $1,000,000 in 2002, and all the way up to $3,500,000 in 2009. The tax bite itself will also gradually decline.

The estate tax will be repealed altogether in 2009. But, since the entire tax law expires in 2011, the estate tax will come back. This proves that Congress does have a sense of humor, but leaves donors and their advisors with a fundamentally confused picture down the road. At press time there was no change in this status, but this will be one of the Obama administration's first major decisions.

The central message is the same, however—donors more and more will be encouraged by the tax laws to make their donations on this side of the pearly gates.

trust, you've been paying close attention. The difference is that in a pooled income fund the collective assets are professionally invested and the payout is determined by the performance of the fund, not by a formula against the then-current dollar value of the assets as is true in a remainder trust. So in this way pooled income funds share characteristics with mutual funds.

There are a few other differences too, one of the most important being that the beneficiary must receive the payout over their lifetime, not over a preselected term. And there is some protection for the asset since distributions are limited to the income of the fund so that the asset base will not erode.

Donor-Advised Funds

Donor-advised funds are one of the newest and fastest-growing kids on the block. As financial markets and associated instruments restructure on what seems like a monthly basis, new fund-raising threats and opportunities are sure to pop up. Donor-advised funds, for example, were barely on the radar screen two decades ago. These instruments allow donors to gain the advantages of a private foundation at a lower level of giving and without a lot of the associated expense. Donors gain tax advantages while directing the use of their donations. Today, Fidelity Investments' donor-advised fund ranks as one of the 10 largest recipients of donations in the country according to both the *Nonprofit Times* and the *Chronicle of Philanthropy*.

Shrewd fundraisers know that they are most effective when they can think like a donor. Their best problem solving is done on behalf of those who wish to give more effectively, not the intended recipient of the donations. There is no substitute for learning the financial rules of the game. It's all about cows.

Control

CHAPTER 17

Insurance: The Maddeningly Complicated Art of Covering Your Assets

I f there is a more hallowed temple in all of American capitalism than a successful insurance company, it would be hard to imagine it. And if there is a more complex and counterintuitive part of financial management, no one has discovered it. Few in the nonprofit sector go there voluntarily. Read on, and we'll make it digestible.

All insurance, whether it is health insurance, dental insurance, life insurance, or property insurance, is essentially the activity of providing temporary access to capital for a fee. In the ordinary course of events, both individuals and companies can experience sudden and potentially ruinous financial demands from health crises, natural disasters, accidents, and numerous other perils. Without insurance, these calamities could be financially devastating. With proper insurance, they can be more easily tolerated. Of course, the way that the system works is complicated enough to make a grown actuary cry.

At the outset, an insurance company collects money for nothing since it collects premium dollars ahead of time before it ever pays out a single claim. This is free money, for a while. The lag between when the cash premiums are collected and when the first claims get paid out can be a month, a few months, or even a few years depending on the type of coverage being purchased. Meantime, the money sits there. What's an insurance company CEO to do?

If you said "invest it" you too could be a successful insurance company executive. Insurance companies have a second line of business. In addition to paying out claims, they are big-time investment managers. This means that insurance companies have two distinct ways of making money for their stockholders: profit on the claims, and profit from the interest on temporarily unused cash. With a racket like that, you would have to figure these people would be making so much money they would have to hire cargo planes to cart it around for them.

But here's where it gets interesting (well, okay, mildly interesting). There are lots of other insurance companies out there who have figured out the same thing, and they are all trying to get people to pay them insurance premiums in order to make some money off their claims and off their own investing activities. When the stock market is hot, the salespeople for the insurance companies are tempted to drag premium dollars in the front door no matter what the risk, figuring that they will always be able to cover a slight loss from claims with great investment results. This is called a *soft market*.

At some point the market always cools off. When that happens, the companies reverse course, working a lot harder to make money off their claim payment side and hoping to at least just hold their own as investors. For consumers, this is called a *hard market* because it gets tougher to find reasonably priced insurance, and some categories of insured groups may find themselves getting cut off entirely by the insurance companies newly afraid of what they see as a high risk.

But wait, there's more. In the liability insurance field (*property and casualty* being the term of art), the insurance companies you see are really just spider monkeys. The real 800-pound gorillas of the insurance world are called reinsurance companies. These are the insurance companies' insurance companies.

In practice, the reinsurers who stand behind the primary insurance companies are more like risk syndicators. Their job is to spread all of their primary insurance company customers' risks among even larger pools of capital. They will carve up what looks to you like a whole insurance policy into smaller pieces and arrange to have each piece covered by some larger chunk of capital. The famous Lloyd's of London is not really an insurance company, but rather a kind of market in which syndicators peddle small segments of a big risk to many different people and institutions so that no one bears undue risk alone.

Reinsurance companies tend to renegotiate their own funding and risk profiles on January 1 and July 1. Your policy year may start on October 1, but the economics governing your new premium charges were set three months earlier.

TO INSURE OR SELF-INSURE?

The fundamental question in the access-to-capital-for-a-fee business known as insurance is to what degree you are willing to substitute your own capital for that of someone else. The more you must rely on someone else's capital, the more it will cost, although you greatly help protect and preserve your own capital. On the other hand, the more you rely on your own capital the less it will cost to buy insurance, but the greater your risk of serious losses. So the constant question is whether you buy insurance or self-insure.

Self-insurance cuts across all types of insurance, from property and casualty to health insurance, and it usually works the same way. The core principle is that the insured party puts its own money at risk first, using traditional insurance to cover a smaller amount of risk, or perhaps none at all. This is the same strategy that leads your health insurance company to insist that you cover a deductible each year before they begin reimbursing you for any claims. That deductible saves the insurance company from paying out the first few hundreds of dollars in claims in any given year for each subscriber.

The core principle of self-insurance is that one puts one's own capital at risk in the event of a loss. But there are a few other important aspects of insurance that the self-insuring nonprofit must consider. The most pressing of these is what happens if the worst-case scenario materializes. This is no small calculation. Five hundred people sounds like a lot to participate in an employer's self-insured health plan, but a single disastrous claim such as a terribly premature baby can decimate a self-insured health plan. If a single claim costs $200,000, a five-hundred-person group can wind up paying more than $30 per month in extra costs if that eventuality hasn't been anticipated. That can be enough to sink a small self-insured plan.

Self-insured groups of all kinds get what is called specific stop-loss insurance for these situations. Typically, this type of insurance policy will protect the nonprofit above a preset level for any one claim. So the organization might purchase a stop-loss policy for all claims of more than $25,000. This softens the blow from a huge claim, but it does cost money to buy the insurance.

Aggregate stop-loss insurance protects against large losses in the plan as a whole. If claims are budgeted to reach no more than $300,000 in a group during a single plan year, the employer will purchase stop-loss insurance that will kick in for all losses exceeding $375,000 (the level is usually 25 percent higher than expected claims).

The third broad element needed in a self-insured health insurance plan is an administrator. Insurance is a complex business, and only the very largest employers can effectively run their own insurance company, which is what a self-insured plan requires them to do. Most often, the day-to-day administrative chores are farmed out to a third-party administrator (TPA), which is equipped to deal with the endless cascade of details that a self-insured plan presents.

Risk Management

Are there any nonprofit management subjects more boring than risk management? Nominations from the floor? We'll wait. . . . It's a little quiet in here. . . . Okay, risk management wins.

EXCESS AND SURPLUS LINES

The insurance industry is very clear about what it understands and is willing to insure and what it doesn't understand and, on the whole, would rather not insure. Mainstream industries such as construction, transportation, professional services, and the like are in the first category. Many nonprofit services such as international relief providers, day care, and youth-serving programs are often in the second category.

Odd and little-understood categories of insured organizations are usually served by what are called excess and surplus lines insurance carriers. To the casual consumer the difference is negligible, but one major implication is that many nonprofits that are insured by excess and surplus lines carriers are much more susceptible to volatile swings in the insurance marketplace.

Oh, yes, an obvious question. What *is* risk management anyway? This is one of those questions that would have invited sophomoric answers in an undergraduate exam ("risk management is the practice of managing risks . . ."). But here's the punch line that attracts seasoned managers: Good risk management saves money. It also has the ability to improve quality. Think of risk management as a quiet form of quality assurance.

Look at Exhibit 17.1. The table summarizes some of the common insurance coverages agencies must have in order to provide services responsibly. It shows the type of insurance, the nature of the risk the insurance typically covers, and the management areas relevant to the risk. To improve the quality of services, what we need to do is to get the weight of insurance coverages behind changes in the areas in the righthand column.

EXHIBIT 17.1   COMMON INSURANCE COVERAGE NEEDED TO PROVIDE RESPONSIBLE SERVICE

Type of Insurance	What's Covered	Area(s) Affected
Workers' compensation	On-the-job injuries	Workplace standards, client interactions, qualifications of staff
Corporate automobile	Property and personal injury	Transportation-related issues
Health insurance	Employee health care costs	Human resources management
Life insurance	Employee mortality	Human resources management
Corporate professional liability	Civil actions related to deviations from accepted professional standards	All program delivery systems
Errors and omissions	Benefits and insurance administration	Administrative systems and policies
Property and casualty	Site-related losses and injuries	Site management
Unemployment	Lost wages due to layoffs	Recruitment practices, hiring and firing policies
Surety bonds	Losses due to embezzlement, etc.	Internal controls
Directors and officers	Actions arising from duties as board members and executives	Leadership and management decisions

For example, most workers' compensation claims involve lost time and "soft tissue" injuries (meaning things like torn ligaments and twisted back muscles, not broken bones). Workers' compensation specialists have already demonstrated the link between reduced claims and proper training for employees that must lift as part of their jobs. They have also shown how an inclusionary workforce style helps reduce lost time due to injuries, since injured employees are more likely to return to work in a place that actively asks them to do so. In short, better training programs and more attention to the work environment reduces workers' compensation costs. Not coincidentally, these improvements also help contribute to the quality of services provided.

These are representative elements of risk management, a practice that everyone can support. After all, it's in the insurance company's interests to minimize claims so that they can maximize profits. It's in the nonprofit's interest to manage risks and minimize claims so that they might (I said "might") pay less for their insurance. More important, many of the techniques of risk management also happen to be quite consistent with plain old good management, so there's a possible double payoff.

Funders and accrediting agencies could help by paying more attention to this seemingly obscure area of management. A simple look at an organization's record of workers' compensation claims and associated payouts can tell more about the real human resource practices of a nonprofit than a stack of nicely printed human resource policy manuals. The written record of workplace injuries may be far more revealing than anything that a simple site visit could provide.

How to achieve quality services is a subject that will occupy teams of researchers, philosophers, and data analysts for the next several years (okay, maybe not philosophers). Risk management will elicit yawns, yet it can offer some useful information and some established methods for making real inroads into the question of how to achieve quality services. Too bad it doesn't have a very interesting name.

CHAPTER 18

Internal Controls
for External Goals

When the talk turns to the subject of Bruce the controller, his boss grows effusive:

> Bruce is a treasure. We call him our controller but he's really so much more. He's the first one in the office every morning and usually the last one to leave. He never takes a vacation. Last year I practically ordered him to take a week off and he couldn't do it—he came back two days early. Said he was worried about the new payroll system. He's been around for almost 15 years now, longer than any of the rest of us, and he knows everything about this office. He's never afraid to pitch in and do someone else's job temporarily. I don't know where we'd be without Bruce.

Probably several thousand dollars a year richer. You see, Bruce is an embezzler. This is the portrait of a quiet crook. He works those long hours to keep an eye on everyone else. The reason he can't take a vacation is that if his system is left unattended for any period of time it may collapse. He wasn't worried about the new payroll system, either; he just needed to make sure it didn't accidentally uncover one of his schemes. Sure he'll pitch in to do someone else's job. It keeps him on top of everyone and everything in the office.

Now before you complain that we are picking on old guys, we never said he was old. Actually, he could be only 33, having started with his present employer as a high school student, or he could be middle-aged, or his name could be Angela, who's not a treasure at all but a surly bookkeeper of indeterminate age and questionable competence. Or Angela might not be a bookkeeper, but rather an CEO who routinely makes colossal errors in financial management.

You get the point. A threat to a nonprofit's financial health looks like Bruce . . . or Angela . . . or like you or me. In fact, there is no one portrait of an internal financial threat, no single characteristic that they all have in common. Fraud, error, and bad management operate in a multitude of different ways, and it is the nonprofit corporation's responsibility to prevent or minimize the possible damage. Preventing loss of resources by making errors less likely and fraud more easily detected is the job of the system of internal controls.

Most inside thefts start with relatively small money. Pop culture memorializes gigantic corporate thievery, and that tends to color our perceptions, but the truth is that most frauds are not counted in the millions of dollars. Take a look at the graph in Exhibit 18.1 for some insight into the nature of business fraud in our economy.

Sure, publicly-held companies ("SEC" in the chart, for Securities and Exchange Commission) and their privately held counterparts are firmly up in the six figure range for the median losses due to business fraud, while nonprofits and governmental entities are about half that amount. But remember that the vast majority of nonprofits have budgets well under $2 million, so a six-figure fraud in that size organization can be truly devastating.

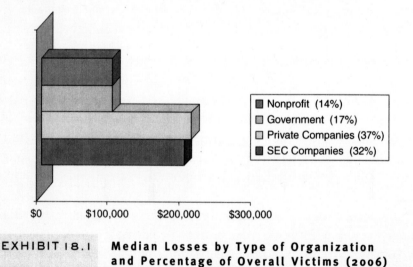

■	Nonprofit (14%)
▨	Government (17%)
☐	Private Companies (37%)
■	SEC Companies (32%)

$0 $100,000 $200,000 $300,000

EXHIBIT 18.1   **Median Losses by Type of Organization and Percentage of Overall Victims (2006)**

Why skim small money? Because it's less likely that one will be caught. Big bangs get noticed, while that steady chipping sound becomes background noise. It's only when the scheme is successful for a while that its dimensions tend to grow.

It's another unfortunate by-product of Hollywood's influence that most thefts are not usually the product of evil geniuses. Fortunately for those who must guard against mischief, there is ordinarily very little originality in thievery. Since most systems have at least a semblance of internal controls, it takes a bit of heavy-handedness to facilitate an illicit transfer. In addition, the theft has to be simple enough to be repeated, or else the money usually won't be worth it.

The Elements of Internal Control

The problem with the concept of internal controls is not that they are vague, but that the phrase encompasses such a wide range of conditions, actions, and systems. Six important elements of an internal control system are:

1. Control cues
2. Policy communication
3. Segregation of duties
4. Record keeping
5. Budgets
6. Reporting

Taken together, these policies sketch the acceptable boundaries for fiscal decisions, govern the way resources are allocated, provide information for evaluation, and define the processes that are to be used in carrying out the organization's mission. In short, they control the organization. We'll take each one in order except for budgets, which was covered in detail in Chapter 12, "Budgeting: Taming the Budget Beast."

Control Cues

Well-known fact number one (okay, well-known among those who get involved with these kinds of things): no single internal control is as important as the culture of internal controls. The best defense against inside people doing illicit things is not a single provision or a specific policy, but the overall message communicated by managers and the systems they put into place. The controller who preaches accountability but leaves the safe door open all day or the CEO who jokes about submitting inflated expense accounts are each corrupting the culture of internal control. It doesn't take many of these instances to send the message that no one gets caught.

Happily, the most efficient means of controlling the nonprofit organization is the cheapest. We call these collected communications "control cues." They are the signals that management and board send about the safeguarding of assets and accurate financial reporting. And they do send them, intentionally or not. No matter what the content, these signals put out stronger messages about what managers value and the level of accountability they demand than all of the computer software or policy memoranda combined.

The reason that control cues are cheap is that they are largely symbolic. Frequently, they consist mostly of not doing things. The CEO does not put her personal mail in the outgoing mail pile to be run through the organization's postage meter: The business manager doesn't leave the door to the safe wide open the whole day even if it is more convenient that way.

On a more substantive level, managers in the adequately controlled nonprofit corporation communicate their expectations of proper control and train staff at all levels in matters of control policies appropriate to them. For example, management letters from yearly audits frequently mention systemic breakdowns in internal controls: These should be corrected as quickly as possible. Appropriate security should be designed and maintained for all computerized records, and so on. Over time, dozens of small cues add up to an overall picture of control and accountability that tend to discourage people from even trying anything underhanded.

Policy Communication

The challenge for the designer of a communication system is to do it as efficiently yet as thoroughly as possible. The stakes are high since a large measure of accountability to external forces derives from how transactions are handled internally. On the other hand, this is one of those areas where reality has outpaced theory. One of the easiest suggestions an outsider such as an auditor can make about a system of internal controls is that it needs a written policy and procedures manual. Unhappily, it usually doesn't

THEFT BY DESIGN

The faith-based fund-raising organization's vice president of marketing and communications had a full-time graphic designer on staff. The designer admittedly had a heavy workload and coped with it as best as she could. The situation was not ideal, but then the designer found an outside source for the overflow and so the work was produced on time and with only a slight budget overrun. The outside designer was especially helpful and produced timely material during the run-up to the group's large annual conference.

It was not until the designer left that the CFO discovered the overflow work was provided by a fictitious company, and that the checks for the work had been cashed by the graphic designer herself. Reviewing the total amount lost, he calculated that it was at least $8,000. He pursued the designer, eventually launching a mini-campaign of letters, certified mail, telephone calls, and emails, but she never responded and he could find no trace of her.

The money was lost, but the organization got a small amount of satisfaction in the end. Reasoning that the graphic designer was guilty of self-dealing even though the overflow work actually got done, they reported to the IRS that the designer had earned an additional $8,000 in consulting revenue from the organization that year.

One more thing. They also overhauled their system of internal controls.

happen that way. The next time that the business staff of the average small to medium-sized nonprofit organization has the time to sit down and carefully document its internal control policies and procedures in a three-ring binder with color-coded tabs will be the first time. Larger nonprofits have to maintain some form of internal control manual in order to simply survive, but it is remarkable how often the official documentation is lacking or out of date.

The fact is that few nonprofit corporations actually maintain such policies and procedures manuals, and yet many have as good a system of internal controls as one could wish. The reason is that they have an effective system of communication about changes in policies and procedures, it just doesn't happen to take the form of a manual. Improvements in communication technology over the past few years have helped a lot in this regard, as have organizational changes that the technology has facilitated. The fact that many nonprofits have small business office staffs doesn't hurt either, since they are better able to communicate with each other without layers of bureaucracy.

Today, technology such as computer networks, voice mail, and fax machines can accommodate an organization's need to communicate widely while remaining highly flexible. The real challenge is to make use of each form of communication while keeping the content coherent and retrievable. The three-ring binder with carefully typed tabs specifying all aspects of the accounting system may be history, but the need for communication will always be with us.

Segregation of Duties

Think of an accounting system as a series of vulnerable areas or pressure points susceptible to leakage and distortion of results. These points are natural and inevitable, and they represent the areas where breakdowns in control are most likely to occur. It is not inappropriate to think about an accounting system as though it were under permanent siege by forces that would corrupt its processes and divert its assets. The analogy to a castle is tempting except that, unlike a castle, an accounting system is endangered far more by those from within than by those from without.

Embezzlement is a loner's crime. Big bank robberies takes gangs, but gangs in a back room are hard to put together and even harder to maintain. Thievery from the ledger requires patience and a certain amount of planning, and the best way to keep it going is to wholly dominate a segment of business operations. The point of internal controls is to insert a system of checks and balances that make that domination harder and to increase the likelihood of detection should it occur.

Inside financial crimes tend to be unoriginal. Crooks don't usually innovate (happily)! Sophisticated computer capability sometimes makes the crook's job easier and faster, but the broad outlines have stayed the same. In the end, unauthorized entry is unauthorized entry whether it occurs in a safe or a computerized bank file.

One of the easiest and clearest ways to thwart those bent on financial crime is to break up the various duties so as to make it nearly impossible for any one person to gain the kind of total dominance over a portion of the system mentioned earlier. This segregating of financial duties creates a network of safeguards at the various pressure points that makes it much more difficult to coordinate and expand fraudulent activity or to accidentally lose assets. It is still possible for a determined embezzler to steal from the nonprofit via even a single pressure point, and human error can play terrible tricks on the strongest of systems. As a result, the system of internal controls has to be vigorously maintained and routinely updated to take into account new developments in the nonprofit's financial life.

There are any number of potential weak spots in an accounting system. Fortunately, for each one there are one or more things that the careful manager can do to minimize the risk. Preventing loss is a lot easier and less expensive than coping with it, so here are some not-so-rare scenarios along with tips on preventing them at the end of each segment.

Making Segregation of Duties Work in a Nonprofit Setting

There are many other duties whose components can be segregated in the typical nonprofit organization. For instance, custody of securities is a major issue for nonprofits fortunate enough to own some and is one reason why portfolio management is best entrusted to professional money managers. There will also be many other duties unique to a nonprofit organization that will need to be split up in order to help ensure adequate control.

SCENARIO

WHO MAILS?

I hope they give me the job of sending out the mail. Boy, would that make my scam easier. It would be a lot nicer to know when those payments for the fake invoices were going out. Better control, you understand.

PREVENTION

Be sure that the person who mails is not the same person who writes the checks and signs them.

OPENING THE MAIL, RECEIVING CASH

Sure, I realize that opening the mail is not the most exciting job. But I don't mind. This is an old, established, excruciatingly wonderful organization that gets lots of support from lots of different people. I see big foundation checks rolling in from time to time, and some money from the government. But what I really like are the contributions.

Like this one, for example. Handwritten envelope. Shaky writing—probably someone older and not inclined to make trouble. I slit open the envelope and spot a ten dollar bill. I slide it under some papers on my desk. It'll go into my wallet later today. It's only ten dollars, they'll never feel it. They never send thank you notes, so the donor won't know it's gone. Besides, if they ever ask me about it, I'll just lie. Do it again in a week or so, maybe for a bigger amount then.

A few years ago they also let me receive cash for the organization. I made a lot of mistakes at first, and then I realized that an intentional mistake now and then can accomplish as much as an accidental one. I know opening the mail and accepting cash is pretty boring stuff but I don't mind . . .

PREVENTION

Recruit and hire employees with a focus on proven honesty. Train staff in proper techniques of handling cash and recording donations. Replace any long-time mail handler at least temporarily and monitor cash intake to see if it changes. Use an imprest fund for petty cash, meaning a locked box (with only two or three authorized key holders) always containing the same amount of money in some combination of cash and receipts; for example, if I take out ten dollars in cash, I must replace it with ten dollars in receipts. Use prenumbered receipts and monitor their usage. Restrictively endorse checks upon receipt and list cash received. Use a lockbox for collections (a service offered by a bank in which donors or payment sources send money directly to a bank's post office box number). Bond—take out a specialized type of insurance—any employee handling cash or other assets.

APPROVE PAYROLL

I'm not going to tell you my name since that would blow my cover. Let's just say that I don't have to work real hard for my paycheck. In fact, I don't even have to work at all. Don't get me wrong—my paperwork is in order, and the bookkeeping office thinks I'm just one of hundreds of hardworking stiffs in this nonprofit. As far as all the records are concerned, I'm golden. It's just that I don't have to do anything to get paid.

I am part of a small office several miles from the central office headquarters. They say we're outstationed to another nonprofit's programs in the building, which really means nobody knows what we're doing except that we're doing it outside of the normal central office and program locations. It started a few years ago when this organization took over a group of scattered programs with lousy administrative systems. I have a cousin who is pretty influential around town and apparently someone owed him something. Nobody figured out what was going on then, and as long as nobody from this business office talks to anyone at the program they probably never will . . .

PREVENTION

All supervisors must have full knowledge at all times of staff, their salaries, and work expectations. A position control system backs up this level of knowledge by specifying authorized levels of staffing, budgeted amounts, and details of the actual staffing complement. A position control system is practically mandatory for any nonprofit employing hundreds of employees. It can be as simple as a computerized spreadsheet or as elaborate as a module in an accounting system. Plain communication helps, too. Business staff and direct service staff need multiple opportunities to communicate, and a framework for identifying and researching unexplained variances from budget. Middle managers in charge of programs need to know exactly what personnel they have been allocated and why, and they should be held accountable for how they use them.

CREATING FINANCIAL RECORDS

Me, I like detail. The more the better. I especially like details like how a transaction gets entered in our books, and the amounts recorded on bank deposit slips. You can call me Albert or Randall, if you prefer. I also answer to Charles and, of course, John. These are all my friends, and during the course of a year most of them turn up in our financial records. Sometimes they have checks made out to them or their companies, and other times they just appear in our records to cover some other deal I'm working.

None of my friends are real, you see. Instead, I think of each one as extensions of my personality. I am an artist, you might say, a creator of financial fictions, and this nonprofit's books are my canvas. It helps that I have responsibility for entering lots of transactions as they occur, and for reconciling the records with our bank accounts. Keeps me in control of the loop, and everybody else outside of it.

PREVENTION

Separate bank statement reconciliation from the completion of deposit slips. Separate the processing functions such as receiving and preparing for recording a transaction from the actual recording of it. Require approval for interfund transfers.

Still, this is a book for those who rely on systems of segregation of duties, not for those who must create them. The power of segregating duties is clear, and the wise manager will use it carefully.

The real obstacle to effective segregation of duties in a nonprofit setting is not so much lack of knowledge as it is lack of people. A very rough (emphasis on *very*) rule of thumb is that for nonprofit organizations with revenues greater than approximately $3 million, it should take one to two full-time equivalent (FTE) financial people plus an additional 0.25 to 1.5 FTE per million dollars of revenue thereafter, with the rate of additional staff tailing off at the industry's typical economic size (see Box).

ECONOMIC SIZE

The consistent inability to handle routine administrative tasks may be a signal that a nonprofit is operating below its field's desirable economic size.

Some nonprofits cannot afford to have the level of business expertise on staff that they really need. While one reason is the chronic underfunding of administration by funding sources and some managers themselves, another reason may be that the nonprofit is not of a sufficient economic size.

In order to open its doors, any nonprofit must invest in a fixed amount of administrative equipment and personnel. In most cases, this implies computers, telephone systems, an office, and personnel. Most nonprofits allocate a small percentage of each incoming revenue dollar to meet these needs. More sophisticated and varied demands on the financial and administrative systems mean higher fixed costs.

If those financial and administrative needs are costly—if, for instance, the nonprofit requires complex software and high-level accounting personnel—the only way to get those things if the allocation percentage stays the same is to increase the number of revenue dollars. At the point where there is a reasonable balance between the amount of programming delivered and the adequacy of the financial and administrative systems is the economic size.

We know what happens if the nonprofit is below the economic size—it will be unable to perform properly and with financial accountability. What we don't know for most fields in which nonprofits are active is whether it is possible to miss the economic size by being too large. Much more research is needed here.

Unfortunately from the perspective of controls, most nonprofit groups under $3 million in revenue have one or fewer people identified as financial staff, and it will usually be someone concerned with keeping the financial records, not managing them.

It is impossible to segregate duties when one person does it all. In those circumstances, it is necessary for another individual, most likely the CEO, to take on complementary control duties. Happily, it is possible to achieve a reasonable degree of segregation even with two people. With more people, it becomes that much easier. *The Nonprofit Management Reports* (Third Sector

Press) developed a very useful set of sample duty allocations for two-, three-, and four-person offices. These are reproduced in Exhibit 18.2. A matrix for pinpointing weaknesses in internal control is on the accompanying Web site. 👆

EXHIBIT 18.2   SEGREGATION OF DUTIES

Two-Person Segregation

Business Manager	CEO
Post accounts receivable	Sign checks
Mail checks	Sign employee contracts
Write checks	Custody of securities
Post general ledger	Complete deposit slips
Reconcile bank statements	Perform interfund transfers
Post credits/debits	Distribute payroll
Give credits and discounts	Reconcile petty cash
Approve payroll	Record initial charges and pledges
Open mail/receive cash	Approve employee time sheets
Disburse petty cash	Prepare invoices
Authorize purchase orders	Complete check log
Authorize check requests	
Approve invoices for payment	

Three-Person Segregation

Bookkeeper	Business Manager	CEO
Post accounts receivable	Prepare invoices	Sign checks
Reconcile petty cash	Record initial charges	Sign employee contracts
Write checks	and pledges	Custody of securities
Post general ledger	Open mail/receive cash	Complete deposit slips
Reconcile bank statements	Mail checks	Perform interfund transfers
Post credits/debits	Approve invoices for payment	
Give credits and discounts	Distribute payroll	
	Authorize purchase orders	
	Authorize check requests	
	Approve employee time sheets	
	Approve payroll	
	Complete check log	

	Four-Person Segregation		
Bookkeeper	**Clerk**	**Business Manager**	**CEO**
Post accounts receivable	Distribute payroll	Complete deposit slips	Sign checks
Reconcile petty cash	Open mail/receive cash	Give credits and discounts	Sign employee contracts
Write checks	Record initial charges and pledges	Prepare invoices	Custody of securities
Post general ledger	Complete check log	Approve payroll	Approve employee time sheets
Reconcile bank statements	Disburse petty cash	Approve invoices for payment	Perform interfund transfers
Post credits/debits	Authorize purchase orders		
	Authorize check requests		
	Mail checks		

Record Keeping

The actual pathways of information flow are contained in the financial record-keeping systems the nonprofit maintains. In principle, a recording
system is pretty simple. It keeps track of money and assets coming into and
flowing out of the organization, and it makes sure that all documentation
of the flow is summarized in the general ledger. In practice, the details can
get quite complex, but the underlying principles don't change. Exhibit 18.3
shows the relationships among the various parts of the record-keeping
system.

Czar Nicholas Alexander was said to have sighed on his deathbed, "I
never ran Russia; a thousand clerks did." Most nonprofit CEOs feel the
same way about the financial operations of their nonprofit. For that matter,
so do many financial managers. The record-keeping system is just that—a
system. It is of necessity a gigantic commodity processor, and its commodity
is financial transactions. Nobody can be said to run it in the same sense that
one runs a piece of heavy equipment or an automobile. At base it is nothing
more than small units of information going through proscribed processes in
carefully determined steps. The systemic aspect consists of trying to get the
same results every time that one starts with the same type of input.

If one were able to turn a financial record-keeping system into sound, it
would probably be like thundershowers on a tin roof. Just like thundershowers, financial transactions keep coming, the pace intensifying around

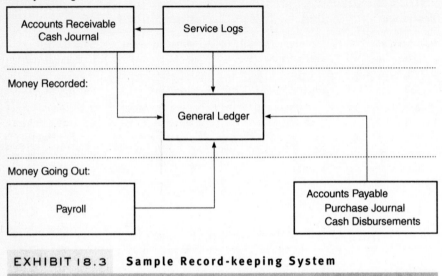

EXHIBIT 18.3   Sample Record-keeping System

certain times of the day and periods of the year. There is no respite when overseeing a financial record-keeping system.

This nonstop pace dictates that each transaction be handled rapidly and accurately or else the entire system bogs down and eventually stops altogether. It also means that the way to judge a system is via whole groups of transactions, not by how well it does on one or two transactions. But there is an ironic twist to evaluating a financial system. A large majority of transactions in any organization of substantial size recur along similar lines, and it is a straightforward matter to compose a system for processing them. Some percentage of transactions, however, are unusual or nonrecurring, and these must be handled quickly and effectively because otherwise the entire system bogs down. It can be said that the mark of a good system is one that can handle volume without being so imprisoned in routine that it cannot cope with variety.

Banking regulations require personnel in key financial positions to take two successive weeks off each year, the idea being that any illegal schemes they may be running will collapse while they are away . . .

How to Monitor the System

For the nonprofit executive or manager assigned responsibility for a financial system but despairing of his or her ability to control it, there is a reassuring and effective method of getting the job done. *Let someone else do it.* Seriously, there is a considerable amount of outside help available to perform some of the record-keeping functions or to help shape how they are performed, and a secondary payoff is that this simplifies the control function. Here, in no particular order of importance, are some of the ways the smart manager can leverage outside help to maintain proper internal controls.

Use a Payroll Service

Thanks to a steady accumulation of laws, regulations, conventional practices, and competitive strategies, preparing any organization's payroll has become an absolute swamp. Just getting the correct withholding amounts for each employee is a challenge in itself, especially with changes in calculating withholding amounts. Contracting it out is usually a good idea. In fact, there are only two types of nonprofits that may have a good reason for doing their own payrolls: the very small who can't afford even an extra dime, and the very large that can afford to staff their own internal payroll departments. (*Note to the small:* Find the dime. *Note to the large:* Stop kidding yourselves.)

Large national firms now compete to provide payroll services to nonprofit organizations of all kinds. Some banks are also still in the payroll service business, although others have lost their enthusiasm for it. And in every major city, there are local payroll service bureaus catering to a particular niche. Often, these bureaus operate independently for some period of years and then are purchased by one of the national firms.

What all of these companies have in common is that they are the ones that deal with the rapidly changing laws, regulations, and schedules that one must master in order to pay American employees correctly today. Due to the nature of the payroll business, they must compete on price and then service. It adds up to good value and reliable accountability for the practicing manager.

Finally, it should be noted that payroll service companies typically offer a wide array of options for using their services, including sophisticated electronic linkups between the user and the bureau's computer system.

Increasingly, there is little reason for the average nonprofit entity to go it alone in this crucial area.

Accounts Receivable Management

For a few nonprofits, accounts receivable (A/R) may be another candidate to let outside services manage. Often, when invoices must be prepared according to strict guidelines and the nonprofit expects to submit large numbers of them, the stage is set for outside expertise in the billing process.

Sometimes this expertise is a service that looks like a payroll service bureau. Volume makes it all work, since the billing service can achieve economies of scale. Sometimes it takes the form of specialized software, operated with or without the continued involvement of the billing specialists.

Cash Management Services

Banks are the traditional providers of cash management services, and with the changes in the banking industry and the technology of information processing, there is a dizzying array of cash management tools available to nonprofits. It is possible for a bank to take such a strong role in a nonprofit's cash management that the nonprofit's personnel almost literally never touch cash or make any day-to-day cash management decisions other than to request specific amounts of money for operations.

Suppose consumers mail in their payment to a designated post office box. This is a "lockbox" service, in which the bank opens the envelope and deposits the check into a specially designated account. At the close of business that same day, the account could be "swept" clean of cash above a predetermined level, with the excess going to an overnight deposit account paying interest at a market level. Automatically—or upon receipt of a signal from the organization—a certain amount over a designated level is removed from *that* account and placed into a longer-term instrument paying higher interest rates. Those funds and others on deposit can be electronically transferred to a field office or other recipient. All of this happens without any substantive staff involvement until transaction records are received for reconciliation. Naturally, these types of arrangements are more suitable for larger organizations, but even smaller groups can take advantage of some of them.

Application Service Providers

Application service providers, or ASPs, are offspring of the Internet. As such, they are still relatively young and gangly. Still, they offer promise for the future.

Here's the way an ASP works. A software company, instead of selling you their package, allows you to license it for a certain number of users. The software remains on their computer, not yours, and you access it and your accumulated information via an Internet connection. They keep your data secure and separate from everyone else's, and you pay a monthly access fee based on usage.

An ASP offers nonprofits many advantages, including avoiding a capital investment, constant upgrades, lessened need for technical support, more sophisticated application support whenever necessary, and a more powerful application. They also come with some disadvantages, such as the need for multiple high-speed Internet connections, the fact that one may have to pay for more firepower than needed, and the possibility that the ASP company might go out of business abruptly.

MAINTAINING THE SYSTEM

Once a system of internal controls has been assembled, it must be maintained. Most of the changes in its components will be small—a different person starts generating invoices, someone else covers for an absent cash management accountant and never relinquishes the duty—so it may be hard to spot new breakdowns in internal control. Aside from the most important technique of hiring a qualified accounting professional to oversee the accounting system, there are two things nonprofit managers can do to stay on top of the control environment. One is the yearly management letter, and the other is to structure an effective system of financial reports.

The Management Letter

The fastest and most routinely available route to guidance about improving internal controls should be the corporation's annual management letter. An accompanying piece to the annual audit, the management letter is a potentially excellent source of information about how well the system is operating because it is the system of internal controls that can give the outsider the highest degree of comfort that what management presents is in fact what is truly happening.

Typically, the management letter is written with a bit more candor than can be found in the formal financial statements. The idea is that, although the auditors are supposed to report to the board of directors, the management letter is their opportunity to spell out directly to management the improvements that the auditing team feels can be made. It is the only context in which management, the nonprofit's governors, and qualified outside observers can explicitly discuss the heart of what might be called the accountability infrastructure.

The management letter serves as a kind of punch list for repairs to the financial management system over the next 12 months, so it should be quite explicit and practical. In the nonprofit world, it can also serve as a political document in the sense of mediating between board and staff concerns. The bulk of references in a management letter should originate with the auditors, but on occasion they will include a point raised by staff that would have greater importance when coming from outsiders. Whatever their origins, the real message about management letter points is that they should be dealt with by management, preferably within the next 12 months.

Reporting

Put away the printouts. Trash the memos. Forget about the special reports. You only need five financial reports to control the average nonprofit corporation. Breathtaking advances in information processing technology allow us to create a virtually infinite variety of reports, but for high-level oversight it's hard to beat the basic five: balance sheet, revenue and expenses, aged accounts receivables, cash flow projection, and utilization reporting.

Most of these reports have already been covered elsewhere in this book and need little or no elaboration. The balance sheet will be unaudited, and it should be delivered monthly. Revenue and expenses should be reported by program on both a budget-to-date and year-to-date basis with some form of index to allow quick location of trouble spots. For instance, the final column in the report could be a percentage variance from budget, or whole dollar differences from budget-to-date figures.

Aged A/R reports are essential for any organization that does a substantial amount of billing. Also done monthly, the aged A/R reports show the classes of revenue (or the actual outstanding invoices, if practical) and the amounts of each type outstanding for 30, 60, 90, and more days. Cash flow projections need to be updated at least quarterly if not more often. Finally, most agencies need some form of utilization reporting. Unlike the other four reports, this information varies greatly according to the services provided. It may be enough for a museum to know how many people paid to attend its summer exhibit, for example, while a health center must have detailed information about the different sources of payment its consumers use. There is little alternative, but for each type of nonprofit to develop homegrown utilization reports unless they are stipulated by some funding source or a particular format is routinely accepted in its industry.

CONCLUSION

No one in any business entity likes to lose money through error, waste, or fraud, but nonprofits must be doubly cautious because of their fiduciary responsibility. Nonprofit financial and accounting systems have natural weak spots, and the goal of a system of internal controls is to prevent loss or to maximize the chances of detection if loss does occur. Nonfinancial managers need not get enmeshed in the details of running the system of internal controls, but they do need to see that it is maintained. Knowing the components of internal controls helps, as does knowing where to look for information.

CHAPTER 19

Enron Spawn

Nonprofit organizations have always been expected to adhere to a high standard of ethical behavior, but in recent years the bar has been raised two notches. This bump up was caused by three factors. One was the Sarbanes-Oxley law; the second factor was the less well-known rules published by the U.S. Government Accountability Office (GAO); and the third is the new crop of charity watchers. The central paradox is that the widely known Sarbanes-Oxley law was designed primarily for publicly held companies and therefore has mostly secondary effects on the sector, while the nearly invisible GAO regulations and the charity watchers have a primary effect. We'll sort this out later in the chapter. Together, they are likely to achieve for nonprofits exactly what was intended for Sarbanes-Oxley to achieve for all publicly held corporations: a restructured relationship between the entity and its auditors, and greater transparency with its constituencies.

Sarbanes-Oxley (also known as SOX and SarbOx) was passed in direct response to the wave of corporate accounting scandals and questionable financial practices of the Enron era. Ironically, the GAO revisions had been in the works long before that time. Philosophically they owe their roots to the concerns about auditor independence that Arthur Levitt, a past chair of the Securities and Exchange Commission (SEC), had raised in the late 1990s. Both trace their origin to the same policy question: What is the best way to ensure that the audit function will remain truly independent?

Auditor independence is important for obvious reasons, and it can be compromised in less than obvious ways. The central concern in these matters is that the external auditors may lose the outsider's perspective during the audit relationship and end up in a relationship with the audited organization that could in some way impair their ability to render impartial judgments. This can happen most readily if either the audit function is mishandled or consulting services performed by the auditing company are improperly designed or delivered.

A handy way to think of the underlying principles of independence is to use four standards as a measuring stick. Auditors lose independence if they perform services that cause them to:

1. Audit their own work
2. Create a mutuality of interest with the client
3. Make management decisions
4. Become an advocate for the client

These four conditions bear a little further description. Auditing their own work is obvious . . . most of the time. But it's easy to overlook it when the organization's books are in bad shape and the auditor first must help the client get the books in order. At some point during major record reconstruction (exactly where it is hard to say with complete certainty), the books and records effectively become the product of the auditor, not the client. Alternatively, in small organizations, if the auditors also close the books each month and do bank reconciliations or similar work, they too have lost their independence.

A mutuality of interest can exist in the case of situations such as contingent fees or business relationships. The latter are more likely to occur among large audit firms and large clients and might typically involve one group selling the other's products or services.

Making management decisions in place of management is a clearer violation of the standards. Financial management requires many day-to-day decisions among competing choices. Auditors usually advise their clients and have no power to implement their recommendations. However, if the audit firm assumes responsibility for a sensitive part of the operations such as information technology design or managing internal control systems, the auditors will quickly lose their independence. Unlike the mutuality of interest, this is particularly likely to occur in small- or medium-sized non-profits without adequate financial staff who naturally want to turn to their auditor for help.

Finally, providing legal services or expert witness services for clients can impair independence. This, too, is more likely in large and complex nonprofits even though the principle is applicable in all contexts.

Many of these situations will arise only in special circumstances, but the general principles are valid, so an audit relationship that strays into one of these areas is out of bounds.

The GAO regulations:

- Deal with nonaudit or consulting services
- Apply only to nonprofits receiving more than $500,000 in federal funds
- Base policy on principles, not rules as has often been the case in the past. For example, one of the GAO independence standards is as follows: "In all matters relating to the audit work, the audit organization and the individual auditor, whether government or public, should be free both in fact and in appearance from personal, external and organizational impairments to independence."
- Hold the independence standard to be based on two fundamental principles:
  1. Auditors should not perform management functions or make management decisions.
  2. Auditors should not audit their own work or provide nonaudit services in situations where the amounts or services involved are significant/material to the subject matter of the audit.
- Also stipulate that nonaudit services must meet additional tests; for example, the people performing the services should not work on the related audit, an audit organization's work must not be artificially reduced to make it look like less of a conflict, and the services must be documented and must meet certain quality assurance safeguards.

Under Sarbanes-Oxley:

- Certain nonaudit consulting services are prohibited from being performed for a client by its audit firm.
- All tax and consulting services must be preapproved by the audit committee.

- Partners must rotate off an SEC engagement after five years (it used to be seven).

- Audit committees must disclose the name of at least one "financial expert" member.

- Most personal loans to the company's executives are prohibited.

- The auditor must report on the company's internal controls.

- Company executives must vouch for certain reports and controls.

SOME PREDICTIONS

While the GAO regulations have a direct impact on nonprofits that receive substantial federal dollars, Sarbanes-Oxley has had a more far-reaching yet subtle impact. This may seem odd, considering that all but two of its provisions apply exclusively to for-profit, publicly held companies (whistle-blower provisions and record retention policies apply to all corporations). But because Sarbanes-Oxley has grudgingly become the de facto standard for for-profit executives on their home turf, when they sit on nonprofit boards they wonder why it shouldn't be applied there as well.

There is considerable evidence that a cultural shift is in fact occurring. For example, the accounting firm Grant Thornton in 2003 found that 56 percent of all respondents to its survey were somewhat familiar or very familiar with Sarbanes-Oxley, but just a year later that number had grown to 83 percent. In 2003 only about 24 percent of all nonprofits surveyed had a written conflict of interest statement. In 2007, 78 percent did.

There are some obvious and not-so-obvious trends likely to emerge as this new emphasis on accountability settles into the end of its first full decade. Some likely candidates are described next.

Audit/Consulting Split

The unavoidable conclusion one must draw at this point is that nonprofits will begin to use different firms for their consulting services than they use for their audit services, although this is not necessarily required in the majority of cases. This split is what many advocates and federal officials intended for the for-profit corporation, of course, and now they sometimes explicitly do require it. Where it is not required, the step of getting audit committee's preapproval will at least slightly discourage management from this course of action. Why would managers stir up a potential controversy on the board level if it's possible to get the same thing accomplished just by going to another provider?

There are two ironies in this probable outcome. The first is that nonprofits generally never engaged in the kinds of practices that with regard to for-profits gave rise to serious concerns about auditor independence. For instance, in the technology boom years of the prior decade it was not unusual for the large accounting firms' consulting practices to have significant numbers of employees outsourced to their clients' financial software implementation projects, looking like the client's employees but in reality being on the payroll of the audit/consulting firm. Most nonprofits simply don't have the scale of operations that makes that kind of arrangement either necessary or financially feasible (although, again, small or rural agencies have sometimes used their auditors for financial management consulting services even though that practice has always been very close to an automatic violation of auditor ethics).

The second irony is that this auditing/consulting split was, for different reasons, already in the works at the major accounting firms even before the events of the past few years. Most of the large firms had already spun off their technology implementation practices well before the corporate accounting scandals, and smaller firms usually didn't have consulting practices of a similar scope anyway.

Rise of the Trophy Financial Nonprofit Board Member

Some may read with surprise the Sarbanes-Oxley requirement to have at least one "financial expert" on the audit committee. Weren't for-profit corporations' audit committees packed with financial experts anyway? Not necessarily, it turns out. In any event, it will now be part of the culture that nonprofit boards of directors will be expected to have at least one bona fide financial expert. This means that CPAs, corporate internal auditors, and financial watchdogs will become the new class of trophy board member, as nonprofits feel compelled to reassure funders of their financial oversight capacity.

Good Internal Controls Part of Board Expectations

Nonprofits with a large amount of federal funding are already used to their auditors reporting on their internal controls, but many other groups are not. As this becomes a requirement for for-profit firms, their executives serving on nonprofit boards will want to make sure that the internal controls are in good shape there, too. This means that cultural groups, advocacy organizations, and nonmainstream nonprofits will be pressed to concentrate some time and attention on strengthening internal controls.

Nonprofit CEOs Held More Accountable

Sarbanes-Oxley requires the publicly held corporate CEO and other executives to sign off on the financial statements. While there is no comparable provision for nonprofits, the idea has now been implanted in executive culture that the CEO and other senior types have personal responsibility for what goes on in their organizations. Look for this to be translated to the nonprofit sector. There have been some congressional attempts to formalize this practice in the sector, although nothing yet has stuck. Even in the absence of formalized requirements, the subtle accountability wedge driven between the CEO and CFO by Sarbanes-Oxley (both must sign sensitive public reports) will likely carry over to the nonprofit sector as well.

Rise of Principle-Based Auditing

The real sleeper development in all this may be that auditing becomes less rules-based and more principles-based. Many experts are trying to push it in that direction anyway, arguing that strict rules-based auditing encourages too narrow a focus, which facilitates the kind of accounting scandals that arose in the first decade of the new century. As noted, the GAO rules themselves can be read as a miniature experiment in regulation based on principles rather than rules. Most of the rest of the world has already adopted this approach in the International Financial Reporting Standards (IFRS).

THE NEW INDUSTRY OF CHARITY WATCHING

They're watching you.

They have earnest names and they have figured out a way to measure you based on one or more criteria for success. They appear in the popular press whenever some non-streetsmart nonprofit management team commits a blunder. They offer up a pithy quote or two and then they go back to their computer screens. You know who these groups are: the charity watchers (cue the eerie music).

Really. Charity watchers have fashioned a mini-industry out of publicly available information on nonprofit public charities. And the truth is, we need them. Explicit government oversight of public charities is, in all honesty, lax. One can count on a single hand the number of state government charity oversight officials with anything more than a bare-bones budget and systems that are even close to being adequate. As a sector, this has to be one of the most honorable and accountable, but there are always a few bad guys sprinkled here and there. Auditors require a certain level of disclosure, but sunlight really is the best disinfectant and that's what the charity watchers supply.

At the same time, it's not pleasant to be rated, especially by a distant presence whose only exposure to your organization is likely to come from a megabyte of data and no in-person contact. Moreover, some no doubt harbor the suspicion that charity watching is more about the watchers than it is about improving the charity world. In the end, however, these are quibbles. Publicly held companies know that their stock prices are partially at the mercy of analysts, some of whom never leave the comfy world of lower Manhattan to see the companies they rate. Why should it be any different for public charities? Considering that lax corporate rating practices helped facilitate the 2008 Wall Street crash, this is not much of a rationale. However, since we are likely to see reform in that area that strengthens the value of rating services, it would be wise to prepare to adapt the lessons that come from this area.

In any event, the watchers are with us, and streetsmart managers will find ways to deal with them. Based on our experience, there are four ways of coping with the watchers. Each has its own logic, and each can offer a different set of solutions to the potential problems caused by the watchers.

Data Presentation

Is there anyone in the voluntary sector with more than about six months' worth of experience who believes that the IRS Form 990 doesn't matter? Unlike the personal Form 1040, the Form 990 is considered an informational return because no money is expected to change hands as a result of the information it presents.

Sure. Tell that to the nonprofit that didn't get a grant because the donor didn't like the organization's percentage of administrative spending. The publicly available Form 990 has become the information currency of the nonprofit sector.

Take the quick calculation that many have learned to make. Divide line 45c by line 12 to get the management costs as a percentage of revenue. This is a guide to overhead costs for the reporting organization, but if you throw in fund-raising costs on line 44d, the percentage climbs. Overhead costs like these are becoming the acid test for some donors and funders. Everyone knows that overhead costs take away from programs and services; so everyone knows that the higher the overhead percentage, the less efficient and therefore less worthy is the organization. The point is reinforced by some of the watchers' rating methods.

This dynamic tension is probably permanently enshrined in the nonprofit sector. So the expense information had better accurately represent your organization, or it could carry a high cost. In our experience, most nonprofit board members and executives alike sincerely wish to keep administrative costs low, as do the charity watchers. But that doesn't mean that they report those costs accurately.

Internal inconsistencies can derail a Form 990. Combine those with untutored analysts, and the stage is set for a public relations gaffe. For example, one major newspaper pulled a large sampling of Form 990s and printed an analysis of which ones raised the most dollars from the public. But in at least one case a reporting entity mistakenly called government funding "public contributions." The newspaper accepted the declaration uncritically even though the organization's small and accurately reported fund-raising expenses would have meant its cost of fund-raising was an absurdly efficient 1 percent!

Of course, if one's management expenses are high for legitimate reasons, well, that's just the reality and everyone will have to find a way to be comfortable with that, including the watchers. But eliminating sloppy or misleading reporting should be a natural first step.

Allocation Methodologies

Direct costs have the benefit of being traceable to specific services, programs, or types of spending. But many costs cannot be directly attributable to any program or activity and must be allocated according to some reasonable formula. Management and general costs from column C on the second page are classic allocations. Sometimes it is possible to allocate a cost directly to the management function. For instance, a bookkeeper is virtually always going to be a management cost of some sort. But other allocations are not so clear-cut, and ultimately they tend to be a judgment call.

Allocations also have a way of working themselves into everyone's consciousness, where they take on more credibility than they sometimes deserve. For instance, one well-known public charity consisted of a large central office, where most of the programming and management tasks were carried out, and several small satellite offices, which were largely direct-service and a bit of management. Many years earlier, when the charity watchers didn't exist, the organization started lumping the satellite direct-service operations into administration because it was easier that way. This greatly inflated the administrative costs, which never mattered much—until the watchers came to town. Lowering the charity's ratios was largely a matter of correctly segregating direct-service costs from administrative costs.

When They're Right (Darn It)

Then there are the times when the watchers get it right—you *are* inefficient. If that's the case, how you report the financial results is largely irrelevant. You've got work to do.

Many managers see inefficiency in two dimensions, like a mathematical formula—if you want one part of the formula to come up, you have to push down on another part. Rarely is inefficiency that simple. For example, if you really do spend too much money on fund-raising, chances are that it's your fund-raising model and your related cultural expectations that are to blame. It may have worked to base your fund-raising on special events 10 years ago when the organization was small, but to get to the next level it will take a complex effort involving a new organizational strategy, staff retraining, donor management, and serious cultivation efforts. This is a major undertaking, and it's the right thing to do for the organization. Just don't expect it to show up in the watchers' ratings for a while. In the meantime you at least have a case to make based on your constant improvement.

Communication

Throughout the process of dealing with an unfavorable charity watcher rating, try to keep the channels of communication open. Some watchers are more amenable to this than others. It never hurts to try to open up lines of communication with a watcher. Some allow nonprofits to place additional information on their Web sites. In general, more communication with the watchers and your constituencies is better than less. If nothing else, you have more of a chance to shape the dialogue and be less reactive.

In some instances, nonprofits use independent parties to do things like conduct an objective analysis of a charity watcher's score or to model a situation to identify the true drivers of a low score. They can also act as intermediaries between an organization and a watcher.

Charity watchers have become part of the fiber of the voluntary sector. They serve a useful function—even if aggrieved managers may not always feel that way. So streetsmart managers will find ways to manage this new development just like they manage so many other things. And there's a certain symmetry to this. Who else is going to watch the watchers?

CHAPTER 20

Management Controls: Toward Accountability for Performance

W e end the book with a glimpse into the future. Conventional ways of thinking say we should close with a safe, straightforward discussion of management controls in the nonprofit environment. We should talk about responsibility centers and cost centers and profit centers and all of those other pieces of financial terminology that serve mainly to complicate the obvious. We will do that. But we need to move beyond conventional thinking in order to position nonprofit institutions to function well in the future, and that challenge is by far the more important one for this final chapter.

Nonprofit organizations reflect the environment in which they were created, and for years the same command-and-control approach that won wars, mass-produced billions of dollars' worth of consumer goods, and built millions of housing units in this country and around the world served the industrialized world's nonprofits quite well. Management controls were the linchpin that made it all work. Managers exerted their influence on a nonprofit through a system of explicit controls, and the organization moved forward in a linear fashion. Things didn't change much, and when they did, it was usually in a reasonably predictable fashion with plenty of notice. Nonprofit financial management systems were essentially an afterthought, designed with a minimalist's brush and expected to run to keep up with programs' evolution.

MANAGEMENT CONTROLS CIRCA 1980

The conventional formula for management control pivots around the idea of responsibility. Certain points on the organization chart are designated as responsibility centers, meaning that whoever is in charge of that point must either produce something or make something happen. Typically, those in charge are given responsibility for producing profits ("Profit Center"), controlling costs ("Cost Center"), or generating revenue ("Revenue Center"). If circumstances warrant, a fourth category for managing investments might also be added (or it might be considered a profit center). Different organizations may use different language to define these functions, but for the most part they all mean essentially the same thing.

Within each responsibility center, the tasks may or may not be broken down into smaller units of responsibility, and so on until we reach the smallest possible unit of functional responsibility. Management's job is to plan the work of each unit, set the direction, organize all appropriate resources, and then control them. The impact of the organization is equal to the sum of all the individual functions controlled by the responsibility centers.

This style is suited to the nonprofits that the old national economy spawned: sprawling universities, complex museums, large site-based programs for the mentally ill and mentally retarded, and large hospitals. These types of nonprofits all require a major investment in property, plant, and equipment and the people and control systems to keep them running.

Throw out all of that conventional thinking for the future and start over again. In the industrialized economy, it was enough simply that these types of institutions existed. In the future, they will also need to perform. Government as a provider of direct services has been in retreat for decades. The commercial sector must strip down and compete in a global economy. What's left is a steadily increasing middle ground that must be tended by honest brokers, the time-honored role for nonprofits. But this time those brokers have got to produce in a different way, and to do so, they must reorient their financial systems from command and control to performance.

BEYOND MANAGEMENT CONTROLS IN THE TWENTY-FIRST CENTURY: HOW TO DO IT

As society demands greater emphasis on performance and as nonprofits struggle to respond, there is a key fact that may or may not be reassuring, depending on one's perspective: *We are all making it up as we go along.* This is not a commentary on the competence of our overall performance but rather an acknowledgment of a sobering reality. We simply have not demanded that nonprofits organize for and deliver performance up to this point, so we are not all that good at it.

Plus, the landscape is shifting rapidly. Government at all levels must deal with shrinking resources and increasing demands on them, and the nonprofits that they work with are being forced to change accordingly. The health care system, a major chunk of our total gross domestic product, must soon undergo massive changes to cope with aging baby boomers, and no one yet has the slightest idea how it will all turn out. Higher education will eventually have its day of change too. The one constant in these and other settings is that there will be a greatly increased demand for performance.

The obvious questions are: How do we do it? How do we organize for performance? How do we even define performance? What is the connection between the resources that go into a nonprofit and its performance? What is the proper role of the funder? The consumer? The manager? One key element of this admittedly broad question is the work of financial people, especially the CFO. We will spend some time trying to tease out the future role of the CFO.

MESSAGES

Nonprofits of all kinds can move beyond simple management controls and toward a performance orientation. The first critical ingredient is a clearly articulated mission. Having an understandable and widely accepted mission focuses an organization and makes decision making easier. It becomes an organizing principle as well as a foundation for measuring progress.

The nature of information gathering and processing must change in any organization the closer it moves to outcome-based management. Financial information typically takes up the greatest concentration of data processing resources in most nonprofits. In the future, it will have to share the power with outcome measures.

Performance-based nonprofit management will stress performance comparisons, known as benchmarks. The quantum leap that microprocessor technology took in the 1990s has made individualized benchmarking much easier. All that is needed now is the emergence of centralized authorities such as governments, trade associations, research groups, and private advisors to develop and disseminate benchmarks for use by their constituencies.

Performance-oriented nonprofits routinely and consistently ask consumers what performance means and how they are doing it. Surveys, it is safe to predict, are going to proliferate in future years until we figure out better and more efficient ways of soliciting formalized and statistically valid feedback from users.

The nonprofit committed to performance will also flatten itself. The traditional pyramid hierarchical style organization no longer works for most nonprofits. In its place is a flatter organization, made possible by improvements in communication technology and made necessary by the economic squeezes of the past decades and the latter part of the first decade of this century. It no longer takes as long to get information from one level of the nonprofit to another, and this eliminates the need for at least part of the formerly intervening level of management at the middle of the pyramid. At the same time, executive levels will take a more direct role in managing internal performance standards, in part because funders will demand it and in part because there will be fewer managers to do it anyway.

Finally, the serious nonprofit manager will look for generally accepted performance standards and will eventually seek outside validation of its performance. Right now, few such independent verifiers exist. Accrediting and licensing bodies fill part of the void, but only a small part. Universities, research groups, and consultants are workable sources of performance verification at the moment, but in general there is a real lack of independent expertise available to conduct performance reviews. As funding sources increasingly ask for details on what was accomplished as opposed to the more traditional focus on what was spent, the traditional financial audit may even take on a more outcome-oriented flavor. It is even possible that an entirely new class of performance-verification entities will be invented to meet the demand for independent attestation of results, somewhat similar to the circulation confirmation services that newspapers and magazines currently employ.

How to Prepare—The CFO of the Future

As stated earlier, the practical implication of the preceding chapters is that the financial role in the average nonprofit is changing. Here's a trail map of what those changes will probably look like.

A More Co-Equal Role for the CFO with the CEO

Study the proceedings of the high-profile corporate corruption trials from the early years of the twenty-first century, and you'll notice a subtle change. For the first time, the CFO of each of these companies has been accorded status as a near-partner with the CEO. The financial person who formerly was nearly invisible to the casual observer has been placed side-by-side with the individual responsible for the corporation as a whole.

This is emblematic of a parallel change in the nonprofit sector as well. Many of the similar changes in the IRS Form 990 will put more pressure on the chief financial person to help design and maintain systems than ever before. Implicitly, this suggests that regulators expect more from financial staff than previously.

For many nonprofits, this amounts to little more than an external recognition of reality. Many nonprofit CEOs long ago discovered that it was in their interest to have a strong, competent, respected CFO who acts as a partner in formulating strategy and reporting to the board of directors. What could be different for nonprofits is that that financial partner, who used to operate out of sight of most outsiders, may be called into the spotlight more regularly in the future.

Greater Separation between the CEO and the CFO

Ironically, this external effort to link the CEO and the CFO in financial accountability may also create a little daylight between them. Currently the IRS Form 990 that nonprofits file each year is considered an informational return with little at stake even for the person who signed it. But the IRS now requires things such as explicit confirmation of management policies, oversight of compliance activities, and so forth.

With little at stake before, the CFO who was so inclined was able to defer his or her responsibility to the CEO in these matters, who in turn didn't even need to think about whether to accept it. But as demands for an explicit acknowledgment of basic governance, programmatic, and financial accomplishments grows, the streetsmart nonprofit CEO will demand personal assurances that the work has been done before signing off. This will set up the possibility for a pointed inevitable internal dialog about whether the organization has accomplished its minimum expectations. Which, of course, is exactly what regulators intend.

What will really occur here could be a forced choice between professional standards and administrative expediency. Experienced, professionally trained CFOs, especially those with a credential such as a CPA, have a professional duty that goes beyond their immediate employer. Increasing the demand for accountability from the nonprofit CFO, even if indirectly, will increase the likelihood that in some cases the individual will feel it necessary to say no to the CEO, the board, or whomever in the organization may ask them to violate the standards of their profession.

Greater CFO Involvement in Technology

Most nonprofit managers probably correctly regard Sarbanes-Oxley as a somewhat distant federal law not directly related to nonprofits but which has an indirect impact. But one of the biggest implications of that law's implementation is that financial managers are being drawn headfirst into matters of information technology to an unprecedented extent, and one of the most time-consuming aspects of the law is its insistence on certain standards in electronic financial controls.

The same will be true in the nonprofit arena as the tenets of Sarbanes-Oxley are accepted as the gold standard and board members see the indirect applicability in a nonprofit setting. This effect could be hard to spot, since it will be couched in terms of the need to ensure that controls are sound and up-to-date, that policies are being followed, and so on. It is the practical implementation of seemingly innocuous provisions that will bring the CFO into the technology realm to a greater degree. You may have internal controls in place, but since so much of your record keeping is electronic, how can you be sure that they are working as intended? In the future there will be certainly be electronic filing and updating. Will electronic filing be a relief or a nuisance? These are just some of the technology-related matters that will force their way onto the CFO's plate in the future.

Greater Need for CFOs to Think Strategically

What distinguishes a truly outstanding CFO from an ordinary one is his or her ability not just to keep the information flowing accurately but to think strategically. Budgeting is currently one of the most common areas in which a nonprofit CFO is called upon to think carefully about the financial future, but this is a somewhat narrow demand since the budget horizon is often only a year and allocations are frequently limited by either the funder or by the way it was done last year.

Thinking strategically means having financial input into decisions ranging from what revenue sources to pursue ("Foundation A gives smaller grants but allows us to draw down money when we need it, thereby improving our cash flow") to capital improvements ("Installing a new boiler system will lower our heating costs by 35 percent, partially offsetting the cost of financing it").

This is one area not driven by increased interest in accountability. Good CFOs already do this kind of thinking, of course, but as nonprofits grow larger and more complex, the need for moving beyond simple accounting and reporting will grow as well.

Meet Your New CFO

It's a safe bet that the nonprofit CFO of the future will look just like the CFO of the past, with higher expectations. Small nonprofits will want to look for someone who can move beyond simple bookkeeping toward managing and controlling financial affairs. Other nonprofits will expect their financial function to take on greater internal importance and move toward more compliance with external accountability demands. All nonprofits should expect the financial function to receive more external scrutiny and to be able to articulate a new balance with the CEO. All organizations can expect an emerging role for technology in internal financial matters, necessitating a CFO more skilled in managing information electronically. And the prized catch for a streetsmart CEO will be a financial person who can do all of the above, and whose eyesight extends years into the future, not just the next twenty feet.

A Financial Management Cultural Primer

One aspect of the global economy is that the United States's nonprofit sector increasingly welcomes people with no previous knowledge of it, either because they have spent their energies in the for-profit world or because they are from another country. Although this book has been written as simply and accessibly as possible, it still assumes a certain level of familiarity with American cultural, legal, management, and political practices. The purpose of this appendix is simple: to answer anything about a topic in the book that a self-deprecating person in this position might refer to as a "dumb question." We organize it as a kind of glossary, by chapter, to make it easier to use as a reference guide for anyone whose use of the book might otherwise be hampered by seemingly obscure references (including anyone needing a quick refresher on a topic).

CHAPTER I

Gross Domestic Product—A measure of a country's economy that tries to encompass the total market value of all the goods and services produced during a given period, usually a year.

Trade associations—Nonprofits that are formed for the explicit purpose of advocating on behalf of the interests of what are usually member corporations from a specific industry that join voluntarily with the hope of supporting industry-wide actions. Trade associations can be found in industries as diverse as telecommunications, hospitals, biotechnology companies, and veterinary practices.

Accountability—You'll see the word a lot in this book, for two reasons. The most important reason is that accountability to the general public (from whence all those tax breaks come) is at the heart of what nonprofits are all about. For another, accountability has been high on the list of big public stories for many years, starting with the savings and loan debacle in the late 1980s and continuing to the Enron scandal and on up to the subprime meltdown and Wall Street crash of 2008.

Great Society—A period in American history during the mid-1960s under President Lyndon Johnson when a variety of health and social welfare advances were made at the federal level and began to cascade down to the state level. It was similar in its overall approach and philosophy of government to the New Deal, a group of federal actions taken under President Franklin Delano Roosevelt in the 1930s.

Entitlement program—A governmental benefit given to consumers if they meet certain criteria, usually backed by force of law. Social Security, a government-operated retirement savings system, is considered an entitlement because it is available regardless of need or personal situation. Contrast this with means-tested programs, which are available only if the individual meets economic criteria, such as fitting a definition of poverty.

Grantmakers—A broad colloquialism that generally refers to private foundations and other entities that exist solely to give sums of money (grants) to entities and individuals for specific purposes.

Chief Financial Officer (CFO)—A high-ranking individual in an organization, nonprofit, or for-profit, whose responsibility is to oversee the entity's financial matters. CFOs are typically found only in medium to large organizations. Small entities often have a counterpart named "business manager," "director of finance," or something similar.

Corporation—A legal overlay on what might also be called a company. Corporations are legal structures. Only a government entity can grant corporate status. Corporations can be organized as nonprofits or as for-profits. Contrast corporations with partnerships, which are less formalized arrangements.

Tax-exempt—U.S. governments impose taxes on many things, one of them being the profits of corporations. A nonprofit corporation is tax-exempt. Tax-exempt status is granted by the Internal Revenue Service (IRS) to corporations that meet certain requirements.

CHAPTER 2

Chief Executive Officer (CEO)—This term typically refers to the topmost paid person in the organization. In nonprofits it is often synonymous with "executive director," which was a more widely used term in the past and which is still used more by small nonprofits. This term has gained more favor because of its more corporate sound, and is sometimes used interchangeably with or in addition to "president" (a term that used to refer more frequently to the chief volunteer officer of the nonprofit).

Visiting Nurse Association (VNA)—a kind of health care nonprofit that specializes in offering medical care in patients' homes instead of the hospital.

CHAPTER 3

Certified Public Accountant (CPA)—A professional designation given to an accountant who has met certain work-related qualifications and has passed a test designed to verify the accountant's level of knowledge. Sometimes this term is used imprecisely to refer to a very good or highly qualified financial person.

CHAPTER 6

Audit—An examination of an organization's financial books and records by an outside, independent, qualified examiner. Technically the term refers to the complicated process of assessing key elements of the organization's financial record-keeping, and then offering an opinion as to whether the information reported by management can be relied upon by outsiders. The term is also used more generally, and inaccurately, to refer to just about any evaluation process conducted by an outsider of the books and records of an entity.

CHAPTER 7

Accounting—The general practice of keeping financial books and records for an entity. Some assume that these systems are run entirely by and with accountants but, especially in small organizations, trained accountants are in the minority—if they exist at all. Instead, these systems use bookkeepers, clerks, and other administrative personnel to process financial data. Accountants are usually best used for higher-level tasks requiring deeper knowledge. Accountants functioning as independent contractors may also help run systems, as in small nonprofits when an outside accountant (not the auditor) comes in once a month to close the books on the transactions accumulated in the previous month.

CHAPTER 8

Indirect costs—Also called "administrative costs" or "overhead." In the nonprofit world, where transparency is the norm, indirect costs have become one way for casual observers to judge a nonprofit's performance. Nonprofits are aware of this. They take steps to make sure that they report low indirect costs. Then, when the nonprofit next door reports lower indirect costs, they go back to their books and find a way to report even lower indirect costs. The nonprofit next door sees this, and you can guess what it tries to do. Eventually everyone gets sucked into a black hole of antimatter.

CHAPTER 9

Auditors—Sometimes people equate auditors with accountants. Auditors have to be accountants, but not all accountants are auditors. Think of auditing as just one of the things one can do as an accountant. Also, some people refer to "the auditor" as though it were a single person looming in the doorway at the end of every fiscal year. In fact, a single person can act as the auditor, or an entire auditing firm can act as the auditor.

CHAPTER 11

Capital—One of the great ironies of nonprofit management is that this decidedly noncapitalist part of the capitalist economy requires its most effective practitioners to out-capitalist the capitalists in order to succeed. The aforementioned noncapitalists can be against capitalism if they wish, but they will find themselves chasing capital a great deal of the time.

CHAPTER 12

Budget—Few management tools are as well known as the budget. At the same time, budgets are greatly misunderstood. Budgets are planning and communication tools. They're also tools of power within a bureaucracy, as anyone knows who has ever worked in an organization where the budget is less well-known than the formula for Coca-Cola. Be prepared to see budgets in all these incarnations.

Legend has it that only a handful of people know the formula for Coca-Cola. The formula—and a first-rate global distribution system—is responsible for the drink's success.

CHAPTER 15

Profit—Americans have an uneasy relationship with profit. On the one hand, it is a key element in a capitalist economy. On the other, it gets associated with all kinds of unsavory things. Nonprofit people are often much closer to the latter reaction. Then they join management and undergo a conversion. Try to think of profit as an economic function, not an ideological litmus test.

CHAPTER 16

Fund-raising—In 1912 the U.S. federal government instituted an income tax. Before the end of that decade the concept of deductions was established, and the two events together created the basis for the current system of tax exemption. This tax-favored treatment of voluntary contributions is the cornerstone of the nonprofit sector. All the glitzy dinners, the walkathons, and the benefit concerts can trace their lineage back to this central proposition.

CHAPTER 18

Internal controls—Whenever one caveman stole another's supply of edible seeds, the victim would hit the thief over the head with a rock. After a while, a smart caveman figured out that he could protect his seeds by putting them in a box with a combination lock on it. This was the beginning of internal controls. The concept first attracted a large amount of attention from normal people in the Enron era. The Sarbanes-Oxley law requires that certain tests be done to make sure that a publicly held company's system of internal controls is intact and effective. Today, financial people generally have a heightened awareness of the importance of maintaining effective internal control systems, as do streetsmart board members.

CHAPTER 20

Performance orientation—Nonprofits are asked about their impact more often today. Funders are anxious to prove to themselves and their constituencies that all that money has made a difference. Municipalities consider taxing nonprofits as a way to replenish their depleted revenue streams. These developments are just illustrations of a rising interest in accountability for results in a global economy where most entities have a diminished tolerance for inefficiency. In many ways, this entire book is just a way of laying the foundation for individual organizations to be able to cope with these new and more intense demands.

Budget Bloopers

Apart from bad formulas, misspellings, and general spreadsheet lapses, there are a number of common errors budget-makers can make. Here are some of the more common budget bloopers other people (not you, now) can make.

Taking prior year adjustments as expenses—or revenue. Prior year adjustments exist to set the record straight. Don't count on them for the future, and they have nothing to do with current year revenue or expenses either.

Using different allocation bases in the same area of the budget. The purpose of allocating expenses is to spread costs evenly around an organization so that it is possible to get a true picture of what it takes to provide each kind of service. If the same kind of cost is allocated based on, say, square footage to one department and allocated on the basis of percentage of department revenue to another, doing so virtually guarantees that costs will be spread unevenly.

Treating capital campaign proceeds as revenue (usually). Like loans, capital campaigns are financing tools, not a source of revenue. One exception is if one explicitly shows part of the capital campaign's total production as being for operating revenues for one or more years (such as when a new development person's salary is funded for three years as part of the campaign).

Mixing capital spending with operating expenses. Capital spending is actually an investment—in effect, you move part of your cash assets to a different line on the balance sheet such as "land, buildings, and equipment." Spending goes in your operational expense line item, whereas investments go on your balance sheet.

Using cash records as sources of historic data. Budgets should be built on data, but be careful to use accrual-based records as your starting point, not cash transactions. Cash records don't capture things like depreciation and may give a distorted picture of when money comes in and goes out because cash data gets recorded when it happens, not during the period to which the related activity related to the cash occurred.

Mixing consultants with payroll staff. Consultants don't get benefits or have their pay reduced by taxes. Mixing consultants with payroll staff overinflates the budget by whatever the related payroll taxes and benefits costs might be.

Showing expenses such as fill-in staff as benefits. The reasoning here is understandable—in order to give the benefit of vacation time off, you have to find someone to work in that slot. But the IRS defines benefits, and costs related to providing the benefits are not a benefit. Put them in the "temporary staff" line.

Posting in-kind revenue without an identical expense of in-kind donations. In-kind donations are often welcome, but they skew budgets if the donations are counted as revenue. If you feel you must do this for management reasons, offset the total of in-kind donations with an identical line (usually calling it "cost of in-kind donations").

Treating loans as revenue. Loans are a financing mechanism, not a revenue source.

For monthly budgets, not taking account of predictable monthly variations. This is one of the most common budgeting errors. Snowplowing will happen only in the cold-weather months, guaranteed. So don't divide the snowplowing line by 12 to get a monthly figure. Divide it by the number of months in the snowplowing season, and put those amounts only in the snowy months. For more precision, massage the numbers to reflect the normal flow of intensity—flurries and small storms in the beginning followed by big storms, followed by small storms and flurries at the end. Think of it as a snow bell curve.

Failure to spread out multiyear grants as multiyear revenues. For budgeting purposes, make sure you project revenues in the year they are supposed to happen. Accounting records don't always produce reliable information for these purposes because of the way accounting rules work.

Budgeting by object code, not by area of responsibility. This is a common mistake made by small organizations. "Object code" is a fancy term for "categories of things you spend money on." If one uses object codes as the basis for creating an overall budget, there is no good way of showing how much this department spends on the object code for food versus that department. At the same time, object codes themselves can reveal useful patterns. So the idea is to use them the way responsibility is distributed throughout the organization—otherwise known as the organization chart.

Offsetting revenues or expenses. In this mistake, the revenue or budget figures are shown after they are adjusted. For example, a fund-raiser may be shown as the product of gross revenues less fund-raiser costs. You gain more precision by showing true revenues or expenses and then showing the offsetting expenses or revenues.

Putting stipends in the employment line. Stipends are not salaries or hourly wages, and they're given to workers such as interns or students. Better to put them into their own line.

Using the Web Site

TABLE OF CONTENTS WITH COMMENTARY

PART ONE: ANALYSIS

Financial Tasks

Different types of nonprofit organizations present different types of financial management challenges. Use this chart to locate your type of nonprofit and pinpoint the corresponding financial pressure points.

Messages from the Balance Sheet

Educated readers can derive a great deal of information from a balance sheet. Here, in summary form, is a guide to interpreting the messages your balance sheet is sending you, plus some suggestions for future action.

Financial Analysis Tools

These financial analysis tools provide managers, board members, funders, regulators, and advocates with an invaluable portrait of an organization's fiscal health. All data needed to complete these financial analyses can be taken from a single year's IRS Form 990.

Financial Definitions

This shorthand chart defines each of the tools used in the Financial Analysis Tools file.

Financial Ratio Formulas

This file shows the actual formulas used in the Financial Analysis Tools file in a manner suitable for reprinting along side the analysis file itself.

PART TWO: ACCOUNTING

Cost Allocation

If you have ever wondered about the true cost of your nonprofit's services, use this form to learn the answers. For maximum benefit, keep the line items to a minimum and restructure the relationship between the "departments" as necessary.

Audit Equation Self-Test

Many nonprofit organizations do not understand what is expected of them as financial managers, and as a result they may produce poor financial audits. Use this file to evaluate your organization's degree of control over the audit process.

PART THREE: OPERATIONS

Cash Flow Projection

Certain information is essential to have on hand when preparing a cash flow project. This time-saving checklist makes gathering the data an easier task.

Cash Flow Forecast

Ask your financial staff to complete this projection on a monthly or quarterly basis. Use the results to plan better use of your cash.

Fringe Benefit Rate Calculation

Fringe benefits are good for employee morale, but they can be expensive. Use this worksheet to find out just how much they cost.

Budget Report

This file can help simplify the chore of budget development for a single program, an administrative and finance department, or an entire organization. It contains formulas designed to build in standard allocation percentages for such expenses as fringe benefits and indirect costs.

Breakeven Analysis

To plan projects or ongoing budgets responsibly, managers need to know the projected breakeven point. The breakeven analysis file automatically calculates it once you enter complete data.

Economic Size Self-Test

The notion that there might be an economically efficient size for a nonprofit to provide certain types of services is just beginning to be understood. This file offers a way to test the influence of fixed costs (an important element of economic size) in a given nonprofit.

Profit Planning

Nonprofits need profit just as much as for-profit organizations need it (they just do something different with it). The Profit Planning Package translates the ideas about desired profit size in the text of this book into a single, easy-to-use spreadsheet.

PART FOUR: CONTROL

Internal Controls Self-Test

How effective is your system of internal controls? This handy matrix will spot potential weaknesses just by filling in the blanks with staff names. Draw a line from each name; wherever the lines cross, you have a potential weakness.

Red Flag/Yellow Flag

This slide show demonstrates how to complete quick analyses of your financial statements using our special Red Flag/Yellow Flag method. Please refer to the Youth Haven Audited Financial Statements in Appendix A when using this file.

Talking Red Flag/Yellow Flag

The content of this file is identical to the Red Flag/Yellow Flag presentation, with the added feature of voice narration by the author throughout.

Financial Analysis Using Calculations

For those willing to calculate a few formulas, this file offers invaluable information about your nonprofit's financial health. Please refer to the Youth Haven Audited Financial Statements in Appendix A when using this file.

Talking Financial Analysis Using Calculations

The content of this file is identical to the Financial Analysis presentation with the added feature of voice narration by the author throughout.

INTRODUCTION

The files on the accompanying Web site are saved in Microsoft Excel 97-2003 and Microsoft PowerPoint 97-2003, In order to use the files, you will need to have spreadsheet software and presentation software capable of reading the files.

SYSTEM REQUIREMENTS

- IBM PC or compatible computer
- Windows 95 or later
- Microsoft Excel 97 or later

   Users who do not have Microsoft Excel on their computers can download the free viewer from the Microsoft Web site. The URL for the viewer is: http://office.microsoft.com/downloads/2000/xlviewer.aspx

- Microsoft PowerPoint 97 or later

  This download is for users who don't have Microsoft PowerPoint; it allows them to open and view PowerPoint 97 presentations: http://office.microsoft.com/downloads/9798/ppview97.aspx

Note: Many popular spreadsheet programs and presentation programs are capable of reading the files on the web site. However, users should be aware that a slight amount of formatting might be lost when using a program other than what is specified.

USING THE FILES

Loading Files

First, download the files from the website and save them to your computer on an appropriate drive and directory. To use the files, launch your spreadsheet program or presentation program. Select **File, Open** from the pull-down menu. Select the appropriate drive and directory. A list of files should appear. If you do not see a list of files in the directory, you need to select **EXCEL DOCUMENT** or **Presentation and Shows (*.ppt; *.pps)** under *Files of Type*. Double click on the file you want to open. Edit the file according to your needs.

Printing Files

If you want to print the files, select **File, Print** from the pull-down menu.

Saving Files

When you have finished editing a file, you should save it under a new file name by selecting **File, Save As** from the pull-down menu.

USER ASSISTANCE

For technical support, please visit http://www.wiley.com/techsupport.

To place additional orders or to request information about other Wiley products, please call (800) 225-5945.

Index

CPSIA information can be obtained at www.ICGtesting.com
Printed in the USA
BVOW00n2213020913

329916BV00016B/20/P